STORYMAKING
in Education
and Therapy

This Book is dedicated to the life and work of:
Leif Kongsrud
Herman Straatman
and
The Wandsworth Group of Students.

STORYMAKING
in Education and Therapy
by Alida Gersie and Nancy King

Jessica Kingsley Publishers
London
and
Stockholm Institute of Education Press
Stockholm

© 1990 Alida Gersie, Nancy King and Stockholm Institute of Education Press

First published in 1990

First published in the United Kingdom by
Jessica Kingsley Publishers Limited
118 Pentonville Road
London N1 9JN

ISBN 1 85302 519 4 (hardback)
ISBN 1 85302 520 8 (paperback)

First published in Sweden by
Stockholm Institute of Education Press
Box 34103
S-100 26 Stockholm
Sweden

ISBN 91 7656 195 X (paperback only)

Graphic production: ORION GRAFISKA Malmberget Sweden
Printed in Great Britain by Billing & Sons Ltd, Worcester

British Library Cataloguing in Publication Data

Gersie, Alida
Storymaking in education and therapy.
    1. Medicine. Psychotherapy. Use of tale analysis
    I. title II. King, Nancy
    616.89'14

ISBN 1 85302 519 4
ISBN 1 85302 520 8 pbk

ACKNOWLEDGEMENTS

We wish to acknowledge the encouragement, interest and support which we have received from the following colleagues who are also friends:

Dr. Ofra Ayalon - Haifa University, Israel,
Dr. David Hart - Jungian Analyst, Boston, U.S.A.
Dr. David Herbert - Central School of Speech & Drama, London.
Dr. Sue Jennings - Dramatherapist/Anthropologist, London.
Michael Shackleton . Osaka Gakuin University, Japan.
Stig Starrsjö - University of Stockholm, Sweden.

We gratefully acknowledge the help offered by our respective institutions:
Hertfordshire College of Art & Design, Division of Arts & Psychology, U.K.
The Honors Program of the University of Delaware, U.S.A.

Our special thanks and gratitude are extended to:
Dr. Leon Campbell, University of Delaware, U.S.A.
Dr. Walter Allan Last, the Open University, U.K.

Without their support, care and trust, our work could not have happened.

Alida Gersie, U.K.
Nancy King, U.S.A.

CONTENTS

MYTHS AND STORIES

Trickster:

Healing:

Return:

THE STRUCTURES

Beginnings - The Structures

General structures
An exploration of ''In the beginning''
An exploration of answers to the question, ''How come?''

The stories

Passages - The Structures

General structures
Crossing the threshold
Blessings in disguise

The Stories

Knots - The Structures

General structures
An exploration of knots
Exploration of knots using drama

The stories

The Tree - The Structures

General structures
The tree as symbol of myself
The mystery within a tree

The stories

Trickster - The Structures

General structures
    Exploring Trickster
    Creating a trickster

The stories

Healing - The Structures

General structures
    A circle of blessings
    A healing place and person

The stories

Return - The Structures

General structures
    Going and coming
    A journey's end

The stories

Preface

From time immemorial and around the whole world man has, in multifarious ways, tried to find rich experiences and deep and comprehensive knowledge to increase the ability to understand reality, not least concerning oneself and other human beings, and to try to understand life's purpose and meaning. We humans also have the desire and the possibilities, not least in creative form, to carry experiences and knowledge further to others. In this connection myths and related stories have shown themselves to be a valuable form of circulation for experiences and deep knowledge.

In the myths we meet gods, heroes, animals and forces of nature who in a timeless world seek to throw light upon man's eternal questions. The stories we speak about here often contain descriptions and explanations of man's and life's origin and meaning. They also touch on questions about the creation, about gods and rites as well as about the material and spiritual culture. We especially encounter myths in these religions which see the evolution of the world as a cosmic drama. According to common belief, myths tell something essential about the universe's and life's creation, condition and end. Rites and cult ceremonies have often depicted that which the myths tell.

Many researchers have tried to elucidate the origin and meaning of myths. At the same time they claim that myths fill a widespread human need and that they belong to the human culture. Many researchers also mean that the myths can help man with explanations where customary knowledge and research have failed.

Offered in this book are a number of well chosen myths and stories related to them. They have been brought from different parts of the world.

The two authors, Alida Gersie, therapist and teacher from the U.K., and Nancy King, professor of drama from the U.S. have together and over many years worked with myths in a number of different ways and in most cases with a marked element of creativity. They have also worked this way abroad. Thus, Nancy King has been with us at the educational drama department on many occasions. Her work has received great attention from colleagues and teacher students.

The fine choise that the authors present here has been put together with much interesting information about how the texts came about, what they mean and how they can be used in different contexts. We are also offered a great number of choice exercises and suggestions on how one, with the help of creative and drama-emphasized exercises along with dialogue, can reach deeply into the different myths.

We, at the Stockholm Institute of Education, and particularly we at the Department for Educational Drama, are thankful, glad and proud that the two authors chose to allow us to publish their book. We hope that many will discover this book and that the readers derive from it everything that it has to offer, not least the value it has for their work amongst others.

Stig Starrsjö
Lecture in Educational Drama
at the Stockholm School of Education

PART 1

CHAPTER ONE
INTRODUCTION

People tell myths and tales as a way of making sense of their world. Stories pass from one generation to the next bearing witness to the ordering of knowledge, providing the distilled wisdom of each age for those to come. Groups of people gather around a fire, listening as the storyteller shares tales which instruct, heal, entertain and mystify. The listeners and the storyteller participate in an experience which connects them to their family, tribe and nation, through past and present, towards the future.

Although people in many parts of the world still tell stories, we in the Western world generally began to be deprived of hearing the ancient tales when we no longer needed to depend on fire for light at night. With the coming of gas and electricity, the work day was extended and books could be read at night. Later, radio and television became primary vehicles for instruction and entertainment. For the most part, storytelling stopped except for the stories told to children at bedtime.

We believe that hearing and telling stories stimulates the imagination. The production of images by our inner eye cannot be compared to the absorption of prescribed images with which television programs present us. When the inner eye is closed we lose the capacity to generate dreams, ideas and visions; our ability to imagine begins to atrophy. We become receptacles and reproducers, deprived of contact with our original and unique voice. This deprivation can become apparent at any age, especially when the imaginative resources with which we were endowed as children begin to wane. The time comes when we want and need to rekindle our birthright vitality.

In our search for solutions to this predicament, although we accept the premise that our bodies need a certain amount of physical activity in order to remain healthy, there is still a reluctance to recognize that the imagination, one of our psychic functions, also needs exercise. This primal source of vitality, which nourishes our creativity, requires stimulation and use in order for us to experience well-being.

Stories, necessitating the use of imagination connect and express fantasy and reality. They are simultaneously plausible and unlikely. Whenever a story is told, teller and listener embark upon a journey of inner and outer exploration. Through the process of connection with the story's content, we are able to discover the personal meaning it has for us. Our psyche is nourished by the evocation, stimulation and expression of actual inner imagery. The awareness of self is enhanced through exploring these images in drama, movement, sound, writing, talking, painting and sculpting.

Traditional tales express essential human experience. By allowing the myth to resonate within us, stimulating our personal expressive abilities, we are enabled to learn to connect our personal experience to the experiences of the human race. We become active witnesses to the past — realizing our present — transforming our future.

Stories speak through images which embrace the paradox of possible and impossible, the likely and the desired. Whenever our perspective on the future is narrowed by the reality of our current possibilities, the dreamer inside us is deprived of a voice. The rebirth of the dream, which inspires our existence, is accompanied by a re-emerging desire to share our story.

STORYMAKING in Education and Therapy is a book which includes myths and tales from all over the world, grouped around seven themes. These themes are reflective of all forms of human experience. We suggest ways in which these myths and tales can be used to develop our authentic voice, and how this expression can be communicated to others who are engaged in the same task. Even though most of the mythmaking structures are designed for use in groups, individuals who have followed them on journeys of their own have found them stimulating and exciting. A group, however, provides its members with the opportunity to share ideas, to acknowledge and enjoy difference. Alternative points of view can be welcomed for they offer new possibilities of engaging with experience.

The book is written for teachers, therapists, pastoral counselors and group workers, as well as for the individual reader. We believe that the material provided will be of use to those who work within the purposeful formality of educational and therapeutic settings; a formality with which explorations need to be encouraged and made possible.

The book: STORYMAKING in Education and Therapy is divided into three parts. In the first section, we discuss the nature of myths and tales. The second section includes seven themes explored in seven chapters, each comprising an introduction, six tales and twenty myth-making structures. The themes we have selected to work with in this book are: Beginnings, Passages, Knots, The Tree, Trickster, Healing and Return. Although the stories within each theme might be placed in other themes, depending on how one interprets a story, the order selected represents one clear usage. Notes for facilitators are offered in the third section. Specific uses of the material in this book are discussed, as is the development of necessary boundaries. We indicate some of the differences between educational and/or therapeutic practice when using the material in this book.

The authors: Who are "we"? Alida Gersie is a Dutch woman whose lifelong interest in myths found its initial expression when she translated creation myths as part of her studies at the University of Amsterdam. After moving to London to continue her work in arts education and creative therapy, she was invited to teach a course in comparative mythology as part of an adult education program. Although her initial teaching method was traditional, (introducing myths followed by discussion) she recognized that all of the issues raised through studying myths were of great importance to her students. Through much experimentation, exploration and discussion, she realized the importance of active, expressive, interaction with mythic material.

Drawing on her therapeutic studies and practice and extensive arts education experience, she created a way of working that resulted in improved access to personal creativity, imagination and expression and which proved to be satisfying to the participants even though they had differing levels of education, arts training and expressiveness. People who "could not paint", painted. Those who "could not write", wrote. Everyone discovered levels and layers which had hitherto been unknown. The students worked within a group which gave support, provided questions and served as audience. The activities in this book are in large measure derived from the London adult education mythmaking workshops.

From these beginnings, her myth work in the United Kingdom has found a place in various educational and therapeutic institutions whose programs include: special education, arts therapy, social work and language development. Alida Gersie is on the faculty of Hertfordshire College of Art & Design, courseleader of the Postgraduate Dramatherapy courses. She also works as a freelance consultant in storymaking in the United Kingdom, Holland, Israel and the USA.

Nancy King, born in New York City, author of three published books and many articles on theatre education, drama, movement, arts education and creativity, is currently on the Faculty of the University of Delaware teaching myth and expression in the Honors Program. Her initial education centered on physical expression through the use of dance, movement and theatre (playwright and director). Her continuing interest in telling and writing stories and plays which explore myths and tales led to her initial collaboration with Alida Gersie.

After the first participation in the London workshops, Nancy King returned to her work as Professor of Theatre and began to integrate myth work into aspects of her teaching and writing in the USA, Canada, England, Denmark and Sweden. She too saw the liberating effect it had on participants. People found new sources of energy through their group experiences and were amazed by their unexpected abilities to create in a variety of media. The work gave expression to feelings, ideas and thoughts which were discovered and uncovered in the process of creation. Not only were participants more able to express inner activity, they also were able to use mythmaking techniques in a wide variety of professional activity.

The University of Delaware initially provided a grant so her work using myth and expression with a variety of groups, people and programs could continue. Today, students in the Honors Program, as well as interested students and faculty from all areas within the University, are offered the opportunity to work with myths and tales as part of the University of Delaware's commitment to the use of imagination, creativity and expression as an important part of university education.

Our work in England, the USA and other countries has led many people to ask for written material for use in their own professional practice. STORYMAKING in education and therapy is our response to these requests. The book represents the thoughts, feelings and ideas of two people coming from different cultures, backgrounds, education and experience who have developed material which embraces all their multi-faceted difference. STORYMAKING in education and therapy is offered to readers to encourage many journeys into myth for anyone willing to be a sojourner.

A young woman lying under a tree is awakened by the roar of a tiger. She stands up and sees, in the distance, a ferocious tiger running toward her. Seeing no place to hide, she runs away from the tiger as fast as she can. The increasingly loud roar of the tiger tells her she has little time in which to find safety. She looks around and notices a cliff and runs to it. As she comes closer she sees two strong vines growing down from the face of the cliff. Just as the tiger is about to swipe her with his paw, she jumps over the edge of the cliff and holds tight to the two vines.

As she catches her breath, she watches the tiger above her settle down and fall asleep. While looking around, she hears the roar of a tiger. Puzzled, she looks up and sees the tiger is still asleep. Then she looks down and there, below her, is another tiger, roaring as loudly as the first.

While clinging to the vines she hears a gnawing sound just above her right ear. She looks up and sees a small mouse chewing on the vine. Then she feels something graze her left ear and, looking up, sees a tiny black mouse nibbling on the other vine.

Comforted by the sturdiness of the vines and the small size of the mice who take turns gnawing, she nestles against the vines and smells a delicious smell. Looking around, she notices a luscious, ripe plum just within her grasp. She reaches over, picks it and becomes totally lost in the moment, eating the plum.

A Tao story

CHAPTER TWO

MYTHS, TALES AND STORYTELLING

Myths, tales and legends

Stories are where reason does not go. Multitudes of stories are created yet few survive the process of telling and retelling. Each has a beginning, middle and end with a theme connecting various events into a more or less meaningful whole.

The ancient tales, which describe what happened in the beginning of time, are called myths. Their origins dwell within the soul and bloodstream of a people. The more recent anonymous tales, which have been passed on from one generation to the next, can be gathered under the collective title of folk or fairy tale. Even though the events and happenings in these stories may seem illogical or uncanny, the tales possess inherent reality which we somehow recognize. They reverberate within us. Legends continue to speak of historic events, a real happening "once upon a time". The historical memory may have long been forgotten and the original description altered beyond recognition, yet the legend continues to display its roots in reality, to relate a kind of truth. We may ask what is truth in the face of centuries of retelling? The answer lies with experience; as long as a tale is told, it has meaning (truth), will evoke response and can be understood.

Those who repeat myths, which are sacred to their people, emphasize the crucial importance of the eternally unchanging. An old rabbi spoke to his son who was copying a passage from the Torah and said, "My son, be careful in your work and do not change one title or word, for in so doing you would change the whole world."

For whenever we tell a story we continue the process of creation. Although the specific words of a folk tale or legend are not of great importance, each word of a myth matters. They are chosen words, selected because of their precise ability to represent the elusive intangible. Their sequence must not be altered because in so doing, we dare to change the universe. Mythical words are sacred. They evoke the original intention which inspired creation. They contain the seeds of all that can be known about the events in the beginning. Their utterance is their mystery; their recording and translation although sometimes a careless deed, is more often, the devoted response to the imposition of divine duty.

Some tales are accessible to anyone who is prepared to listen. However, others can only be told to those who have shown their willingness to become responsible adult members of their group/tribe. Some communities celebrate rites of passage by requiring initiates to undergo tests involving exposure to stress and fear. The successful completion of these rites assures those tested of the right to be told the group's sacred stories. The elders know that the newly initiated will deal with the new insights and information with courage and responsibility.

Even in societies without formal rites of passage, attaining a particular age or status may be marked by the telling of certain stories or events which influenced our lives or those of our family members. A new light may be thrown onto some previously unclear or mysterious interaction. The teller of the tale, the conveyor of history, usually has specific reasons for choosing to tell a particular story at a given time and place. The story might be told to affect a decision, to safeguard important family history or prepare family members for an impending death. The listener is judged to have reached "the age of understanding" and the telling conveys that the listener has now achieved this new status. Whether the teller intends to purge, console, guide, or instruct, the tale itself carries content which is relevant to teller and listener alike.

The one who listens is exposed to the impact of the tale. It is possible for one's whole life to be changed by a story told at a crucial time by someone whom we respect and trust. For the effect of a tale rests not only with its content, but also in the timing of the telling, and abides above all within the relationship between teller and listener. This is what the ancient people knew. Such is the power of stories.

A people's accumulated experience led to the construction of rules for guidance as to when to tell which story, to whom and under which circumstances. These rules safeguard listener as well as teller and protect the potential for instruction and inspiration which the tale contains. Out of all the functions which stories fulfill, these two stand out with clarity and continuity. Instruction implies the possibility of development, the necessity of creating structure. Inspiration celebrates the acceptance of the spirit, the possibility of change.

Each story is an emblem of existence, the symbolic representation of someone's interpretation of reality, of the interaction between inner and outer world. Although stories may be the container of ideas, knowledge, experience and insights, more than these, they connect with our longings, dreams and need for hope.

The meaning of story and tale

The word story has come to imply a narrative, an account of events. Its etymological roots link to a Greek word which means to know. Tale finds its basis in "taal", language or speech (talk). Thus both story and tale reflect and indicate our ability to use language to gain knowledge of life and to communicate the process of inquiry and outcome. Stories and tales are the product, the end and therefore, paradoxically, the beginning of our journey towards understanding.

The relationship of teller and listener

With your inner eye imagine two people sitting near one another. One is telling a story, the other is listening. In the space between storyteller and listener images will arise. Characters will be created who engage in battles, encounter other beings and overcome difficulties. Both people will "see" the story and yet each of them sees their "own" story. The shared tale is no more and no less than a private possession. The words are collective, the imagery individual. Whenever we listen to a tale we prepare ourselves to be introduced to the process of creating structure and we open ourselves up to be inspired. When the space between us and another is filled with words of intentional sequentiality, we take inside us the energy which is attached to the verbalization. The power of words extends beyond the power of content, it is also the power of repeated usage, of association and of intent.

But whatever the situation or context, the storyteller always recounts the tale by the grace of the one who is willing to listen. Whenever the attention of the listener is no longer held by the content or the telling of the tale, the teller will have to woo the listener so that the tale can be continued. When the audience listens, the storyteller can share images, emotions, experiences and ideas which are given to the listener for reflection, knowledge and response. Telling a tale enables each of us to know ourselves as someone who has a voice which is worth listening to, someone who can be heard and understood.

Each story is re-created in the interaction between teller and listener. It is their relationship which causes a particular tale to come to life. The ebb and flow of the listener's concentration and attention influence its dynamics. The relationship between teller and listener is always intimate. The closeness is generated by the interconnection between the one who tells and the one who listens. By the act of sharing highly individual or collective, symbolic material with another to whom this same symbolic structure matters, a special, fragile bond is created which lasts for as long as the story is allowed to continue. The potency of a story is derived from the investment teller and listener have in its relevance to the actual experience and interpretation of their own lives.

Any tale told is like a journey remembered. In the act of telling we allow another human being access to our experience of life, our inner world, the journey on which we have been. Once the words are spoken, the teller knows that the tale will have a new life of its own, one which is independent from the teller. From then on the tale is as much the listener's as it is the teller's. This is why no matter how often and how faithfully a teller tells a tale, it can never be told exactly the same way twice. The audience, situation, time, personal history and above all, the moment, effect the communication and determine the bond which needs to grow. Each tale is told only once; once and for all. Thus although a tale may be old beyond memory, it is always new; the same, yet permanently different.

When we listen to a tale we become peeping Toms in a world where the laws of "reality" give way to the laws of fantasy, where inspiration gives birth to the spoken word and where fact is born from fiction. We move out of the here and now and into the there and then. We suspend our awareness of the present and allow another reality to enter consciousness. The outer eye may register a familiar room or people but the inner eye generates images of unfamiliar worlds and beings. The storyteller becomes the guide through this unknown realm. The listener surrenders, trusting that the once-known world will continue to exist during the time of storytelling and that we can return at will to the room with its known dimensions and contents. We take a substantial risk...

In listening we show that we are prepared to make space for someone else's expression of their experience. But, more than making space, we indicate that we wish to participate in their journey. Thus, we allow the outside in, enabling it to become part of our own life experience. New insights and concepts may well be introduced and these can be frightening. Although we need to surrender to the unknown of the tale, we can only do so if we trust that our guide knows the way.

"Please tell me a story"

Have you ever wondered why so many children want to hear a story at bedtime or why adults so often read before going to sleep? We suggest that apart from wishing to delay the moment of falling asleep by clinging to the known of consciousness, the story performs the function of reassuring the recipient that the unknown can become knowable, that the road between the known and the unknown can be traveled both ways.

Stories are often told in times of transition. One common occurrence is the transition from wakefulness to sleep. On other occasions it may be at the beginning or end of the school day or during times of travel. During the period of time before falling asleep we are in transit from light into darkness, togetherness into aloneness. We are about to travel from one kind of known world to the next which is unknown; we may not like it at all. Tucked in between the sheets, safe in our bed, we can encounter scenes of intense dramatic power. We leave the events of our daytime existence and travel barefoot into the unknown world of sleep and dreams and nightmares.

How many of us feel truly comfortable with this experience of letting go? What kind of shortcuts do we use to limit the transitional period of time? The story at bedtime can be both remedy and treatment. When we look at the type of stories people have wanted to be told in this time of transition we can detect a common pattern. For these stories invariably introduce us to the unpredictable and the unexpected. They offer advice and help the listener become acquainted with strange events, with the struggle between bad and good, with sudden twists of fortune and unwelcome guests.

A participant in a mythmaking session recalled the type of tale she enjoyed hearing when she was a child. This is what she wrote:

> "My uncle was my favorite storyteller. Whenever he and my aunt visited I would beg to be told a story. Not just any old one, but more about monkey. This monkey lived in a bell tower in a little village. Near the bell tower was a church with a high spire. At night monkey flew between these two. On his journey he would see what was happening in the village and then he would plan what to do. He would go into action. The most amazing things happened. Yes, he was my favorite."

An unusual being was introduced into her world — a flying monkey — who could see, plan and intervene. The tales at bedtime assure us that our heroes can defend themselves, that helpers do appear, and that after defeat resurrection is possible.

Whenever we find ourselves in transition chances are that questions will arise about origins and causes, purpose and meaning. If we go in search of answers it is likely that we will attempt to formulate a response by logic and reasoning, through repeated experimentation. But what do we do when we find no satisfactory solution? We may try to forget our questions or we may turn to stories hoping that they will contain some insight and comfort.

A mythmaking participant recalls:

> "I remember a time, just after an awful fight with my mother. My aunt came to visit and saw that I had been crying. She invited me to go for a walk and as we walked, she told me a story about a lovely Russian princess named Petrushka. I still remember my aunt putting her arm around me and the feeling of being drawn into a new and magical world. Her stories eased my thoughts about the fight and gave me the sense that there was something special which only she and I shared."

Stories offer more than consolation, they provide encouragement to continue the formulation of questions rather than to abandon the search. Through identification with a hero or heroine, who shows the degree of patience, wit and courage needed to surmount setbacks, we learn to face our own fear and loneliness. Untethered by the constraints of reality, yet within a plausible structure, our story characters explore alternative actions until an answer and a way out is found.

Meanwhile, the listener's imagination has become engaged. Listening to the gripping tale we think about questions posed, problems created and approaches and resolutions which hold us captive to the process of solution. When the story is completed the listener may experience a sense of conscious realization about analogue questions and attempts to find an answer.

Thus, stories are gatekeepers between our inner and outer worlds. The known world is the starting point, the connection with a reality which we can identify and recognize. In the process of its unfolding, the tale develops a story line which contains and explores the unknown. A story is a guide because it takes us from resting place to adventure, through misfortune to culmination and the end. The listener walks metaphorically, hand in hand, with the storyteller, inside whom, the tale finds a temporary abode. When the journey is completed, we the listeners, emerge revitalized. The imagination has nourished and inspired our motivation which in turn contributes to realization and solution. We gain strength by identification with a story character who initially had the will to persist and who found the courage and strength to prevail.

The thread of wonder

In our imagination we can create an inner world of great delicacy, spun out of the threads of human experience and dreams, whatever the age of the spinner. However, we can only visit this inner world if there is a point of embarkation, the expectation of arrival and the trust and knowledge that we are able to return to the place of departure. We see this in the play of healthy children when a child interrupts the playing to re-enter, often abruptly, the "real" world. The interruption may be to invite an adult to come visit the enchanted place or to ask for a token representation of "abandoned reality" in the form of food or an object. If the child's invitation to visit is accepted, the grownup needs to be prepared to suspend disbelief for the moment and to function within the code of conduct of the imagined environment. "Don't sit there, that's where the princess is sleeping," says the child, pointing to an empty cushion on the floor. Nonetheless, the presence of the adult visitor will remind the child that the journey from the real to the imagined land is both possible and repeatable which can be reassuring. The invitation conveys more than the need for "reassurance", it also indicates that guests are welcome to share the child's inner world. Little does the child know that those who have lived for many years sometimes lose access to their ability to weave a web of make-believe, that their dreams may lose potency and experience of the world can cause a thickening of the fragile threads of wonder.

In the act of imagining we create a separation between our current, actual situation and one that we imagine as an alternative. The space which is thus created, enables us to reflect upon our actual situation; to shed light upon it. As long as we are identified with an experience we cannot see it nor can we illuminate it. Distance is needed. There are many ways of creating space through reflection, therapy and education. Using the imagination to create space is effective because of its multi-dimensional and multi-functional qualities.

The multi-dimensional quality of imagination makes it possible for us to reach the darkest corner of our being, to reveal our most hidden longings and capacities (at least to ourselves). The multi-functional aspect of imagination helps to resolve, reconcile, energize, stimulate and encourage. In itself, the imagination is neither good nor bad, it is the function which we give to it which determines its usefulness.

At times, however, the confrontation between experienced reality and the potential of dreams can be too painful for a person, especially when reality is only a threadbare version of the longed for potentiality. A young woman who worked as an activity therapist in a day center for mentally ill adults experienced this when she introduced an "IF" game to her clients. Participants were asked to respond to questions such as, "If I were rich, famous, brilliant.... I would...." She wanted them to write down how such a situation would come to pass, what it would feel like, how it would affect their lives. She noticed that the group became more and more silent, obviously reluctant to play her game. Then, one man burst out:

"Don't you realize Miss that we don't wish to play this game? It hurts too much, far too much. Can't you see we're nowhere near any of these things? It's too painful. It's cruel. I won't play this any longer." With that, he put down his piece of paper. Other group members followed, repeating his words, "It hurts too much."

When we suffer a substantial amount of mental pain, it is difficult to tolerate an imaginary world, especially if attempts are made to establish connections between daily life and what is made manifest in a fantasy. This dilemma can be resolved by taking more or less exclusive refuge in the dream world, thus denying the existence of what is too bad to be endured. If one is forced to persist, to find a solution, the individual may take refuge in madness. To remedy this, we can refuse to imagine, or we can choose to imagine only what can be kept entirely separate from what and how the world is "known" to be. This allows us to operate on parallel trails of fantasy and reality which neither interconnect no interrelate. Any overlaps in content between the experienced real and the imagined remain unexplored. Here, the imagination is active but deprived of its usefulness. At the same time, we lose access to our imagination which we will need if we want to make our "dream of life come true".

The imagination not only reflects our experience and longings, it also harbors our potential which has the possibility of becoming manifest but which is currently latent, beneath the surface. If our actions and deeds belong to the world of realized potentiality, then our dreams and longings dwell in the realm of potential actuality. The questions then raised are, "How can what is potential become actual and how can we translate our dreams into our actions?"

A key to the understanding of this process might be in the use of the word potential. Potency evokes images of power and sexual prowess and is related to the Latin word "possum" which means "I am able." "Able" is connected with "to have". Thus we see how potent has come to denote powerful. Those who are aware that they have (something) and are able (to make use of whatever they have) are the ones who experience themselves as potent and are described as powerful by those who know them. In our imagination we potentially achieve and experience what may seem to be inaccessible to us in our real world. We all need to find the energy to begin and to continue the process of actualizing our potential. Traditionally, stories have been used to serve this purpose. They trigger and nourish the imagination. Through a process of vicarious stimulation, they nurture the individual's ability to bring about change.

Listen to these tidings

Some stories are homemade, based upon the teller's real or imagined experiences, thoughts and feelings. Others are tales from places near and far, author unknown or known. A few are even said to be handed down by the gods themselves. Although there are many reasons why a story is told, there are even more which relate to its creation.

Sometimes we nurture our inner tales because they are an image, a potential of sequentiality, no more than a shimmer of thought. Others are the stories of real life events, of what we saw and felt. The quality and intensity of emotions attached to these tales affects how often and when they can be told. Circumstances may also dictate the kind of tale to be told. Those which are less intense, less intimate, may arouse a sense of relief, delight or inspiration in the listener. Others, distract, inform, console or help us to imagine walking in the footsteps of those who have gone before.

The Bushmen of the Kalahari desert say that without a story of one's own, one hasn't got a life of one's own. All people need to find and express their own story in order for each person's life to qualify as a life of one's own, a truly individuated existence. The act of storytelling then, is more than a way of "using language to narrate an event". It also becomes a process through which we give form to our experience of life and affirm our individuality by expressing our knowledge of the world. When we make up tales, which we create for our own sake, or in response to a request, a new inside-out tale is created. When we give voice to our experience of the interaction and confrontation between inner and outer world, we create an inner tale which can be composed of memories, experiences, knowledge and/or reflections. All of these are special and particular to the individual and therefore, always a symbolic re-presentation of the creator.

When we listen to the words, "Once upon a time..." the response evoked within us will be indicative of the type of memories we have of storytelling.

We may remember being slightly bored, totally entranced or positively outraged. Whatever our association, when we listen to someone who talks about an actual life experience which occurred at a real point in time, we have a different experience than when we hear an imaginary tale with time unspecified and place unlocated. The further away in time and setting a story happens, the more it becomes a tale which resides in never-never land. Whenever we listen, the degree to which we are able and allowed to identify with the story characters, matters and colors the listening process.

Over-identification with another person's real life story is often experienced as a substantial intrusion. For it removes the ownership of an event as if the listener, in the process of identification, diminishes the occurrence and the intensity of what happened. Although this may be a relief when our tale is one of woe, our response changes when we wish to be the sole owners of what happened and are only prepared to share its occurrence but not to dilute the energy generated by the experience. At this time someone else's identification with our story is an undesired phenomenon because it has an attenuating effect.

However, when we listen to a "Once upon a time..." tale listeners are allowed and encouraged to identify to their heart's content. No one will stop us nor will a code of acceptable behavior prevent us from identifying with an imaginary or legendary character. On the contrary, the tale is told precisely for this purpose. We are encouraged to experience a whole range of events vicariously and thus broaden the base of our existence.

Therefore, we can expect that a tale told in a time of illness will substantially differ from a story told in a time of plentitude. The storyteller's choice will depend upon the perceived needs of the listener. The listener's willingness to pay attention depends in turn, on the fulfillment of their needs.

"Hark, hark ye people. Listen to these tidings." These are the first words of the Icelandic Edda. They arrest the attention and evoke a sense of apprehension. In order for the teller to be able to tell, there has to be someone to listen. Someone has to have the desire to hear. We are all aware of the different styles and qualities of listening we have both received and given (intense, focused, half-hearted, dismissive, judgmental, open-minded). Whatever our style, it always influences what can be said. Although the listener is never responsible for what the teller is able to express, the form of listening nonetheless exercises influence. The weight and value we attach to this phenomenon depends on how we view the relationship and patterns of interaction between people.

When we listen to a story similar processes are at work. Whether we have requested a tale or accidentally stumbled across a storyteller, the quality of our listening always guides and directs the process. What we desire to hear determines, in part, what we are likely to hear. In the process of telling we allow another person access to our knowledge and experience. We demonstrate our willingness to share what we have discovered and we make it available for comment, response and possible rejection. Although we can make attempts to ensure that the listener will react in a predetermined manner, there are no ways to assure a particular reaction. The teller always takes this risk.

The power of silence, of not sharing, relies on the perception of untested, assumed strength which the listener projects onto the non-teller. Thus, it might be tempting not to tell our tales, not to know our lives in the presence of others. However, once the telling starts and the silence is ended, both teller and listener enter a new stage where the dream of potentiality is completed and is replaced by actuality with real possibilities. When we converse we share and when we share we become accessible, public and available.

Once we have decided to break our silence we need to know when and how the story we tell begins and ends. We require delineation. We need to reach an agreement about the differences between ordinary talk and story talk. The ritual words "Once upon a time, in a place not very far from here but not so very near..." convey that the story has begun in earnest. But any other words, setting a similar tone, will also do, for what matters is the transposition in both listener and teller, from a predominant awareness in the here and now, to an engrossed sojourning in the there and then. We have to set the boundary which delineates the real world from the one described in the tale. At a later stage this boundary will function as a safeguard against intrusion and flooding with unconscious mental imagery into our real-life events and experience. The creation of demarcation can be of crucial importance if fantasy and reality become too intertwined.

The tension which is generated between the existing and the possible is enhanced by the awareness of difference. The knowledge of the relationship between what was, what is and what might be inspires and guides our action in the present in relation to our anticipation of the future. A frightened person is more likely to let go of his or her clinging determination to hang on to the real in order to embark upon an imaginary journey when clear limits are established and no doubt exists as to what is what. The boundary of an indicated, and therefore anticipated beginning provides this safety and thus is habitually used in traditional tales. Traditional endings such as, "May they live happily ever after" or the following (from the Russian THE FLYING SHIP) serve to tell us that the story is finished.

> "You asked for a story, and now I've told you one. Not too long and not too short, just the distance between you and me. I'd happily tell you more, but that's all I know."

Me-me-and-more me

When a story continues to be told generation after generation it acquires the special quality of distillation. Although in the process of retelling, the outer edges of a story might be changed, its essence is preserved and safeguarded so that the basic knowledge contained within its tale can be communicated. When a tale loses its potency and changes are made to the tales's structure, the original tale ceases to exist and a new story is born.

"Distilled" stories, usually called folk or fairy tales, contain our knowledge and experience of the world. The metaphors used can be retranslated into personally significant, symbolic language but this is not necessary for these tales are understood by us at the level of meta-language. When the listener no longer connects with the metaphoric language used, the story will not be retold or remembered. The tale will cease to exist in living memory and will have played its role in a phase of human development. Sooner and later other stories will take its place.

There will, however, be occasions when a people (probably a scriptless, non-technical community) wishes to communicate across distance (in time and place) and also wishes to preserve continuity of content. Then, ways and methods have to be developed which insure that the knowledge or message does not get lost or distorted beyond recognition. How can this be done?

Gesture and some type of language must be designed to provide a degree of consistency when the message moves between sender and receiver. (We need to create not only continuity of signal but also continuity of signal-reception and interpretation.) Signs external to the human body, such as symbolic objects, carved or painted images and ultimately script will be used. For without these, knowledge can only be transmitted across time and place when the person who possesses the knowledge is physically present. This means that individuals who "know" have to be protected and well looked after. Once their mortal body perishes the knowledge they own will disappear with them unless they have ensured a timely passing on of their knowledge to another person.

The ones who have this knowledge are often placed in a special position within their community. Even though the precise nature of these positions varies from people to people, a common requirement placed upon such persons is the recitation of the history (time specified, place located) and the story (time unspecified, place unlocated) of the people. In the act of recounting, their knowledge is shared, though still protected, by the one whose responsibility it is to remember. Through the act of listening the knowledge can be absorbed, and redistributed, depending upon the degree of responsibility the listeners take for safeguarding its content. In these situations, listening will be closely connected with the ability and the need to remember. The emphasis will be on accurate recall, not on personal inter-pretation of the content received.

Then another difficulty arises. The greater the number of people who know, the greater are the chances that disagreements will develop regarding contents and importance. This happens not only because everyone adds their personal insight, experience and preference to the knowledge received, but also because memory distortion is likely to occur. When the information has been made public, the sharing and discussion of its content become possible. Consequently, variations in recall are noted. These likely disagreements decrease the value of the knowledge and may ultimately lead to its being discarded. If only a few people are initiated into the knowledge then at least there will be no public discussions about what is remembered. The chances of distortion remain unchanged but the authority of the knowledge remains undisputed for the extent of the misremembrance and personal modification is hidden. The limitation of access to information was and is a powerful tool for manipulation and the safeguarding of power depends upon it.

We can see why a scriptless, non-technical community has to find adequate means to maintain and distribute the accumulated wisdom and knowledge of generations of living. One of the common solutions is to differentiate between knowledge and beliefs which need to be shared by all, those that need to be accessible to most, and that which can/must be known only by the select. The distribution of knowledge can thus be divided into public, personal and private spheres, both in terms of the information/content received (outside-in) and of what is sent (inside-out). Continuity is created by the insistence upon periodic repetition of the acquired knowledge and by placing emphasis upon the absolute importance of accurate recall.

A community which honors the preservation of the known will emphasize the timeless, repetitive quality of life. The changing phases are considered to be illusions of the temporal, only the eternal example contains the essence. Each story is perfect and therefore requires perfect repetition. Why change the whole world?

When a community acquires the ability to communicate across distance and through time through secondary message carriers (enduring symbols and signs) it gains a variety of ways of preserving continuity. Knowledge can then be disseminated rapidly and simultaneously across time and place. The danger of this increased availability means we may lose the precious contact, both direct and physical, with people who possess the knowledge and we also might lose our awareness of people (including ourselves) as containers of knowledge.

The writer James Joyce paraphrased the word memory into me-me-and-more-me. Does a shriveled awareness of self as container of knowledge, a shrunken memory, lead to a diminished sense of self? It is clear that talking, listening and memorizing take on different functions once the capacity to read and write is developed. The potential loss of the actual presence of the "One Who Knows" (in the West this may be the parent of a child) may well be one of the explanations for the difficulties some of us have experienced in acquiring or training literacy skills. For written language and spoken language are in a relation similar and comparable to transitional object and primary object. Consequently, the human being will experience the very same emotions and resistances which emerge when the transition from the one to the other has to be learned. Not wanting to be able to acquire new knowledge, not being willing to learn to write (to communicate across time and distance) may simply convey our wish to continue in the presence of the One-Who-Knows for just a little longer.

Storytelling may satisfy our need to remain connected to what we perceive to be an important source of wisdom. At the same time, through the process of nurture and vicarious excitation, we can also encourage the one who is reluctant to go forward, to take a deep breath and move.

The stories in this book

The myths and tales we have chosen to share in our book have been selected and placed by us in their respective chapters and sequence because we believe these choices exemplify aspects of meaning inherent in the story. We are, at the same time, aware that no story can have only one meaning, that other interpretations of story, theme and meaning are possible. Ultimately, our selection results from the need to choose and the need to stop, for the time being, our constant preoccupation with reading new stories. In the process of writing this book we have accepted that the writing stops and the work continues. May your source of fascinating stories be continually replenished.

PART 2

CHAPTER THREE

BEGINNINGS

Beginnings are difficult. Implied in the process is choice, a road not taken. Whenever we begin the "dreamtime" comes to an end and we mourn the loss of the potential, forfeited when the actual beginning is made. In our dreaming, the possible always seems larger, more substantial and complete when compared to the actual. This comparing increases our awareness of limitation, of the impossible, and of time passing. The imagined can be perfect; the actual forces us to face our imperfections. The imagined is forever; the real lives within time and physical space, a contained and confounded actuality. What is, differs essentially from what might be precisely because of this quality, the ending of a dream.

Can you recall the feelings you had when you awoke from a beautiful dream. Even though our daytime existence may be satisfying and rewarding, the sense of loss we experience as our dream disappears can be overwhelming in its sadness. It is almost as if we have been expelled from paradise, from the Eden where we freely communicate with other beings, gods and creatures without the constraints of separate realities; the place where there is food in abundance and an absence of pain, disease and suffering. Paradise is where no questions are asked about our origins or our destination for we belong and have the undisputed right to be who we are, where we are. No justification is ever needed because the essence is the being, not the direction of the being. Thus, paradise is an eternal, never changing refuge of permanent bliss.

Creation contrasts sharply with paradise. Paradise *is*. Creation embodies the process of realization. Through this experience of becoming we discover a different mode of being than the one we knew in paradise. There we knew ease, plenitude, and certitude, the universal monologue. In the process of creation, a dialogue begins. The confrontation between our being and acting ends the stage of unified dreaming. We enter the phase of potentially discordant action.

When creating we become vulnerable, accessible, and recognizable.

Whereas the dream is private and hidden, the action is public and overt. Through creation in context we become accountable. We can be held responsible for what we make and for the process whereby we give form to content. This, in turn, increases the anxiety about beginning the process of creation and may contribute to a preference for hibernating in the dream.

"In the beginning" indicates how sometime and somewhere a process commenced leading to a realization which in turn resulted in further unfoldings until at a certain time the process temporarily halts. The creator needs to make a further choice when the main flow of creative energy indicates numerous new possibilities. Then the new potential lures the creator towards a return to the dream. This is a vital return if the process of realization is to be inspired by the perfection of the possible yet it is a dangerous one if the consequence is a return to non-action. Conception and creation require wakefulness; the exercise of choice and the continuing application of consciousness.

As we travel in the unknown and uncharted territory of creation it is possible for us to journey with a predetermined goal in mind which functions both as compass and director of the passage. Traveling in this manner allows for neither lingering nor meandering. Destiny equals our destination. However, another type of journey also beckons. We may choose, instead, to travel slowly, moving off the beaten path, without clear direction and with little awareness of where we are going or where we hope to end. The purpose of traveling in this instance might be in the process itself. We may be driven not by the expectation of ultimate and prospective rewards, but by the expectation of intrinsic satisfaction and its inherent value. We continue even though we recognize that losing our direction for the sake of variety may cause us to lose our way. Either way of traveling, both the one with single focus and the one with no clear purpose may cause the traveler to miss the journey all together because of the expectation of a promised land.

In both instances the travelers travel. The first is a journeying "towards", the other a wandering "with". Both ways of traveling require the travelers to be aware of the purpose of their specific undertaking, albeit awareness of a different kind. For each side road presents the travelers with a possibility and therefore, a choice: the problem of the road not taken. The decision will be based on their reasons for embarking on their journey (even though these may have long since been forgotten), on what they currently wish to do and need, and upon dreams of future satisfaction. In the moment of decision making, past, present and future meet one another. They illumine the traveler with what was, what is and what might be; each burning with a different intensity. The creator of the journey must decide which road to take in order to continue the process of creation. In the moment of decision making, in the process of becoming and thus creating, the lure of the slumbering, inactive dream is overcome. The energy of creation is allowed to unfold into manifestation and consciousness.

Whether we focus on the process or are goal oriented, in the act of creation we always face the difficulty of beginning. The first step out of the dream into reality, out of fusion into separateness requires energy. This force can be generated by longing, despair, fear, belief or hope and requires our courage and the conviction that acting and unfolding is the preferred process. For when doubt enters, as it will (sooner or later) the strength of this conviction is needed if we are to continue the often painful and seemingly futile process of creation. We have to find the courage to combat the hopelessness and fatigue that steadily accompany the creator. No process of creation is ever a simple straight-forward and unchallenged triumph of order over chaos. Each time the abstract is transformed into the concrete, possibility into actuality, we stand eye to eye with doubt and selfquestioning. We often wonder about the purpose and the meaning of the transformation of the possible into the actual. We face the temptation to return to the dreamtime where we can slumber undisturbed by manifest forms and can suckle to our heart's content the never-ending stream of unconsciousness.

"In the beginning" means that we will encounter an awareness of our aloneness, of isolation and of loss. However, these feelings fueled with hope and longing can bring forth determination, ultimately leading to the enactment of creation. At any time during this process, the unfolding may cease, resulting in an attempted return to the enfolded state, where the dreamtime will continue until a new emergence or glimmer of longing once again gives birth to a renewed beginning.

Myths of creation reflect the sensations of emptiness, loneliness and longing. They lead us through many ways of giving form to the possible, to enable all of us "to make our dream of life come true". To facilitate the conversion of our dreams into our realities, we can recount the beliefs and knowledge of the process by which the world as we know it has come to be. Thereby we are both instructed about the qualities and characteristics of these processes, and inspired and consoled when the wish to surrender to unawareness becomes almost overwhelming.

"We wait in darkness! Come, all ye who listen, help in our night journey. Now no sun is shining; now no star is glowing; come show us the pathway. The night is not friendly; she closes her eyelids. The moon has forgot us, we wait in the darkness." Thus the Iroquois chant during their initiation rite when the young boys are enabled to leave their childhood days and companions behind in order to enter into the presence and therefore, the duties and responsibilities of the adult men of the tribe.

"We wait in the darkness", is an aspect of a stage of change, of growth and therefore of loss. In leaving behind what is familiar we venture forth, on faith and/or belief that the next stage is necessary, desireable, or an improvement. Creation takes place through and largely in spite of mankind. We often wait in the darkness, dreamers in the folds of the timeless, until we awaken to the reality of embodied temporality, separate but not isolated, unique but not rare. Then we experience how, "from the conception the increase" commences. "In the beginning" myths of creation reflect how the mystery, the possible and the explicable are united in the process of dream realization.

The Stories

Mantis and the flower   *Beginnings/Bushman/Africa*

In the time before time, when earth was covered with water, Bee carried
Mantis over the water trying to find a place of solid earth for him. Bee flew
and did not see any dry land. Just as he grew so tired he was not sure he
could continue, Bee spied a flower on the water, its petals cupped open. Bee
flew down and gently put Mantis into the flower. So began Mantis, the First
One, Maker of Fire, Keeper of the Dream.

The shared myth of the one that became two   *Beginnings/India*
                                                        Upanishad

In the beginning this universe was nothing but the Self in the form of a man.
It looked around and saw that there was nothing but itself, whereupon its
first shout was, "It is I"; whence the concept "I" arose. (And that is why,
even now, when addressed, one answers first, "It is I!" only then giving the
other name that one bears.)

Then he was afraid. (That is why anyone alone is afraid.) But he considered: "Since there is no one here but myself, what is there to fear?"
Whereupon the fear departed. (For what should have been feared? It is only to a second that fear refers.)

However he still lacked delight (therefore we lack delight when alone)
and desired a second. He was exactly as large as a man and woman embracing. This Self then divided itself in two parts; and with that, there were a
master and a mistress. (Therefore this body, by itself as the sage Ya-
jnavalkya declares, is like half of a split pea. And that is why, indeed, this
space is filled by a woman.)

The male embraced the female, and from that the human race arose. She,
however, reflected: "How can he unite with me, who am produced from
himself? Well then let me hide!" She became a cow, he a bull and united
with her; and from that cattle arose. She became a mare, he a stallion; she

an ass, he a donkey and united with her; and from that solid-hoofed animals arose. She became a goat, he a buck; she a sheep, he a ram and united with her; and from that, goats and sheep arose. Thus he poured forth all pairing things, down to the ants. Then he realized: "I, actually, am creation; for I have poured forth all this." Whence arose the concept "Creation" (Sanskrit srstih: what is poured forth").

Anyone understanding this becomes, truly, himself a creator in this creation.

Creation   *Beginnings/Maori/Polynesia*

The first period: of Thought

> From the conception the increase
> From the increase the thought,
> From the thought the remembrance,
> From the remembrance the consciousness.
> From the consciousness the desire.

The second period: of Darkness

> The knowledge became fruitful;
> It dwelt with the feeble glimmering;
> It brought forth night:
> The great night, the long night,
> The lowest night, the loftiest night,
> The thick night, the night to be felt;
> The night to be touched,
> The night not to be seen,
> The night of death.

The third period: of Light*

> From the nothing the begetting,
> From the nothing the increase,
> From the nothing the abundance,
> The power of increasing,
> The living breath;
> It dwelt with the empty space, and produced the
>   atmosphere which is above us,
> The atmosphere which floats above the earth.
> The great firmament above us dwelt with the early dawn,
> And the moon sprung forth;
> And the atmosphere above us dwelt with the heat.
> And thence proceeded the sun;
> They were thrown up above, as the chief eye of heaven:
> Then the Heavens became light,
> The early dawn, the early day,
> The mid-day. The blaze of day from the sky.

*During this period all was dark — no eyes.

The fourth period: of Land

> The sky above dwelt with Havaiki,
> And produced lands:
> Taporapora
> Tauwarenikau
> Kukuparu
> Wawau atea,
> Whiwhi te Rangiora...

The fifth period: of Gods

> Ru; and from Ru, Ouhoko;
> From Ouhoko, Ruatupu,
> From Ruatupu, Rua tawhito;
> From Rua tawhito, Rua kaipo;
> From Rua kaipo...&c.

The sixth period: of Men

> Ngae, and from Ngae, Ngae nui;
> From Ngae nui, Ngae roa;
> From Ngae roa, Ngae pea;
> From Ngae pea, Ngae tuturi;
> From Ngae tuturi, Ngae pepeke,
> Ko Tatiti, ko Ruatapu,
> Ko Toe, ko Ruatapu,
> Ko Toe, ko Rauru,
> Ko Tama rakeiora...&c.

Maheo   *Beginnings/Cheyenne/N. Amer. Indian*

In the beginning, Maheo, the Great Spirit lived in the nothingness that was. There was nothing to see, nothing to feel, nothing to hear.

Although Maheo was not lonesome he wondered what good is power if it is not used? He created a large body of salty water. Maheo knew this water contained life, all life.

"I will create beings to live in the water," he said. All manner of fish, shellfish and sea creatures swam in the water and rested on the muddy bottom. In the darkness Maheo could taste the salt and feel the cool water.

"I will create air beings to live on the water." And now there were birds swimming and living on the surface of the water. In the darkness Maheo could hear the birds spreading their wings and splashing in the water.

"Now I want to see what I have created," said Maheo. He watched the light begin to move from black to gray to gold until the light filled the world. Maheo looked and saw the great beauty all around him.

The birds came up to him and said, "We do not mean to complain but sometimes we get tired of swimming. Is it not possible for us to fly in the air?"

Maheo nodded and soon birds were flying.

One of the birds came back and said to Maheo, "We are not ungrateful for what you have given to us but when we are too tired to swim or fly, we would like to rest and build our nests on a dry, solid place.

Maheo agreed. "My power has made water, light, air and the peoples of the water. If I am to continue creation I must have your help."

The people of the water, in one voice said, "Tell us how we can be of help."

"One of you must find some land. Who among you wishes to try?" In turn, the biggest, the fastest and the smartest water birds tried. Each flew high into the sky, then dived down into the water's depths. They came back and brought nothing.

Then a little coot paddled up to Maheo and said, "Sometimes, when I swim down in the water I think I see something. May I try? I will do the best I can."

Maheo answered, "This is all anyone can do. Go with our blessings." The little coot gently dipped beneath the water surface and he was gone for a very long time. When he finally reappeared he swam toward Maheo without saying anything. As he reached the outstretched hand of Maheo, Coot opened his mouth. A small bit of mud dropped out of Coot's mouth onto the hand of Maheo.

Maheo smiled and said to Coot, "Go in peace little brother. You have done well." Maheo kneaded the little ball of mud until it began to grow. Soon there was more than Maheo could hold in his hand. He saw no place to put the mud. Once again he gathered the water peoples and said, "We must rest this mud on one of you. Who will offer?"

All of the water creatures came but none was strong enough to hold the mud. Only one person was left. Maheo said, "Grandmother Turtle you are very old yet there is none but you. Will you help us?"

Grandmother Turtle slowly swam to Maheo and waited calmly while he placed the mud on her strong back. The mud pile became a hill and soon Grandmother Turtle could be seen no more. Maheo gathered the others to him and said, "The earth is our Grandmother." Then he told his power, "Grandmother Earth shall be fruitful. Help me my power." Soon there appeared trees and grass and flowers and seeds. Maheo thought the Earth Woman the most beautiful of his creations.

"Earth Woman must not be alone," he said. "I will make her something from myself to let her know that I am near and that I love her." Soon Maheo created the first man and the first woman to live on Grand-mother Earth. After the first spring a child was born and soon there were many children.

Maheo put animals upon the earth to feed the people and to provide them with tools, shelter and clothing. Maheo is always with us. He is everywhere, watching his children and all of his creation.

The sacrifice to make the sun   *Beginnings/Nahua/Mexico*

There was no day, only darkness. The gods met to decide how to bring light
to the world. One god, Tecciztecatl, offered his services thinking that such
a task would be an easy thing to do. But the other gods thought differently
and looked around for a second volunteer. None of those assembled made
a move. Each in turn explained in great detail why such an offer could not
be forthcoming. Finally, all those assembled looked at the god who remained silent; a thin, scabby god to whom the others paid scant attention. They
said to the god, sitting quietly, covered with scabs, "You shall be the one to
help light the world." Honored, Nanautzin agreed.

The two gods spent four days in prayer and preparation. Tecciztecatl, a
proud god, offered brightly colored feathers instead of old, dead branches;
gold pebbles instead of hay, and thorns made of rare jewels to replace those
of the cactus. He offered red coral in the shape of thorns instead of thorns
dipped in blood followed by fine quality coral.

Nanautzin offered nine green reeds tied in bundles of three instead of old,
dead branches and hay and thorns dipped in his own blood. In place of coral he gave scabs from his own sores.

The other gods built a huge tower in which they prayed for four nights.
After the great fire had burned for four days, and after all the offerings had
been burned, the gods assembled in two lines on each side of the fire and
spoke to Tecciztecatl: "Tecciztecatl, jump into the fire." He made ready
to jump but the fire was huge and the heat was great. Four times the gods
spoke: "Tecciztecatl, jump into the fire." Four times Tecciztecatl tried
and failed.

It was decreed that no one might have more than four chances in which
to jump so the gods spoke again: "Nanautzin, jump into the fire." With all
the courage he possessed, he closed his eyes and thrust himself into the fire.
When Tecciztecatl saw the little scabby god's bravery he found the courage
he needed. He threw himself into the fire.

The poorest of the gods had shown the way. The Sun owed its life to the
great voluntary sacrifice.

The separation of God from Man *Beginnings/Togo/Africa*

In the beginning God and Mother Earth lived so close together that there was very little room to move about. God began to be annoyed when he was knocked on his thigh by a woman grinding with her pestle. In order to get away he had to go a little higher up. His annoyance increased when the smoke of the cooking fires hurt his eyes and he had to go still higher to get away from it. Much to his great irritation, in some places people used him as a towel to wipe their dirty hands. But the worst insult of all was when an old woman took a small bit of him each time she made soup. This forced him to go so high people could no longer touch him. From then on, all they could do was to look.

Beginnings - The Structures

Theme: BEGINNINGS
Focus: An exploration of "In the beginning"
Length: 50 minutes

Paint: A picture of a small part of the earth as it might have looked "in the beginning".

Paint: On a new sheet of paper paint a picture of a creature who inhabits this particular part of the earth and the place wherein the creature dwells.

Write: Describe this creature's first hesitant awareness of its environment using first person singular.

Share: The writings.

Discuss: The way in which these paintings and writings connect with your life experiences.

Reflect: On the entire session.

Theme: BEGINNINGS
Focus: An exploration of answers to the question, "How come?".
Length: 50 minutes

Write: A "how come" question in the style of: How come snails carry their houses on their backs? How come fish don't have legs? How come bananas are curved?

Collect: Questions and redistribute them.

Write: An answer to the question in story form explaining how it came to be that......

Share: The stories.

Reflect: On the patterns which emerge from the way answers have
              been given to the questions.

Text: MANTIS AND THE FLOWER
Focus: An exploration of endlessness and its opposite.
Length: 50 minutes

Paint: On one half of a sheet of paper create the image evoked by
              the word "endless". On the other half, the image of the word
              which you believe to be the opposite of endless.

Associate: Write down any words which you associate with these two
              words, endless and its opposite.

Divide: The group into two groups. One group will explore
              "endlessness", the other group will explore "limits".

Explore: Each group will find their own ways of playing with their
              word for five minutes. The groups then exchange words and
              explore the second theme for five minutes.

Tell: "Mantis and the flower."

Set up: An imaginary line in the room. Designate one end
              "endlessness", the other "limited".

Move: Each group member, one at a time, finds a place along the
              line which becomes a continuum from limited to endless-
              ness.

Tell: Each group member, one at a time, tells one effect that their
              choice of place on the continuum has on people and what
              people need to know and/or learn in order to make optimum
              use of this effect.

Share:	Any experiences evoked by participation.
Reflect:	Upon entire session.

Text:	MANTIS AND THE FLOWER
Focus:	An exploration of "silent time"
Length:	1 1/2 hours
Recall:	The means by which you woke up this morning and how you discovered what time it was.
Share:	Your experience.
NOTE:	From here on the group will work in silence.
ASK:	Group members to remove their watches and to place the watch before them. If necessary group members can share watches.
Look:	At the watch for two full minutes. Witness the passing of time.
Write:	As much as you can remember of what you thought during the two minutes.
Paint:	An image of TIME without painting images of clocks, or other time keeping devices.
Create:	In groups of 3, share your paintings (no talking) then on the basis of what you sense from the paintings, create in silence, using movement, a representation of your work. Move silently. (7 minutes)
Return:	To your watch and look at it for one minute only.
Write:	Again record what you can remember.

Share: With full group your writings.

Tell: "Mantis and the flower."

In pairs: Move in silence and present a movement exploration of the
            text to your partner.

Write: For three minutes about anything that comes to mind.
            (These remain private.)

Share: In large group any words which emerge from and relate to
            your experience.

Reflect: Upon the entire session.

Text: MANTIS AND THE FLOWER
Focus: An exploration of "moments of an encounter"
Length: 1 1/2 hours

Paint: A picture of a flower....the only flower.

Move: One by one, leave the circle.

Represent: In movement represent in some way the idea, a great emp-
            tiness. You can use objects if you so choose, but remove
            these before the next person starts.

Walk: Around the room avoiding eye contact. Become aware that
            your quiet solitary walking will be punctuated by moments
            of encounter.
            Witness what needs to change within you so that you may
            enable these moments to occur. Allow them to happen.

Return: To circle.

Paint:	Contemplate where on a large sheet of paper you will place two small dots. Paint the dots on the paper.
Tell:	"Mantis and the flower."
Look:	At your paintings of the only flower and the two dots.
Write:	At the top of the paper, the sentence, "So began Mantis, Maker of Fire, Keeper of the Dream". Add whatever else presents itself to you.
Read:	Your writings to the group.
Response-task:	While listening to the writings work with your paintings, adding whatever seems appropriate. Tell the one who has shared, what you have done.
Reflect:	Make connections between your various pieces of work, the text and your experience.

Text:	THE SHARED MYTH OF THE ONE THAT BECAME TWO
Focus:	An exploration of "inter-connectedness"
Length:	50 minutes
Move:	In a circle. One person initiates a movement, the others repeat it. Someone else initiates a new movement, the others repeat it until everyone has initiated a movement.
Move:	In pairs, without making any arrangements as to who leads or follows, experiment with: - shadowing your partner's movement; - mirroring your partner's movement; - amplifying/minimalizing partner's movement; - altering your partner's movement.

Return: To circle.

Tell: "The shared myth of the one that became two."

Write: One sentence from the story, as you remember it, which resonates within you. Think of a human situation which you can recount where you can end your telling by using your sentence. Write the story.

Sequence: The sentences in relation to their positions in the text.

Tell: The stories in this sequence.

Ponder: The material contained in the stories and their connection with the text.

Reflect: Upon entire session.

Text: THE SHARED MYTH OF THE ONE THAT BECAME TWO

Focus: An exploration of "I, you, they"

Length: 1 1/2 hours

Write: All the personal pronouns on a sheet of paper (I, you, he, she, it, we, you, they)

Design: On a new sheet of paper draw the personal pronouns in such a way as to clarify their relationship to one another, both through their relative positioning and the design of the writing.

Move: To a place someone in the room and settle the direction of your gaze. Do not establish eye contact with anyone. (Sit or stand.)

Speak: Softly, repeating the various personal pronouns without changing your body position. Experiment with altering the volume and pitch of your voice as you repeat the pronouns. Witness your feelings.

Move: Your head, neck and shoulders to free them.

Speak: The pronouns as you move and establish eye contact. Witness your feelings.

Move/speak: Feel free to move around the room and to be with or near other people while you speak. Explore what happens. Return to circle.

Tell: "The shared myth of the one that became two."

Sculpt: With clay around the theme "It is I" for 15 minutes.

Write: When you have finished sculpting take some paper and write about whatever comes up. (This will not be shared.)

Share: Bring your pronoun painting and sculpture into the circle. Reflect upon the experiences which the work evokes in you. Connect reflections with the text.

Reflect: Upon entire session.

Text: THE SHARED MYTH OF THE ONE THAT BECAME TWO
Focus: An exploration of uniting through separating
Length: 1 1/2 hours

Move: In a group to create the smallest possible group huddle. Freeze for a few seconds. Now create the largest possible group huddle maintaining only the lightest contact. Freeze for a few seconds.

Explore various ways to move from one huddle to the other (fast, slow, rolling, smooth, jumping, alone, in pairs etc.).

Write: Collectively, on a large sheet of paper, write down ANY words you choose.

Improvise: In groups of 3, create by yourself, a brief movement or drama improvisation around the following words: create, avoid, transform. These words are the only words to be used and may be repeatedly spoken aloud as part of the drama or movement.

Share: Improvisation with each other.

Tell: "The shared myth of the one that became two."

Write: A few thoughts that come to mind. These will not be shared.

Recall: Any memory that springs to mind at this moment.

Write: This memory.

Share: Memories.

Reflect: Upon entire session, making connections between your various experiences.

Text: CREATION
Focus: Moving through myth
Length: 50 minutes

Distribute: The text.

Read: The text aloud at least three times.

Divide:	Into small groups and choose one of the six sub-groups in the text with which to work. Each person will work with two periods (not necessarily sequential).
Discuss:	Each group has 10 minutes to discuss their part of the text.
Improvi-sation:	Each group has 10 minutes to prepare and rehearse an im-provisation (movement or drama). Each group will create a transition so that each group will share their work with no intervening directions or words and will create a transition for the sharing from one group to another. The last group creates the ending.
Share:	Improvisations.
Re-read:	The text at least three times.
Reflect:	Upon the session.

Text:	CREATION
Focus:	To look at the light within the dark
Length:	1 1/2 hours
Read:	The first two periods of the text.
Paint:	Group members choose one "night of a certain kind" as described in the Second Period of Darkness. On a long sheet of paper they each paint their image of this particular kind of night. Several members may choose the same image or finish more quickly than others.
Move:	To a circle around the painting.
Talk:	About what is evoked by the painting for each group member.

Write: For 5 minutes using whatever comes to mind. These writings remain private.

Sit: In pairs. Touch each other's hands. Establish eye contact.

Move: Slowly let your hands lead you into a dance. The dance may involve your whole body or only a part such as the head, arms or trunk. Complete your dance.

Look: Establish eye contact and carefully look at your partner. Notice the reflection of light which we all carry with us. Allow your partner to look for that which is light within you.

Distribute: The text.

Read: The text to the group.

Paint: A picture evoked by the text or a part of it.

Share: Whatever you wish to contribute.

Reflect: Upon entire session.

Text: CREATION
Focus: To dwell with distant glimmering
Length: 1 1/2 hours

Recall: A starry night.

Share: Your memories.

Respond: In one word to the question: "What made you notice this night sky?". Remind yourself of this word.

Paint: A painting which reflects this word.

Place:	Your painting somewhere in the room so others can see it.
Look:	At one another's paintings.
Write:	When you see a painting somewhere in the room find a sentence or a few words which seem to be evoked by the painting. Write the words, phrase or quote on a piece of paper and leave it near the painting.
Read:	The writings near your painting.
Arrange:	The writings into a seemingly meaningful pattern.
Read:	From the conception the increase.
Write:	Add whatever sentences you think necessary to make a complete text for your painting.
Read:	These texts.
Share:	Memories, feelings evoked by the texts.
Reflect:	Upon the entire session.

Text:	MAHEO
Focus:	In praise of quiet support
Length:	50 minutes
Tell:	Maheo
Distribute:	Copies of text to group members.
Reread:	The text.
Select:	A scene which creates a profound impression within you.

Paint: Your response to this particular moment.

Write: In five sentences or less, write a song of praise for one animal in the text.

Encourage: Group members to choose different animals, especially those who may not have played important or active roles but simply witnessed the attempts.

Read: Your writings.

Reflect: Upon entire session sharing what the work evoked within you.

Text: MAHEO
Focus: An exploration of response to creation.
Length: 1 1/2 hours

Recall: An experience of swimming or diving. If your experience was frightening remind yourself of the way in which you came through.

Write: About your experience.

Response-task: On a sheet of paper create as many spaces as there are group members. While listening to the memories being shared, draw/paint in each space an image of sky and water.

Share: Your memories.

Write: Word associations around the word "power".

Response-task: While you listen to the telling of the text feel free to doodle, write or draw.

Read:	The text.
Select:	On the basis of your doodles, writing or drawing select three key moments in the development of the story.
Paint/clay:	Create three images in paint or clay which represent these three moments.
Introduce:	Your unit of three images to the group.
Response-task:	Consider your "water and sky" response paintings. Add whatever feels appropriate after you have listened to each group member.
Share:	Whatever comes to mind about why you made these additions.
Reflect:	Upon entire session.

Text:	MAHEO
Focus:	An exploration of "I need your help".
Length:	1 1/2 hours
Write:	At the bottom of a page the sentence:I need your help.
Write:	On a new sheet of paper record all the feelings you might experience were it you who spoke these words.
Response-task:	Create as many small pieces of paper as there are people in the group. When a group member has read his/her writing make a small (symbolic) gift for the one who needs help.
Read:	The writings.

Look: At the gifts.

Read: The text of "Maheo" up to the point "A small bit of mud dropped out of coot's mouth onto the hand of Maheo".

Write: What happened to Coot on the journey to find the mud.

Read/Share: The stories without comment.

Read: The rest of the text.

Look: At the gifts given earlier.

Select: One that feels pertinent at this moment.

Share: Choice with group.

Reflect: Upon entire session making connections between the different areas of the work.

Text: THE SACRIFICE TO MAKE THE SUN
Focus: An exploration of letting go
Length: 50 minutes

Move: Go and stand near a table, chair or wall. Touch it. Change your touch into holding onto. Hold on as if it were a matter of life or death. Now let go.

             Repeat the process somewhere else in the room with another object. Stand, sit or lie.

Move: In pairs, stand near partner. Establish fingertip contact. Take each other on a walk which begins slowly but gradually increases in tempo. Maintain only fingertip contact. Prepare to let go.

Witness your preparation and then let go.

Repeat experience with new partner using eye contact only. Again prepare and witness letting go.

Write: The words "holding on" and "letting go" on top of a sheet of paper.

Response-task: Place a crayon or felt tipped pen somewhere on this sheet of paper and draw or doodle without lifting crayon or felt tipped pen off the paper.

Read: The text.

Draw: Complete your drawing/painting in whatever way you desire.

Reflect: Upon entire session sharing feelings and/or thoughts evoked by work.

Text: THE SACRIFICE TO MAKE THE SUN
Focus: Reflections on sacrifice
Length: 1 1/2 hours

List: Any words which come to mind in relation to the word "sacrifice".

Write: Complete the sentence: Sacrifice requires...

Paint: Create a group painting involving whatever these words evoke.
Work without comment.

Select: One word from list.

Write: The word on your paper in as many ways as you can. Then use at least five of the other words and incorporate them into sentences which you write down on the same sheet of paper.

Present: Your writings to the group in a manner which reflects your content.

Tell: The text.

Return: To the group painting.

Share: The material evoked by the individual presentations, the group painting and the story.

Reflect: On entire session.

Text: THE SACRIFICE TO MAKE THE SUN
Focus: An exploration of "I can't go first".
Length: 1 1/2 hours

Recall: A time in your life when you did not dare or wish to do something. Then, when someone else did go, you followed the example.

Write: About the memory.

Response-task: Create as many spaces on a sheet of paper as there are group members. When a group member shares her/his story write in each space one word which suggests what you imagine might have prevented the person from taking the initiative (pride, fear etc.).

Share: Memories. If wanted, feed back to the memory teller what you perceive.

74

Select: One or two of the "initiative-stoppers".

Improvise: With a partner a brief presentation called: "The different faces of....." (prudence, fear etc.) Use both partner's words.

Present: Your improvisations.

Tell: The text.

Talk: With partner about the text and its relationship with your presentation.

Reflect: With full group on any thoughts and feelings which arise from the work as well as on the entire session.

Text: THE SEPARATION OF GOD FROM MAN
Focus: An exploration of irritability
Length: 50 minutes

Tell: "The separation of God from Man."

Paint: An image of the word "irritation".

Write: A list of several things which irritate you in a minor way. Record at least 6 or 7.

Move: Each group member in turn mimes one personal irritation. The group says what they think is being presented.

Interview: A person for 2 minutes. Ask about irritating habits he/she might have. Partner can only answer yes or no. Reverse roles.

Draw: On a sheet of paper a small representation of the various irritating habits your partner has admitted to.

Write:	On a separate piece of paper a one sentence statement in praise of irritating habits.
Share:	Representations with partner.
Reflect:	On entire session.

Text:	THE SEPARATION OF GOD FROM MAN
Focus:	An exploration of: "So you want space?".
Length:	1 1/2 hours
Draw:	An area in the place where you live which is overcrowded.
Draw:	A picture of what this area would look like were it to be well organized.
Walk:	Around the room. At first use the entire space then restrict yourself to less and less space. Begin to bump (gently) into other people without apologizing or commenting. Continue walking until you are physically unable to move.
Move:	Away from this tight group of people. Go and sit with your back against a wall and look at the others. Register what this feels like.
Write:	About some thoughts and memories which come to mind as you did these activities.
Response-task:	Look at everyone's drawings. For each drawing write one statement which you remember or imagine has been said by people in positions of authority about the situation represented in each drawing. Leave these statements near each drawing.
Read:	The statements which have been left near your drawing.

Select:	One or two which are relevant at this time.
Share:	With the group reasons for choice.
Tell:	The text.
Paint:	An image evoked by the word "mingle".
Share:	Paintings.
Reflect:	Upon entire session.

Text:	THE SEPARATION OF GOD FROM MAN
Focus:	An exploration of "withdrawal is the only answer".
Length:	1 1/2 hours
Paint:	Image evoked by the word "withdrawal". Use only half a page.
Write:	About various situations in which you notice you withdraw.
Drama:	In groups of two or three design a dramatic situation in which one person is left with few other choices than to withdraw.
	Rehearse and work out other possible behavioral options.
Share:	Improvisations.
Write:	Briefly about your experience during the improvisation.
Tell:	The text.
Reflect:	Upon similarities between God and Man's responses and the improvisations.

Read: Your writings.

Paint: Rework your withdrawal painting in any way that seems appropriate.

Share: Some thoughts about this process (reworking the painting) with the group.

Reflect: Upon entire session.

Questions focusing on beginnings

1. How do you explain the beginning of the world?
    How did you come to make this decision?

2. What part do you play in the creation of your own life?
    How much do you think/feel you are in charge of your life.
    Who (what) affects this? How?

3. What do you see as the most important aspect(s) of beginnings?

4. What stories of creation were told to you as a child?
    Who told them to you? Under what circumstances?

5. If you have children, how do (did) you explain the creation of the
    world to them?

6. What stories explaining the birth process were you told as a child?
    How old were you when you discovered how babies are born?
    How did this information affect you?
    If you have children, how did you explain the process of birth to
    them?

7. Have you ever thought there was a time when you gave birth to
    yourself, a new self, different from your old self?
    What were the conditions precipitating the rebirth?
    How did you experience the rebirth?
    Who and/or what helped the process?

8. What words do you associate with the process of creation?
    How do these words connect with you? With your work?
    What feelings do you associate with the process of creation?
    Do these feelings ever change? Under what circumstances?

9. Have you ever been called creative or uncreative?
    How did this affect you?
    How did the labeling come to exist?
    What are your options in regard to current labeling?

10. Given the notion of inner and outer space, how do you go about their creation/recreation?

11. What have you created for yourself.

12. What have you created which exists independently of you?

13. If you could create anything or anyone, what would you create? How would you do this? If a place, would you share it? For how long would you like to remain?

CHAPTER FOUR

PASSAGES

This too shall pass. The words can be spoken with urgency, with more than an overtone of despair. When the pain is nearly unendurable, we long for the realization that life cannot remain like this forever, that change is the essence of life. This too must pass.

But there are other occasions, when our souls are touched with light, with delight. Then, the utterance of the statement, this too shall pass, bears witness to our wish to hold on to the moment and heralds the awareness of the unavoidable reality of change. Then, we can experience a sudden and seemingly unpredictable sadness, in the midst of pleasure and love, when we recognize that this too will pass. We cling to our hope that there is a promise of lighter times when the pain is severe, yet this hope becomes our nostalgia as we long for the continuation of delight.

The passing and the constant confront us whenever we stop and reflect upon our experience, on the events of our life. "Plus ça change, plus c'est la même chose." (The more it changes, the more it stays the same.) Is this what we perceive when we allow our thought to move beyond the here and now of the moment, into the there and then of the life we lived, the lives others lived before and around us?

We can attempt to decipher what is constant within the changing, try to discern patterns where we seem to be confronted with a chaotic profusion of impressions and experiences. The closer we look, the greater the intimacy, the less we see. We feel the moment and the intensity and there is no place for thought. The supremacy of feeling envelops and surrounds us. Tomorrow ceases to exist simply because it does not exist. Yesterday has long since departed to wherever it belongs. All we know and feel is expressed and manifested solely in the present, the one reality we can wholly experience, when we identify with it.

The statement, "This too shall pass," indicates a sense of distance, a temporary loosening of the ties between us and our experience. Identification ceases and reflection begins. In the space thus created tomorrow and yesterday become possibilities, almost tangible realities. Time starts to open up and pulsate in our awareness of passage. Whether we conceive of the passing of seasons as an eternal dance without beginning, end or purpose, the continuing repetition of patterns, the apparent change of the inherently changeless, or as a linear or spiral journey towards an ultimate culmination, the essence of the awareness of before and after is that space is created which allows for the birth of consciousness.

There are many times in our lives when we simply exist. Not just because of the intensity of our involvement with the events of our lives, but because we do not raise our awareness to the level of reflection. We are, and in so far that we are, we are capable of thought and of perspective beyond the immediate moment. Although our thinking may carry us beyond the present to preparations for tomorrow or thoughts about past choices, an essential component of reflection is missing. This is the quality of overview which comprises and embraces past, present and future.

When we reflect upon the events of our lives, we not only register what has occurred or is likely to happen, we engage in this process for the purpose of evaluation. We take stock in order to prepare our books. We describe income and expenditure and explore cost/benefit ratios so that we will be able to work out a balance sheet, thereby creating the possibility of a realistic assessment of our current situation in terms of both past and present. We acquire the ability to prognose for the future. Our course may remain unaltered or we may decide to change directions, to embark on a totally different journey. Thus, reflection is not a passive process. It is an active engagement in the experience of bringing into consciousness the happenings of our lives, our dreams, abilities and motivations, with all the constraints and limitations we have encountered up to now.

Meanwhile, the sun, moon and stars move along their paths; the seasons come and go. Our attempts to reflect will encompass the constant, continuous movement of time, despite us and beyond us, even as we try to come to terms with our own individual journey through life, with and along the passage of time.

Although the joy of identification with the moment or the sheer drudgery of repetitive tasks can absorb to such an extent that we cease to reflect, there are times in our lives when, willingly or not, prepared or not, we are jolted into a realization of the passage of time and are lifted into reflection and an overview. These moments are our turning points. We are offered the opportunity to pay attention to the occurrences and quality of our lives, to think about all we hope(d) for and hold dear.

Turning points are inherently connected to life. We develop from child and adolescent into an adult. We expect to grow up, to enter old age and then to face the end of life. Yet the final task, the facing of death, can present itself at any point along our journey. It is possible for us hardly to note the inner changes which occur as we grow up and become old. No internal markers need remind us that the process of ageing is taking place. We may continue to feel a never changing "I" although embodied in an ageing skin which does bear witness to the passing of time. Regardless of our outside, inside we may feel as if untouched by the occurrences of our life.

Then, one day, an event will penetrate our slumbering core and raise our awareness of the process of growing up and ageing. At this moment, the never changing eternal child beholds the events of its life. Reflection begins unless the internal eternal one decides that the flux of awareness is too great, too painful, and it returns to the silent, unobservant, everbeing essence of the core. The external changes occur but the inside continues to remain innocent to its impact.

In time, another turning point will present itself for change is happening perhaps as much despite us as because of us. Once again a choice is made. In this way it may be possible to move from turning point to turning point and never to be affected by any. The events of such a life can be many but few its transformations.

What happens if the slumbering core is awakened and we do realize that what was will never be again, that tomorrow will never be as we had hoped? What occurs when we understand that we hold within our clumsy hands only and ultimately no more than the fragile awareness of a tenacious present?

We mourn and celebrate, separate and unite, consume and digest. Finally, we return to live once more within the ordinary, accepted and unquestioned rhythm of our life. We continue, but it is a continuation which is characterized by containment. We embrace the passing and the constant, the temporary and eternal, the tone and tune, the pulse and rhythm.

In the process of mourning and celebrating, of separating and uniting, of consuming and digesting, we internalize the external, affirm the obvious, and transform our slumbering non-consenting core into an essence which lives within. We become aware that passage can be experienced as blessing and/or curse, but that beyond the temporal we encounter the eternal, beyond the fleeting, the permanent. However this permanence and eternity are not separate realities existing outside the influence of the changing. Here the changing is both essence and expression of what is. Becoming is the ever possible quality of being.

When we encounter the timeless and time-bound in the myths and tales collected in this section, we journey with the emotions and experiences of mankind. At times we live reluctantly, some times abundantly. Even as we wish to hide from danger we may courageously prepare to face what can be struggled with in order to overcome fear, indolence or carelessness. We will see turning points which are ignored, or used and then discarded, or integrated and allowed to exercise influence and to touch the innermost of innermost — the deepest layers of being.

The Stories

How man was made again   *Passages/Crow/N. Amer. Indian*

Crow and Raven flew up to the highest branch of a tall fir tree to have a talk. Crow said, "Grizzly Bear ate up all the Real People who used to live here and Great One hasn't made any more. I think we need to have Real People in this world. We must do something about this."

Raven agreed, "Let us call a council and then fly up to Sun to ask his advice." That noon they met with Sun who told them how Great One made the red man. With Sun's information, Raven and Crow went to the Council.

All the animals came and sat in a half circle as they had taught the Real People to do. Cougar, the first to speak said, "Real People should have a voice like mine and strong teeth. They should have sharp claws and be covered with fur, just as I am."

Grizzly laughed, "You are foolish. Real People don't need to shriek the way you do. They need to have four legs or wings." Some of the animals started to say how they thought Real People should be but Grizzly paid no attention to them. "Real People need to be very strong and to move quietly so they can kill without warning their prey." When the animals disagreed Grizzly shouted at them, "I know what Real People need. Didn't I eat up them all up?"

Deer, normally very soft spoken, said in a rather loud voice, "For goodness sake, Real People don't need shrieking voices or sharp claws. What they need are antlers and soft ears which help them to hear the smallest sound."

Mountain Sheep disagreed. "Antlers would be a nuisance in the brush. Real People need horns like mine so they can butt down their attackers."

Owl ignored Deer and Mountain Sheep and said, "I agree with Grizzly. Real People should have wings."

Mole, greatly upset, said, "It's useless for Real People to have wings. If they had wings they might bump into the sun and burn. Real People need to live in the earth where it's cozy and comfortable."

Coyote finally stood up and everyone stopped talking to listen to his words of wisdom. "You have all been talking foolishly. Real People need loud voices but they don't need to shriek like Cougar. Fish have no fur and they get along very well. I'm not at all sure that Real People need four legs or to live in the earth. Real People do need to hold things and to have keen eyes like Eagle's but...."

All of a sudden everyone started talking at once. No one listened to anybody. Not even Coyote could get the meeting back to order. Fox could not stand the noise and shouted, "Enough of this screaming. Everyone get some clay and make a model of how you think Real People should look."

All the animals agreed. They rushed down to the river bank to find the best clay. They worked on their models through dinner and far into the night. By the time they were finished they were so tired they left their creations where they were and fell asleep. Only wise Coyote took care. He put his model on a protected branch. That night it rained. In the morning Sun looked for a model to bake and found just one. Only Coyote's model survived the rain.

When the Animal People awoke, there was Coyote's model walking around. Grizzly saw him and moaned, "Oh no, he has only two legs."

Beaver complained, "He has no tail."

Fox snorted, "He has no fur."

All the animals found fault. Raven and Crow decided they needed to tell Great One how upset everyone was with Coyote's model. They wrote a note explaining everything and then gave it to Eagle. He flew up to the highest cloud and left the letter thinking Great One would be sure to see it here.

That night, Great One read the note and decided to act. He looked at Coyote's model and made some changes. He also taught him to defend himself against Grizzly.

Great One was finished. Yet the animals wondered: how will Real People survive with no wings, no tail, no sharp claws, no loud voice and no fur?

The maiden wiser than the Tsar   *Passages/Serbia*

Once upon a time there lived a maiden who was wiser and more knowledgeable than anyone could possibly imagine. When her father went to the Tsar's palace to beg for some food and money, the Tsar was amazed at his manner of speech. "Where have you learned to talk as you do?" asked the Tsar.

"From my daughter, your majesty," replied the man, humbly.

"How is this possible?" asked the Tsar?

"Necessity and experience have been her teachers," answered the man.

The Tsar gave the man food and money and said, "Ask your daughter to hatch these eggs. If she is successful I will give you fine gifts but if she cannot do it, I will punish both of you."

In despair, the man went home and told his daughter what had happened. She took the eggs, weighed them and realized they were all hard boiled. She said to her father, "Go to sleep, I will think of something."

The next morning she gave her father some beans which she had boiled. She said to him, "Take the plough and oxen and work in the field next to the road where the Tsar is sure to pass. When he is within hearing distance, call out, "Oxen, plough this land so that my boiled beans will grow." Then she told him what he must say next.

All happened as she predicted. The Tsar passed by and hearing what the man shouted, asked, "Silly man, how can you expect boiled beans to grow?"

The man answered simply, "In the same way boiled eggs can produce chickens." The Tsar laughed at the way the girl had found to outwit him.

The poor man went home, relieved that he and his daughter had been spared the Tsar's punishment. But the next day, the Tsar sent a messenger with a bundle of flax. The messenger told the maiden that she must spin it into sails for the Tsar's ships. The poor man wept but his daughter said, "Go to sleep father, I will think of something."

Just after the first cock crowed, she put a small block of wood into his hands. "Tell the Tsar, I will make his sails when he carves all the tools I need from this block of wood."

The Tsar was impressed by the girl's answer but said, "Take this glass and ask your daughter to empty the oceans into it that I may have a larger kingdom." The father went home burdened by the thought of another impossible task for his daughter. "Go to sleep father, I will think of something," she comforted him.

The next day the father gave her message to the Tsar. "My daughter says that she will empty the oceans if you will dam up all the rivers in the world with this bit of clay."

The Tsar, hearing her answer, realized that she was even wiser than himself. He ordered her brought to court. In her presence he asked his courtiers what his beard was worth. Each courtier valued it more than the one before, hoping to impress the Tsar. Then he turned to the maiden who answered easily, "A keg of salt."

The Tsar was pleased and said, "You have answered correctly. Food without salt is food without taste. You will be my wife and we shall be married today."

After the wedding was over, the maiden said, "I have one request to make of you my husband. If you or someone in your court should look upon me with disfavor, I ask that I be allowed to take with me the one thing that I value most." The Tsar, deeply in love with his new wife, signed the agreement in the presence of his ministers.

The Tsar and Tsarina lived in peace for many years. Then, one day, the Tsar became angry at his wife and ordered her to leave the palace forever. The Tsarina asked if she might remain in the palace for the night, promising to be gone by early morning. The Tsar agreed.

When he went to bed she fixed his evening tea as usual but this night she poured a sleeping potion into it. As soon as the Tsar fell asleep she had him taken to her father's house.

When the Tsar awoke in the poor man's hut the next morning he was outraged and yelled, "What has happened? Why am I here?"

The Tsarina answered sweetly, "Here is the document you signed when we were married. You agreed that if I had to leave I might take with me the one thing I valued most. You are all I desire. I am willing to risk my life to show you the depth of my love." The Tsar roared with laughter and took her back to his palace where they lived together for the rest of their lives.

The Serpent Slayer   *Passages/China*

In China, a very long time ago, there lived a huge serpent, too big to measure. It dwelt in a cave on the side of Yung-Ling mountain. The serpent was always hungry and ate any bird, beast, animal or man it could find. All of the villagers living near the side of Yung-Ling mountain were frightened. Desperate, they asked their village magistrate to rid the village of the serpent.

The magistrate could not think of a solution so he hired a sorceress to help him solve the problem. The sorceress told the magistrate to deliver ten oxen and twenty sheep to the mouth of the cave every day. However, as soon as the animals smelled the terrible stench of the serpent they ran away. The marauding continued and the villagers grew more upset. They threatened to go to the King. The magistrate went once more to the sorceress and begged for a way to rid the village of the serpent.

She told him, "You must find a healthy maiden of 14 years. On the first day of the eight month of each year she must be delivered to the serpent. Only then will the plundering cease."

The magistrate was not pleased with the thought of having to find a maiden to feed to the serpent each year. However losing one 14 year old girl seemed a small price to buy the village peace from the dangerous serpent.

For nine years a healthy maiden of 14 years was delivered to the serpent on the first day of the eight month. If, by chance, the serpent ate a sheep or an ox, the magistrate gave the villager a new animal which he bought from money given to him as bribes from rich families who paid to protect their daughters from being taken.

In the tenth year, an eldest daughter of a very poor family gathered her parents and sisters around her and said, "We have no food or money. There are no sons to take care of you in your old age. This year I will go to the serpent. In exchange, I will ask the magistrate to see that you have money to buy food and seed enough to last your lifetime." Her family refused to let her go but the girl, Li Chi, insisted this was the only way to end their suffering.

Li Chi decided on a plan and then went to the magistrate to ask for what she needed. In addition, she petitioned that her services be exchanged for money for her family. The magistrate was relieved not to have to search for a maiden and agreed to her requests.

On the first day of the eight month, after making sure the magistrate paid her family, Li Chi went up to the side of Yung-Ling mountain, taking with her a sword, a hunting dog, flint and food.

Although Li Chi was not sure of the way, she and the dog knew they had arrived when they smelled the terrible stench of the serpent. Quickly, she made a fire, cooked the food and positioned the dog. Soon a delicious smell filled the cave and woke the sleeping beast.

Li Chi and the dog stood near the fire, terrified at the sight and smell of the fearful serpent but they did not run away. Just as the beast was about to strike, they rushed to the other side of the fire and the serpent fell into it. The serpent screamed in pain. Ignoring the dreadful sounds, the dog leapt at the beast and bit out its eyes. The serpent rose in agony and Li Chi raised her sword and cut off its head, stabbing the beast over and over until, at last, the serpent was dead.

Li Chi went into the cave and found the small bones of the nine 14 year old maidens who had sacrificed their lives to save the villagers. Lovingly and tenderly, she wrapped them up to take back down to the village for proper burial.

When she returned there was great disbelief at first. Then, after hearing her story and seeing the bones, the villagers rejoiced and held a huge celebration in her honor. When the King heard of her deed, he invited her to his palace and bequeathed her mother and sisters many fine presents. He made her father a governor and asked for Li Chi's hand in marriage.

The villagers never forgot how Li Chi saved them from the terrible serpent. They told all who passed through of her courage and cunning. Her story became a ballad, the Song of Li-Chi the Serpent Slayer and is still sung, even today, in the village near the cave on the side of Yung-Ling mountain.

The knowledge of the birds   *Passages/Cheyenne/N. American Indian*

There was once a mother and daughter who lived together in a lodge. The daughter cried angrily because her mother refused to let her go out at night. Finally, the mother could no longer listen to her daughter's arguments and picked her up and put her outside.

"Stay out if you must. The owls can have you if they want you." Outside the lodge, perched in a tree, sat an owl, waiting for a small animal to come along. When he saw the girl he flew down, grabbed her with his sharp claws and carried her to his lodge as a present for his old grandfather.

The old grandfather was delighted with his present and told the girl to sleep in a corner. When the sun rose, the girl was told to make herself useful, to collect sticks and branches for a fire. As she worked, a little sparrow told the girl that the fire would be used to cook her. Frightened, she ran back to the owl's lodge; she knew no other place.

The owl said, "That is not enough wood. Go out and get some more." The little girl went out and this time was warned by a flycatcher. Once again she ran back to the owl's lodge and once again they sent her forth to gather more wood. She was sent out for a third time and was once more warned by a bird that the owls intended to eat her. She quickly ran back to the lodge only to be immediately sent out by the owls.

A red tailed hawk came up to her and said, "This is the last time we will warn you. The owls plan to eat you."

The little girl asked, "What shall I do? Where can I go?"

The hawk told her to get on his back and said, "I will take you to a safe place. Then I will tell you what to do." When they arrived, she came to a rock and spoke as the hawk bade her.

"My hawk grandfather, I have come to you for protection. My hawk father, I have come to you for protection. My hawk brother, I have come to you for protection. My hawk husband, I have come to you for protection." She heard a voice which assured her of safety as a large rock rolled away revealing a large cave. She timidly entered as the rock rolled back into place.

When the girl did not return, the old owl knew the hawks had helped her to escape. He flew to the mountain, stopping and hooting three times. Each hoot shook the earth. The fourth time he hooted just outside the hawk's cave. The girl became terrified as she heard the owl cry, "If you don't bring out my meat I will come in and take it."

The hawk grandfather told the girl to open the door just enough to let the owl's head in. As soon as the head appeared, the girl slammed the rock back in place and cut off the owl's head. Following the hawk grand-father's instructions, she used a stick to move the head out of the lodge. Then she was told to gather a large pile of sticks. The girl and the hawk grandfather made a huge fire and rolled the head and the body into the flames. As the owl burned, many pretty things rolled out. The girl wanted to keep them but the hawk grandfather made her use a stick to throw every-thing back into the fire.

They went back to the lodge where the girl stayed until she was grown up. One day, she asked the hawks to help her return to her own people. They agreed to do so but told her if she wanted to have a safe homecoming she must do exactly as they told her. The grandfather made her a red robe and told her to make a boy's leggings and moccasins. The grandfather made her a fine bow and put animal tails onto her moccasins to erase her tracks. When he painted her face red and tied a skin on her forehead, she was dress-ed, not as a girl, but as a great warrior.

Upon leaving, the hawk grandfather gave her a mink to keep inside her robe. "Do not let it go," he said. "Pass the first four villages as you travel. On the evening of the fourth day you will face your greatest danger. You will be offered food by an old woman. Give it to the mink. Then you will be of-fered buffalo meat and that will be safe for you to eat. Keep the mink with you until the old lady who has fed you, threatens you. Then let the mink go."

All happened as the hawk grandfather foretold. The girl fed the first bowl of food to the mink and ate the buffalo meat. Then the old woman said, "You must be tired my grandson. Lie down and rest." She fixed the girl a place to sleep on the men's side and then pretended to fall asleep. When the old woman thought it was safe, she sat by the fire and scratched her leg until it grew into a giant club. As she started to beat the girl to death the girl let the mink out of her robe. The mink bit a chunk out of the old woman's leg and she fell down screaming, "You have killed me."

When the girl saw that the old woman was dead she slept until sunrise. The next morning she travelled until she came to her own village. Everyone came to see the handsome stranger but the girl hung her head down saying, "I am the bad child whose mother put her outside the lodge. I was taken by the owls and had a terrible time but now I have returned."

Her mother came to her with tears in her eyes and each forgave the other. A young man asked if he could wear the kind of clothes that she was wear-ing. The girl thought for a moment and then said, "Yes, but because I am a woman dressed as a man you must also do as you are not. In a battle, if you are told to go forward, go backward instead." This is how the great reputation of the Cheyenne warriors began.

The wooden head   *Passages/Maori/New Zealand*

High upon a towering hill called the Sacred Mount lived two sorcerers, Puarata and Tautohito. They were protected by their carved wooden head which had the power to kill anyone who dared to approach their sacred fortress. News of the wooden head spread to every part of New Zealand. Many people came to try to destroy the powers of the two sorcerers in order to steal the wooden head for themselves. But the loud wail of the head killed anyone who came within its range, even those who innocently wandered along the forest path. Whether people came with large, well-fortified armies or in small peaceful groups, no person came near the fortress and survived.

Eventually, word of the power of the wooden head reached the ears of Hakawau, a powerful sorcerer. He gathered all of his good genii around him and put himself into an enchanted sleep to learn if his magic was strong enough to defeat that of the two old sorcerers possessing the wooden head. He woke, satisfied, and resolved to go immediately to the Sacred Mount. He took with him one friend who was willing to accompany him on this dangerous mission.

They travelled for many miles along the sea coast until they came to a fortified village. Here, people tried to detain them, offering the two friends food and rest. Hakawau refused, saying, "We have just eaten and rested. We are neither tired nor hungry." Saying this, they continued on their way.

When they arrived in the next village the friend began to worry. "I am sure we will die in this place." But they walked safely to the last village before the fortress, the most dangerous village of all. Here they could smell the stench of those who had died. The smell was so terrible that Hakawau and his friend thought this might indeed be the end of both. Hakawau began to repeat his incantations to collect all his good genii around them that the good spirits might ward off any attack from the sorcerers' evil genii. The chanting kept them safe.

Despite their fears, they continued on their way until they came to a place near the Sacred Mount where they could rest without being seen by the watchmen of the fortress.

When he was rested, Hakawau, through his incantations, sent some of his good genii to begin the assault. The evil spirits guarding the fortress attacked the good genii who then pretended to retreat. The evil spirits followed, leaving the fortress unprotected. Hakawau repeated his chanting to send the rest of the good genii to kill any of the remaining spirits of the two old sorcerers.

When they were satisfied that all the evil genii were gone, the two friends climbed up toward the fortress, surprising the watchmen. Seeing this, Puarata hurried to his magic head to call upon it to destroy the two strangers. He chanted, "Two strangers come. Two strangers come. Two strangers come." But the head only moaned a soft, low sound. The good genii had destroyed all the evil genii and the head no longer had the power to destroy.

Meanwhile, Hakawau repeated his incantation as he and his friend climbed up the hill leading to the fortress. When they came to a place where the path divided, Hakawau said to his friend, "You take this path which goes by the gateway. I will show my power by climbing over the parapet and palisades."

When the people of the fortress saw Hakawau climbing, they were angered at his disrespect for the two sorcerers. They shouted angry words to which Hakawau paid no attention. Now he was sure that his magic was stronger than that of the two old sorcerers. Disregarding their screams, he went directly to the holy place open only to sacred persons.

Hakawau and his friend came together and rested for a short time. As they started to leave, the people of the fortress cooked food for them and asked that the two men stay to eat and rest. The two friends refused saying, "We have just eaten and rested. We are neither hungry or tired."

Hakawau said to his friend, "Let us leave immediately." As they left, Hakawau hit the threshold of the fortress. The two were barely outside its walls before every person left within, died.

Beauty and the beast   *Passages/Europe*

There was once a father who had three daughters, the youngest of whom was the prettiest and the kindest. The older two were concerned only with the way they looked and the wealth of their prospective husbands. One day, as the father was leaving to go away on business, he asked each daughter what present she wanted him to bring her back.

The oldest daughter said, "I would like to have a mirror which shows me to be the most beautiful woman in the world."

The middle daughter said, "I would like to have a diamond ring which shows me to be the richest woman in the world."

The youngest daughter said, "I would like to have a scarlet flower." Her two elder sisters laughed at her choice. Even her father asked her to choose a gift of greater value but the girl insisted on the scarlet flower.

At the end of his trip the father went to find the presents for his daughters. He quickly found the mirror and the ring but there was no scarlet flower to be had at any price. Discouraged, he began his journey home. En route, he got caught in a terrible storm and could no longer see to direct his horse. The horse, however, found its way to a magnificent but empty palace furnished with all that was fine and beautiful.

In the dining room a delicious meal was set for one. The father resisted the meal for as long as he could but hunger finally overcame his resistance. He ate slowly but soon consumed all that was before him. Comfortably full, he walked around the palace and came to a bedroom with the bed turned down, ready for use. The man was so tired he lay down and quickly fell asleep.

In the morning he awoke feeling refreshed and after eating a delicious breakfast, searched for his host. Finding no one about, he started on his way home through the garden. There, in the carefully tended gardens was a bush full of beautiful scarlet flowers. The man looked around but saw no people anywhere. He thought one flower would not be missed and took one scarlet blossom for his youngest daughter.

No sooner had he picked the flower when he heard a terrible roar. There in front of him was an ugly, ferocious beast. "How dare you treat me so? Have I not fed you? Have I not given you a bed on which to sleep? What is the reason for this outrage?"

The frightened man told the beast about his daughter's request for a scarlet flower and his failure to find one. "I did not think one flower would be missed," he apologized.

Beast said, "You must die for your crime unless your youngest daughter is willing to come and live with me of her own choice." The man was so anxious to see his family one more time that he agreed to let his daughter come. So saying this, he found himself at home.

His oldest two daughters gave him small thanks for their presents. Upon receiving the scarlet flower, his youngest daughter danced with delight until she noticed the pale face of her father. "What is wrong dear father?" she asked anxiously.

"It is well that you are pleased with your flower. I have bought it for a great price." He then told his youngest daughter, Beauty, all that had happened to him and his promise to the beast. Ashamed at having agreed to the bargain he said to her, "Do not go to save my life. I am old and tired and have lived long enough. I do not fear dying." Beauty ignored her father's words and willingly gave her promise to go to the beast.

In the morning, she set off for Beast's palace on a horse which suddenly appeared outside the door of the cottage. She arrived to find the palace seemingly empty yet everything appeared ready for her arrival and pleasure. Although there were instruments for her to play, books to read, and favorite foods to eat she saw and heard no one.

One day as she was sitting in the library reading she noticed questions appearing on a wall. Beauty answered them out loud, as if she had been spoken to, and then the writing disappeared as suddenly as it had come. After Beauty became accustomed to the writing she asked, "Who is it who writes? May we not talk together?"

The next afternoon when she was sitting in the garden near the scarlet flowers she loved, she heard a deep, male voice ask, "Do you need anything?" Startled, Beauty looked around but saw no one. She told the voice she was well content and then the voice faded away. So it was that each day she entered into conversation with an unknown, invisible person.

The conversations grew more lively and interesting each time they talked. One day, Beauty asked, "May we not talk in person? May I not see you?"

"No," answered the voice. "I am too ugly. I would frighten you so much that you would run away and I would die." Yet Beauty persisted. After many days of asking, the voice agreed to reveal himself. Suddenly, in front of Beauty there appeared a malformed, grotesque beast. In shock, Beauty fainted but recovered in time to see Beast slowly and sadly start to leave.

"Stop," she cried out. "Do not go. You are ugly, it is true, but you took me by surprise. I will soon become used to your looks." Comforted, Beast promised he would return the next day.

So it was that Beauty and Beast spent many delightful hours talking and making music. They grew to be good friends and Beauty was content in all ways save one. She missed her family. Reluctantly, Beast agreed to let her visit but told her she must return to him within three days. If she did not return of her own free will, he would die. Beauty promised and prepared for her visit to her family. The next morning she arrived at her home with trunks of presents and fine clothing.

Her sisters grew jealous when they saw all her finery and decided to change the clocks so Beauty would not know when the three days were up. They pretended to be fond of her and very pleased at her good fortune. Beauty, delighted to receive their affection, spent many happy hours with her father and sisters.

She did not forget her promise to the Beast and kept looking at the clocks to see if it was time to return. Although they showed she still had many hours left, Beauty began to grow uneasy. Finally, despite her sisters' entreaties that she had time and despite her father's words begging her to stay, Beauty left for the palace, worried though she knew not why.

She arrived to find Beast lying near the bush of scarlet flowers, dying. Beauty knelt down crying, "Do not die Beast. Please, do not die." As she embraced him, her tears fell on his face. The tears transformed the ugly beast who had been bewitched by an evil fairy into a handsome prince. The prince and Beauty embraced each other. The friendship she felt blossomed into love. They were married and lived happily ever after.

Passages - The Structures

Theme:	PASSAGES
Focus:	Crossing the threshold
Length:	50 minutes

Paint: Image of push on left side of paper.

Paint: Image of pull on right side of paper.

Write: Any words/sentences that comes to mind.

Paint: Image of threshold.

Write: One or two word answers to the following:
1. Who or what is placed before this threshold?
2. What is name of person/creature?
3. What is gender of person/creature?
4. What is this threshold?
5. Who or what is pushing from the other side?
6. How did the pushing and pulling begin?
7. How long has this been going on?
8. What is the outcome?
9. What happens to the threshold?

Paint: Image of outcome.

List: Any words/sentences that come to mind.

Share: Stories and images.

NOTE: Do not give person/creature same name as one's own. Each question must be answered.

Reflect: On common themes and how stories connect with people's experiences.

Theme: PASSAGES
Focus: Blessings in disguise
Length: 50 minutes

Remember: A time when something bad happened which turned out to have unexpectedly good results.

Paint: Image evoking beginning of experience.

List: Words that come to mind.

Write: Story of what happened.

Paint: Image evoked by end of story.

Share: Images and stories.

Paint: Blessing for oneself.

Paint: Blessing for person sitting to your right.

Share: Each group member in turn give blessing to person on right saying a few words about the gift.

Reflect: On how one recognizes a blessing in disguise, how meaning can be found in the midst of pain and struggle. Personal blessings can be shared if desired.

Text: HOW MAN WAS MADE AGAIN
Focus: An exploration of making and re-making
Length: 50 minutes

Sculpt: In 3 minutes sculpt out of clay or plasticine:
- something "useful";
- knead what you have made into a ball;
- something "unusual".

Give:	Give "unusual" sculpt to person sitting next to you. Knead what you have received into a ball. Hand ball back to person who gave you what they had just made.
Sculpt:	For 10 minutes make something which reflects/ represents the way you are feeling right now. This time you will not be asked to destroy or give it away.
Tell:	"How Man was Made Again."
Reflect:	Upon parallels between your own responses during the clay modelling part of the session and the behavior of the animals in the story.

Text:	HOW MAN WAS MADE AGAIN
Focus:	The relationship between preparation and problem-solving
Length:	1 1/2 hours
List:	As a group, typical difficulties/problems people encounter. Write each suggestion on a separate card. Have as many cards as there are people in the group.
Collect:	Cards.
Write:	For 2 minutes about whatever is evoked by the phrase, "be prepared".
Share:	The writings.
Mime:	In pairs, for 4 minutes. One person mimes a preparatory activity, the other describes what the preparation is for (e.g.cooking-eating, putting a stamp on an envelope-mailing it, dressing up - going out).
Tell:	How man was made again.

Distribute: One difficulty/problem card to each group member.

Tell: The text.

Write: How people can be prepared for this difficulty. What people need to learn in order to cope with this problem and how this learning could happen. Formulate an answer in relation to the particular difficulty on your card.

Share: In groups of 3, share with one another, difficulties/solutions.

Design: In same groups of 3, one simple activity which children could do which prepares them for these difficulties.

Try-out: Activities with the large group.

Reflect: Make connections between the story and how your group solved their task.

Text: HOW MAN WAS MADE AGAIN
Focus: An exploration of competition and conflict.
Length: 1 1/2 hours

List: Ways in which we compete and how we do it.

Drama: In groups of 3 or 4 improvise for 10 minutes around the theme of competition. Explore what reduces/increases competition and how it differs from conflict.

Share: Some of the improvisations.

Tell: "How Man was Made Again."

Ask:	Each group member to formulate in *one sentence,* a reason why the animals did not succeed in creating a model of man together.
Write:	A brief paragraph defending your case that this particular form of behavior lies at the root of most difficulties between people.
Share:	Paragraphs.
Reflect:	Make connections between the story, the declarations, the competition writings and the improvisations.

Text:	THE MAIDEN WISER THAN THE TSAR
Focus:	Keeping your wits about you
Length:	50 minutes

Write:	On a small piece of paper for 2 minutes, a real life situation which could be described by the phrase, "having one's back against the wall".
Collect:	Papers.
Re-distribute:	Papers.
Read:	Predicament described on paper.
Write:	A solution on a separate piece of paper.
Share:	With a partner the predicament you have been given.
Interview:	Partner for 2 minutes and ask questions that will elicit at least 3 solutions including those that may appear to be utterly unlikely. Reverse roles.

Re-read: Your written solution to predicament.

Design: A new solution which reflects the other ideas.

Identify: Difficulties which are likely to accompany this way of solving the predicament.

Rewrite: Original writing under new title of "How to keep your wits about you in a time of difficulty".

Share: Writings.

Tell: "The Maiden Wiser than the Tsar."

Reflect: Make connections between the writings and the story.

Text: THE MAIDEN WISER THAN THE TSAR
Focus: Feelings surrounding acquiesence
Length: 1 1/2 hours

Move: Imitate one another's movements in the style of "do as I do" for a few minutes.

Move: In pairs, standing opposite partner. One person take the other's hands and gently moves partner. Explore a range of movement possibilities. Be careful of partner. Reverse roles.

Move: Stand behind partner as close as possible without physical contact. The person in front moves, the one behind follows like a perfect double. The one in front tries to lose double but just when this seems likely, decides against this. Reverse roles.

Select: New partner.

Drama:	For 2 minutes explore "perfect agreement". A. begins "Do you remember when we.... B. "Yes, that was wonderful." A tries to find a way to make B. disagree with A but B never disagrees, always agrees. Reverse roles.
Paint:	An image of the way you feel right now.
Write:	For one minute about anything that comes to mind.
Tell:	"The Maiden Wiser than the Tsar."
Recall:	One phrase from the story which resonates.
Write:	This sentence at the top of a large sheet of paper.
Write:	This sentence at the bottom of the same piece of paper.
Write:	For 5 minutes write down whatever belongs in between. Fill the entire sheet with words.
Share:	Large page writings. Make connections between your writing, painting and drama.
Reflect:	Upon entire session.

Text:	THE MAIDEN WISER THAN THE TSAR
Focus:	Feelings evoked by "testing" experiences
Length:	1 1/2 hours
Paint:	Image of whatever is evoked within you by the word "test".
Interview:	In pairs, through questions and answers, find out which various tests you have experienced or undergone.

List: The tests.

Decide: Between you which 3 words represent how you mostly feel
                about having been tested.

Write: The 3 words on 3 separate small pieces of paper.

Collect: Papers.

Re-distribute: Papers. Each person takes only one.

Create: An empty space which group members can enter one by
                one. The first person to enter decides where to be, then
                speaks no more than a few sentences beginning with: "I am
                the feeling of…(e.g. trust, hopelessness etc.). To complete
                his/her participation person takes a posture evoking the feel-
                ing expressed. One by one the others follow until everyone
                has had a turn. Hold group sculpture for a few seconds. To
                end freeze first person makes statement about what this feel-
                ing offers a person then moves out of space. Each group
                member repeats this sequence until space is empty.

Write: For 3 minutes whatever comes to mind. These writings will
                remain private.

Tell: "The Maiden Wiser than the Tsar."

Share: In groups of 3, experiences which are equivalent of
                "needing to sleep on it".

Improvise: In same groups of 3, around the theme "test/rest" which
                will convey to other group members some of your ex-
                perience/knowledge.
                Maintain eye contact while improvising.

Re-read:	What you wrote immediately after the group sculpture.
Write:	Whatever you choose to add.
Reflect:	Upon connections between you, the painting, the various writings, experiences and the story, and the unused papers describing how you feel about having been tested.

Text:	THE SERPENT SLAYER
Focus:	An exploration of prevention, help and the combat of danger
Length:	50 minutes
Recall/write:	An experience when you felt/were helped by an animal.
Response-task:	Create as many spaces on a piece of paper as there are members in the group. While listening to the recalling of experiences ask yourself how you can characterize the kind of help given by the animals (e.g. comfort, fun, companionship). Within the space allotted, for each group member, create a small symbol which represents this characteristic.
Share:	These experiences.
Feedback:	Share with the group member who shared his or her experience what you have chosen to represent.
Tell:	"Li Chi the Serpent Slayer."
Ask:	Group members to collect their handbags and to choose a partner.
Explore:	Encourage group members to empty their purses as well as the pockets of their clothing.

Share:	With partner the potential preventative function any of these objects might have (e.g.comb to keep hair from becoming untidy, aspirin to prevent pain from getting worse).
Reflect:	Talk about the links between prevention and help and the combat of danger.

Text:	THE SERPENT SLAYER
Focus:	An exploration of fear and courage
Length:	1 1/2 hours

Write:	Word associations around the words fear and courage.
Write:	About an experience when you were frightened and needed courage.
Share:	Experiences and word associations.
Reflect:	Upon what gives you courage.
Write:	One sentence only which expresses something important in relation to what gives you courage. (e.g. Do not desert me. I never want to forget my strength.)
List:	These sentences.
Tell:	"Li Chi the Serpent Slayer."
Im-provisation:	In groups of 3 find a way of representing the text using the sentences listed in any order preferred.
Share:	The enacted representations of the text.
Reflect:	On connections between the story and the writings evoked by the words fear and courage.

Text:	THE SERPENT SLAYER
Focus:	The various characteristics and consequences of threatening behavior
Length:	1 1/2 hours

Paint: Image evoked by the verb to threaten.

List: Familiar threats made by people you know.

Discuss: In pairs why these threats are powerful and what makes them useful.

Move: Create individual statues of a threatening posture and explore where in the body the threat is located. Experiment with minimum and maximum force.

Sound: In pairs adopt mutually threatening postures. Experiment with adding threatening sounds while keeping body frozen. Explore the effect of closing your eyes while making the threatening sounds.
Unfreeze.

Share: Feelings experienced during these activities.

Tell: "Li Chi the Serpent Slayer."

Write: A few sentences which will be the text for a memorial plaque commemorating her deed.

Read: These texts.

Reflect: Upon the connections between the story and the role of familiar threats. Consider the memorial plaque texts.

Text: THE KNOWLEDGE OF THE BIRDS
Focus: Response to advice
Length: 50 minutes

Paint: Image evoked by word "expectation".

Write: A common piece of advice such as: "Don't accept candy from strangers."

Collect: Advice.

Re-distribute: Advice.

Write: A one page statement. Argue why this is bad advice.

Present: These statements.

Tell: "The Knowledge of the Birds."

Write: Collectively list all the advice contained within the story.

Compare: This advice to that generated by group members.

Paint: Without reference to earlier painting, create another one evoked by the word "expectation".

Compare: Both paintings.

Connect: Make connections between the paintings and the advice generated by the group. Consider the relationship between advice and fear and obedience.

Reflect: Upon entire session.

Text:	THE KNOWLEDGE OF THE BIRDS
Focus:	On danger and being endangered
Length:	1 1/2 hours

Paint: An image evoked by the word "danger".

Look: At everyone's paintings.

Write: On a small piece of paper what kind of danger a particular painting reminds you of. Leave this note near the painting.

Share: Read the notes which have been left near your painting. Select one which feels relevant.

Move: By yourself improvise. Try to embody the danger as well as the sense of being endangered.

Share: Improvisations with the group.

Tell: "The Knowledge of the Birds."

Move: In pairs, select "4 danger points" within the story. Decide who represents danger, who is endangered. Begin by standing opposite one another, about 3 feet apart. Interact for 2 minutes through sound (no real words) and movement. Reverse roles.

Allow yourselves to be guided by the danger points which you have identified.

Avoid physical contact.

Talk: With partner about experience you have just had. Distill the essence of what enabled you to cope with the danger.

Connect: Make connections between the material worked with here and other life experiences.

Reflect: Upon entire session with whole group.

Text:	THE KNOWLEDGE OF THE BIRDS
Focus:	Changing feelings in a time of trouble
Length:	1 1/2 hours

Tell: "The Knowledge of the Birds" stopping after the following points:
1. Once again they sent her forth to gather more wood.
2. Each hoot shook the earth.
3. One day she asked the hawks to help her return to her own people.
4. She fell down screaming, "You have killed me".

Paint: At each stopping point paint an image which represents the girl's feelings.

Share: Paintings.

Paint: In groups of 4, each person makes 4 paintings which represent the way in which the girl developed (grew up) during her journey.

Show: Paintings to 3 other group members.

Write: Imagine the girl 20 years later; much will have happened to her. Write about how she now looks back on her experience with the hawks.

Read: Your writings.

Connect: Make connections between the developmental paintings and these writings.

Reflect: Upon entire session.

Text:	THE WOODEN HEAD
Focus:	Giving in and fighting against the odds
Length:	50 minutes

Recall: A situation in which you felt intimidated and decided not to fight, perhaps you decided to give in.

Write: About this time in your life and the price you paid in doing so.

Distribute: To each group member, as many one inch round pieces of cardboard as there are groupmembers.

Response-task: As you listen to the writings create a symbol for each groupmember which reflects how you feel about each story shared.

Share: Writings.

Tell: "The Wooden Head."

Distribute: "Medals" to each group member.

Reflect: On memories shared and gifts received.

Text:	THE WOODEN HEAD
Focus:	An exploration of protection
Length:	1 1/2 hours

Paint: An image of protection

Recall: A time when you felt protected.

Share: Paintings and memories.

Remember: Songs sung in a time of trouble.

Share: Some of these songs.

Tell: The story of the wooden head up to the time when the magician decided he needs to go and fight the wooden head.

Paint: A picture of the wooden head that kills.

Tell: "The wooden head" up to the place where the magician finds a friend to go with him and he chants the incantation.

Write: A 3 or 4 line incantation which will protect the one who chants it.

Share: The incantation.

Teach: The other group members one sentence from your incantation.

Tell: Finish the story of "The Wooden Head."

Chant: The incantations of the group.

Reflect: Upon session and make connections with personal life.

Text: THE WOODEN HEAD
Focus: Fear and comfort
Length: 1 1/2 hours

Recall: Memories of the kind of people, animals or things you were afraid of as a child.

Write: About the special power (real and imagined) they possessed.

Response-task: As group members share their experiences, create an on-going painting while you are listening which encapsulates your responses to these stories.

Paint: Response to stories.

Share: Paintings. Talk a bit about your responses.

Response-task: While listening to story, doodle.

Tell: "The Wooden Head."

Select: One important moment in the story.

Write: Write about this moment in a few words on the page of doodles.

Place: Response paintings and doodle/text paintings next to one another.

Gallery walk: Group members walk around and look at these.

Write: On a small piece of paper some words of advice/comfort for the painter as if the painter were no more than 7 years old. Leave the writing next to the paintings.

Read: The words of advice/comfort received.

Select: One piece of writing relevant to the 7 year old you once were and one piece relevant to you now.

Talk: Briefly about selected writings.

Reflect: Upon entire session.

Text:	BEAUTY AND THE BEAST
Focus:	Unique and shared characteristics
Length:	50 minutes

Create: A group image of Beauty and the beast. Each group member adds an attribute/quality to the sentence: People call her Beauty because she is..(e.g. kind, pretty with sparkling eyes).

Repeat with the sentence: People call him Beast because he is.....

Write: What you believe you have in common with this Beauty and this Beast. Now write down aspects of yourself which you do not share with them.

Select: One "like" and one "unlike" for both Beauty and Beast characteristic (a total of 4).

Choose: One partner. Make eye contact. Decide who is A and who is B.

Share: For 3 minutes A talks and B listens (does not talk) about the 4 characteristics A has chosen. Reverse roles with no discussion.

Tell: "Beauty and the Beast."

Silent talk: Return to partner. Make eye contact. Share feelings about the story without words.

Reflect: Upon the story, the talking and listening without words, and the shared characteristics.

Text:	BEAUTY AND THE BEAST
Focus:	Family relationships
Length:	1 1/2 hours

Tell: Beauty and the beast up to "They spent many happy hours together.

Write: A letter, at least one page, as if you were Beauty, writing to a member of your family for the first time.

Collect: Letters.

Re-distribute: Letters to each group member. If you get your own letter work with it.

Read: The letter you have just received.

Write: Answer the letter as if you were the family member to whom it has been sent.

Place: Beauty's letter on top, response on bottom.

Distribute: Beauty's letters with response to original writer.

Read: Family member's reply.

Share: Without discussion, letters of Beauty and responses of family members.

Tell: The end of the story of "Beauty and the Beast."

Share: Make connections between the story, the letters and real life experiences.

Reflect: Upon entire session.

Note: A good deal of time is often needed to share the experiences and feelings evoked by this activity. Group members are often baffled by an uncanny resemblance between responses received in the letters and those likely to be received in reality from a family member. One could ascribe this phenomenon to synchronicity, coincidence or unconscious projective identification but regardless of the cause, focus the discussion on the letters and the relationships concerned.

Text: BEAUTY AND THE BEAST

Focus: Family connections

Length: 1 1/2 hours

Give: Each group member a piece of string 6 feet (2 meters) long.

Create: An image around the word "family" using the string.

Place: Creations in a circle a few feet from one another without discussion.

Move: Each group member takes hold of one end of string of their creation and one end of string of someone else's creation. When finished the whole group will be connected.

Without words and without losing hold of the string, improvise movement around the theme of "family" for 5 minutes.

After 5 minutes freeze and drop string ends. Disentangle and walk away from the group. When everyone has left, one group member at a time will go and pick up his/her string.

Speak: As the string is being picked up, group member says 2 or 3 sentences focusing on the theme of "family".

Move:	Return to large circle.
Tell:	"Beauty and the Beast."
Choose:	Each group member decides upon one quality which **Beauty** and Beast possess which enables them to bring their experience to a happy ending.
Share:	Qualities.
Reflect:	Upon the connections between the story and these qualities, as well as the family statements and movement experiences.

Questions focusing on passages

1. What do you know about "rites of passage"?
   Who told you?
   How did you learn about them?

2. What experiences in your life can be seen as a passage?
   How do (did) you mark this?
   How do (did) others in your family celebrate this passage?
   How do (did) friends celebrate this passage?

3. How did you decide you had come of age?
   When did you first feel you had become an adult?
   What did you do or how were you made to feel grown up?

4. What do you foresee as your next passage?
   How will you mark its completion?
   How will you know you have found a stopping place?

5. What are the important passages you think (feel) people must pass
   through on their journey through life?
   How do you feel about your passing through these stages?
   What help do you foresee yourself as having?
   How will you manage if this help is not forthcoming?
   What models do you have for encouraging or discouraging suc-
   cessful passage?

6. What importance do you place on finding resting or stopping
   places on your journey through life?
   How do you find them?
   How do you know if or when you have found one?
   How do you use them?

7. What object(s) do you have, if any, to help you through difficult
   passages?
   How did you find them?
   How do they work?

How do they, if they do, outlive their usefulness?
Do you ever consciously look for an object to help you through difficult times?
What do you look for?
How do you know what you need?
How does it help, if and when you find it?

8.   How do you share your experience of a passage?
With whom are you most likely to share it?
Under what circumstances are you most likely to share your experiences?
How important is it to you to share these?
Are there some passages you are most likely to share?
How do you decide to choose?
What might cause you to change your mind?

CHAPTER FIVE

KNOTS

When we describe a knot we may well end up in a tangle. A knot is, in essence, a common piece of thread or rope which has been turned in on itself and moved in many directions to look like an elevation in space: a pimple on the face of the eternal; a pimple with a purpose.

The knot is an interruption in the smooth flow of a thread and indicates how the simple has been replaced by the complex. It is difficult to visualize the process by which two separate strands have come to be united in a knot, even when only one thread existed in the first place.

When we analyze the creation of a knot we have to internalize a clear sense of direction, differentiated into backwards, forwards, sidewards, left, right and in between. We need to imagine the various manipulations of fingers and hands so that ultimately, the outcome will be reflective of the intention. If we are capable of foreseeing a complex form, while actually perceiving an uncomplicated single piece of thread, we will have reached a highly developed stage of conceptualization.

Suppose that we chance across a knot in a piece of string we intend to use. We ask ourselves, do we want the knot to be where it is? Does its presence interfere with our plans, spoil the presentation or hinder the function? Imagine that we wish to undo the knot. Now we need to be aware of beginning and end, of the construction of the complex manifestation which is the focus of our attention: the knot.

For unless we know where our thread enters and re-emerges out of the tangle, we cannot hope to achieve our aim, a return to disentanglement. We start the process of untying when we have discovered the points of entry and exit, hoping that we are working with a continuous thread. What if it is broken in a place hidden from our eye by the external profusion of fiber?

When we disentangle the knots of our lives we need to trust that out of the mess and the muddle, the internal connections will re-emerge with a renewed clarity of direction. We trust that the contractions in the bends where we have taken short cuts, which later led to strangulation, can be healed and repaired. We hope that the knotted threads of our lives can be restored even though we may miss the varied landscape of elevation beyond the plain.

Although it is difficult to describe verbally how to tie a knot, it is virtually impossible to put into words the manner by which what is entangled becomes disentangled. Whereas knotting requires skill, primarily, unravelling relies on persistence, patience and the ability to follow internal processes, the flow and pattern of loops, bends, twists and turns. For whenever strands have been folded in onto themselves, the uncomplicated and the undisturbed have ceased to be.

A knot is the outcome of disturbance or interference, accidental or intentional, which has left its mark. It is a signal of a happening which occurred in time before our hands touched the strands and took hold of the thread. Therefore, each knot is a messenger of history, of purpose and of possible use. As such, it is a carrier of convention, a container of information. Each knot exists in time, is reflective of a period before the present, when the simple became complex.

We can ask ourselves about its purpose, the style of interaction, cause and effect. Even though the knotted piece of string contains the key to our answer, the essence of the answer resides within us, dependent upon our own knowledge, fantasy and understanding.

Although we may hold in our hands a simple lumpy piece of string, with our inner eye we may see ships and shores, sailors and buoys. We may hear the never ending sound of the wind. The knot is tongue tied. Its maker is the keeper of the private secret or the public knowledge. In the recounting of the tale, the knot need not be untied, for this requires a different form of interaction. Thus, we may retell the story of our life a thousand times but unless we desire and attempt the difficult process of following the thread into the tense and pressured darkness of the knot, it will continue to be a silent reminder of times gone by, events endured or enjoyed, making it impossible for us to truly forget our history.

The more times we encounter a knot and confront its complexities, the greater our chances are to discern patterns. What initially seems to be no more than a chaotic profusion of indeterminate curves and tangles, acquires the quality of intentionality. The apparently unpredictable becomes foreknowable which is the advantage of meeting many knots on our way. If we dare to look at them and explore their structure, on the surface and beyond, we discover regularity and purpose. The seemingly useless becomes potentially and essentially useful.

Thus, although we grow old and marked, we become. Whereas the thread is, the knot is reflective of becoming. The image of the knot contains the illusion of quantity. While looking and wondering we grow to understand make-believe. Rare is the knot which connects more than two pieces of string. Usually it is the simple result of a process of reversal and turning about. Yet, when we look at the knot itself, we are tempted to accept that we are confronted with many, though often it is the one, engaged in an elevated, twisted, frozen dance in response to outside intervention.

The knot assures us of the presence of the one and the other, and of the potentiality for impact; sometimes eternal impact. Thus each knot holds the promise of permanence within the potentiality of temporality. It unites the eternal and the passing, the sacred and the profane.

The inside of a knot is empty. The space it takes is the result of the accumulation of a multitude of twists and bends, short lengths of the very same string. It has no content, whatever its size. It is. Its only function is its possible purpose.

A thread is always shortened by a knot, weakened where it is bent due to additional strain and yet, paradoxically, the overall strength may be increased. The greater the number of knots, the shorter the length of the thread. Is its usefulness therefore reduced? Once again we have to consider the question of the purpose. Wherever we turn we encounter the same issue; the knot within the knot. Unless we discard the string we will have to formulate a way to disentangle the thread. Even rejection is a verdict. The question of purpose is unavoidable.

If we wish to make use of a knotted piece of string we have to understand the knot within the context of its intended purpose. Does it need to be undone? The knot waits, impervious to the threat to its existence. For if the essence of its presence is in its purpose, then the dissolution of purpose requires the solution of the knot. The ancient riddle remains until someone succeeds in resolving the inherent complexity and unriddles the riddle, thus transforming the apparently incoherent into the explicitly coherent. What was stuck becomes unstuck. The riddle ceases to be.

Can what has been done be undone? Can a knot be untied and returned to its former singular state? We can try to undo the knot slowly and gradually, without the use of violent means. But if we fail, we then have to decide whether to use more forceful measures. We can always sever the knot and cut the ties that bind, that link the knot to the thread of its previously uncomplicated, straightforward state. If we hew right through the center of the knot we are left with ravelled ends, numerous tiny pieces of string which have to be plucked and discarded.

Alternatively, we may respect the knot for its complexity and tenacious strength, and cut twice, once on either side. Thus we sever the complex from the simple at the points of ending and return to singularity. In our hands we then hold two separate pieces of string; the end of the continuity stares at us. How will we breech the gap?

Is there no painless way to resolve the problem of disentanglement? We seem to endure either the process of struggling, entering into the strangulating darkness of the knot itself, or we are left holding two disconnected strands, each shorter than the original thread; both damaged.

When we tie a knot can we be truly innocent of the fundamental changes which are brought about by the manipulation of the straightforward which results in the manifestation of the complex with its perplexing difficulties?

A knot embodies nothing. It is no more than the outcome of a series of movements. And yet, once the intricate is created out of the elementary, a return is possible only through the exercise of inherently complex procedures. Each knot, therefore, marks a point of no return. The knot elevates the ordinary to the plane of the special, the unexpected to the expected. It moves from clarity to structured obtrusion to mystery; that which is sacred.

A knot marks an end and another beginning.

The stories

A storm coming *Knots/Cape Verde Islands*

There once lived a lazy wolf who ate everything in sight. Uncle Wolf had a hard working nephew. While Uncle Wolf ate, Nephew dug his soil and planted lots of manioc to last him through the winter. When Uncle Wolf saw Nephew's plants he immediately felt very hungry.

"Dear Nephew, I am starving. Please give me a shoot of your manioc." At first Nephew said no but Uncle Wolf made such a fuss, Nephew finally relented and gave him a shoot.

"I am still so hungry Nephew, surely you can spare just one more shoot." Nephew refused and Uncle Wolf went away, determined to force Nephew to leave his manioc patch.

In the days that followed, Uncle Wolf made such a nuisance of himself that Nephew finally left. Uncle Wolf ate to his heart's content. When Nephew returned and saw that his manioc plants had been eaten he said nothing. Two days later Uncle Wolf saw Nephew busily cutting carrapate. Uncle Wolf watched as Nephew plaited the strands into very strong rope.

"What are you going to do with that rope, dear Nephew?" asked Uncle Wolf.

"Do you not see that very black cloud over there?" pointed Nephew. "A great storm is coming. It will wash away everything that is not secure. I am going to tie myself to that tree over there so I will be safe." Nephew started to tie himself up.

"Oh kind Nephew, please help me. Tie me to that tree first." Nephew hesitated and finally gave in to his uncle's pleas. He tied Uncle Wolf to the big tree, spliced the ends of the rope together and hung them out of Uncle Wolf's reach. Nephew left without another word.

The bones of Uncle Wolf are still there.

How different people came to earth   *Knots/Tupis/Brazil*

Sacaibou, father of all people, walked across the plain and noticed something white clinging to the branches of a tree. As he came closer, he saw that it was a cotton tree and took some seeds. When he returned home he planted them near the river. Very soon the seeds became small trees. Pleased with himself, Sacaibou went off to hunt. When he came home he found that all of the trees had been uprooted.

Once again he planted seeds which grew into small trees. Once more they were uprooted. Sacaibou knew the damage must be the work of his son, Rairou, the only other person on earth. Sacaibou made a plan to punish his son. He found a large, strong armadillo and put some glue on its tail. Sacaibou asked it to go into its hole leaving its tail sticking out. When Rairou came by he tried to pull the armadillo out so that he could eat it for dinner. But Rairou could not pull it out. Armadillo dragged Rairou down, deep into the earth. When Rairou finally freed himself he wandered around, meeting strange people and animals, the likes of which he had never seen before. Eventually, some of the people showed him how to return home.

In Rairou's absence, Sacaibou's trees grew tall and strong. Sacaibou was able to spin the cotton bolls into thread for the first time. When Rairou returned he pretended to be pleased to see his father and hid his desire for revenge. He told Sacaibou all about his journey.

"While I was in the earth I met some kind and loving people. Why don't we bring a few of them up here to live with us on earth?" Sacaibou agreed and Rairou went down into the earth to find the people. Sacaibou spun a thread of strong cotton which he let down into the hole. When he felt something pull on the other end he pulled up the thread. He saw a man and a woman of great beauty.

Quickly Sacaibou untied the thread that held them and let his line down for the second time. When he pulled up the thread there appeared two men and two women who looked rather ordinary. Still, after releasing them, Sacaibou untied the thread that held them and lowered the line for the third time.

It took all of Sacaibou's strength to pull up the thread. At the end of the thread this time were six of the ugliest people Sacaibou had ever seen. He thought to himself that Rairou had made a mistake. He started to say something when the thread was pulled from his hands.

Rairou laughed as he told his father, "Now I have had my revenge. You will never have only good and beautiful people on the earth. There will always be all kinds of women and men."

Rairou danced with delight at the trick he had played on his father. Sacaibou sat on a large stone and watched the sun leave the earth. He wondered about what happened.

Maui muri catches the sun   *Knots/Polynesia*

Maui muri noticed that no matter how hard his people worked, they never had enough daylight in which to finish their tasks. Maui muri said, "There is never enough time for the men to fish in the sea or for the women to cook the food. The Sun-god, Ra, moves too quickly across the sky. I must make Ra move more slowly.

Maui muri and his brothers made a huge rope out of coconut fibers. Then Maui muri lay in wait for Ra. When he saw Ra he tried to throw the rope around him but the rope broke and Ra escaped, flying across the sky as quickly as ever.

Maui muri made a second, stronger cord of coconut husks which he braided into an even stronger rope but for the second time, Ra escaped.

After much thought, Maui muri asked his sister Hina to give him some of her hair. He cut off long strands and braided them into a very, very strong rope. He traveled eastward to wait for the first glimpse of Ra. When the Sun-god appeared Maui muri threw his noose around Ra's neck and held tight. Ra kicked and screamed, struggling in vain. When the Sun-god realized he could not free himself he asked Maui muri what he wanted.

"You must move more slowly across the sky so that we will have more time to do our work. Promise me this and I will let you go." Ra promised, but just to make sure he kept his word, Maui muri left some strands of Hina's hair hanging from the sun. You can still see them when the sun is going down and the last rays of light fill the sky. Since that time, people have had more daylight to do their work.

The spirit who could not make up its mind   *Knots/Canada*

A long time ago, before the world was finished, the people were bothered by a peculiar spirit who tore the roofs from their igloos, spoiled their tools and damaged new clothes. In time, the villagers went to Raven who was busy creating a mountain range to protect plants from the ravages of the north wind. Raven was not pleased to see them and suggested they wait until his work was finished.

"We cannot wait," said one man. "I was fishing from my canoe in the midst of a calm sea when suddenly I was tossed overboard. Just as I thought death was certain, I was thrown back into the canoe with all my fish on top of me."

"Did you see anything?" asked Raven.

A chorus of voices joined the man's. "No one has seen it but we have heard it. When my boat turned over the spirit said, No-no-no' and when I was back inside, with my fish safe, it said Yes-yes-yes'".

"It is as if the spirit cannot make up its mind," said a woman. "It overturns a cooking pot and whispers No-no-no' and then tosses the food back in and says, 'Yes-yes-yes'. It is driving all of us crazy."

Raven said, "I have never seen or heard of this spirit but I will come with you and see what I can do." The people returned to their village with Raven. Suddenly Raven felt something plucking at his head feathers. "Stop that, you're hurting me." The plucking stopped. He looked around but saw nothing except a large shadow on the ground. He knew he had met the spirit. Raven asked, "Who are you? Why do you hurt me?"

Raven heard a soft, "Yes-no-yes-no-yes-no."

"Is that all you can say?" asked Raven.

The spirit answered, "Yes-no-yes-no."

Raven asked, "Where do you come from?"

"I am lost," answered the spirit.

"How is this possible?" asked Raven.

"I have never found a shape of my own," replied the spirit. "When I was a wolf I went hungry. When I was an eagle I was lonely. Can you help me? Everyone else runs from me."

Raven suggested, "How would you like to be a whale? You would be the largest creature in the ocean. You would only have to open your mouth to find food."

"Yes-yes-yes," said the spirit. Raven smiled but just as he was about to make it happen the spirit said, "No-no-no. I would be too tired swimming all day."

Raven said, "If you were a whale you would like to swim." But the spirit would not agree to become a whale. Then Raven suggested the spirit become a beautiful maiden. At first it agreed but then refused.

"A maiden grows old and then no one listens to her." Discouraged, the spirit started to make a hole in a new blanket. "Stop that!" commanded Raven. "Listen to me. I know a place close to here where there is a shaman who is too weak to be of much use. You could easily live inside him and then you would receive the attention of everyone who lives in the village."

"How would I get inside? Suppose the shaman doesn't want me?" asked the spirit.

"Let me take care of that," soothed Raven. "I will tell you what to do. We will wait until he is asleep and then you will slip inside and sleep until you wake up. With your wisdom the shaman will become a great and wise man." Reluctantly, the spirit let himself be convinced by Raven.

Raven and the spirit went to the village. The people there were angry. No one was working. They told Raven, "If we ask our shaman whether it is a good day to catch fish, he will say yes. We go out and then a storm overturns our boats. Nothing he says is true. He is a fool. It is useless to ask his advice."

Raven listened. "Stop this talking and do as I tell you. Go to sleep with peaceful hearts. I promise you that when you wake your shaman will be wiser."

That night Raven and the spirit waited and watched. When the sky was darkest, Raven said to the spirit, "When the shaman opens his mouth, you must enter." The spirit started to quiver with fear and began to protest but Raven said, "If you do not like living inside the shaman you can always leave. Now go in!" Raven sighed with relief when the spirit finally entered into the soul of the shaman.

When the morning fires were bright, the villagers flocked to the shaman. "Will today be a good day for fishing?" asked one.

"Yes-yes-yes. There will be large schools of fish."

"Thank you," answered the fisherman, pleased.

"On the other hand," said the shaman, "You may not catch any."

The fisherman nodded and walked away, still content.

"Tell me," asked a young woman, "Is this a good time to plant my seeds?"

"Yes-yes-yes," said the shaman. "The ground is ready." As the young woman turned to leave, he added, "There may not be rain enough to make them grow." The woman left, thinking how to make sure her plants had enough water.

When all the villagers had gone, Raven asked, "Spirit, are you happy?"

"I am the shaman of this village. I do the best I can for my people," responded the spirit with great dignity. And Raven smiled. He walked among the people, listening to their talk.

"Thank you Raven," said the villagers. "Our shaman has changed just as you promised. He now says, "Maybe the weather will be fair or maybe we will not have a good hunt. Our shaman is never wrong."

Why Imboto is alone in heaven   *Knots/Zaire*

A long time ago people lived in heaven. There were no people on the earth. The people in heaven looked down and saw the earth. They longed to live there.

Imboto, their chief, who lived among the people in heaven said, "If this is what you wish, this is how it must be done. You descend first. I will follow after you." All the people lowered themselves on the cord, down to the earth. Then the cord broke. It fell to the earth with a loud noise.

When Imboto, the last one to descend, looked for the way down to earth to join his people, he saw that it was no longer possible. The cord was broken.

Because Imboto cannot find a way down to earth he becomes angry. When he roars, it rains. He wants to come down to earth with the rain but the raindrops will not give him a chance. Thus he thunders in his fury, "Kulukulu".

The story bag   *Knots/Korea*

There once lived a little boy who loved to hear stories more than you could imagine. He listened to a new story every night before going to sleep. Though he heard many stories, no matter how his friends begged, the little boy refused to share even a single tale.

Hanging on a nail, in a corner of his room, was an old leather bag, tightly tied with a thong. No one thought much about it, yet inside, lived the spirits of all the stories told to the boy. Each time a new story was told, the storyspirit had to go into the bag. It could not leave until the boy told the story to someone else. Because he would not share the stories, the storyspirits could not leave. After a while, the bag became so full the spirits had difficulty breathing. Each time they moved they bumped into each other. When the boy's parents died, an old servant told him new stories and the story bag became even more crowded. The spirits inside were miserable.

When the orphaned boy grew up, his rich uncle arranged a wonderful marriage for him. Servants prepared his clothes and packed his bags to ready him for the wedding procession to the wedding ceremony. While everyone was out, the old man heard some grumbling. He looked everywhere but could find no one. The voices grew louder and more discontented. Through a tiny hole in a paper window the old man noticed that the bag in the young man's room was moving, as if something inside it wanted to get out. The old man stood quietly and listened to the storyspirits make their plans.

One said, "On his way to the wedding he will be thirsty. I will turn myself into a poisoned well. When he drinks of me, he will die."

A second voice said, "Just in case he doesn't drink from your well I will be a field full of luscious looking strawberries. One berry and he will live no more."

A third voice, more angry than the first two said, If he should miss the two of you, I will be a red hot poker hidden in the sack of rice he uses to step down from his horse. One touch of me and he will burn to a cinder."

The voices cheered but were stopped by a furious voice. "In the event you fail, I will turn myself into a snake and hide under his bed. One bite from me and his bride will be a widow." The storyspirits cheered.

The old man was horrified. He loved the young man and wanted to protect him. He knew that no one would believe him were he to tell what he had heard. He knew he would have to make his own plans.

He begged the rich uncle to let him lead the wedding party and made such a fuss the uncle reluctantly agreed. After a short time the young man shouted to the old man, "Stop. I want to drink from this well." The old man pretended not to hear and led the wedding procession passed the well. After a few miles, the young man saw the strawberry patch and shouted, "Stop. I want to eat some strawberries." But the old man urged the horses on at an even greater pace despite threats of punishment from the rich uncle.

At the bride's house, two servants came with a sack of rice for the young man to step on. Just as he was about to put his foot on the sack, the old man came rushing up and pulled it out from under the young man who lost his balance and fell into the dust. The guests were very surprised to see the faithful old man play such an unkind trick. The rich uncle became even more angry and vowed to punish the old man after the ceremonies ended.

That night, after all the festivities were over, the bride and bride-groom went to bed. Suddenly, the old man burst into their room, sword in hand. Ignoring the bride's screams and the groom's shouts, the old man pulled a mat from under the bed. There lay an enormous snake, ready to pounce. The old man hacked the snake to pieces, stopping only when he was sure the snake was dead. Hearing such a commotion, everyone rushed to the bridal chamber to see what had happened.

Knowing that all was now well, the old man told the tale of the unhappy storyspirits. To make sure he was telling the truth the rich uncle ordered the sack of rice to be brought to him. When he looked inside, there was the poker surrounded by charred rice. Then a servant showed what was left of the deadly snake.

The rich uncle asked the old man's forgiveness and offered him a reward for his faithfulness. The young man, who had been silent, now spoke. "It is all my fault. From now on I will tell a story to all those wishing to hear one." And he did.

Knots - The Structures

Theme: KNOTS
Focus: An exploration of knots
Length: 50 minutes

Paint: Image of knot

Write: Answers to the following questions as quickly as possible:
1. What words come to mind when you hear the word knot?
2. What does "To tie the knot" mean to you?
3. What experience did you have with a knot today?
4. Where in your body do you feel knotted up?
5. Where in your body do you feel unknotted?

Move: In groups of 5-8 people, hold hands gently,and slowly move about until the group is totally tangled, knotted up.

Without hurting anyone, explore how much movement can be done in the following ways:
- How many pairs of eyes can you count and acknowledge?
- How high can you move your body?
- How low to the ground can you move your body?
- How many elbows can you touch?
- With how many people can you make physical contact (without letting go of hands)?
- How small can the group make itself?
- How large can the group make itself?
- How can the group move in different directions through space without a leader telling people what to do?

Slowly untangle and unknot the group without unclasping hands. Release hands when the group is in its original circle.

Paint:	Image of experience which leaves the greatest impression on you.
Write:	Phrases or memory that come to mind.
Share:	Images, answers to questions, words, phrases or memories.
Reflect:	Upon entire session.

Theme:	KNOTS
Focus:	Exploration of knots using drama
Length:	90 minutes

The following six knots all have unique characteristics:

Containing knot keeps something in order such as shoes tied, package wrapped;

Restraining knot sets boundaries, limits freedom such as dog tied to post, boat tied to dock;

Linking knot is undone easily, such as slip knot, linked arms...allows relatedness and control for as long as it is wanted;

Strangling knot allows no space for anything else, no untying; presses everything into minimal space with no second chance such as a hanging knot;

Connecting knot joins one thing to another, relates to permanence, continuity, shared responsibility such as chain link fence, lovers' knot;

Helping knot functions as a reminder to measure speed or quantity such as knots per hour, or knot around the finger to remind one of something needing to be done.

Divide:	Into groups of 3-4.
Choose:	One knot that appeals to group members.
Share:	Words and ideas that come to mind within group.
Select:	Words and ideas that appeal to group and lie within group's capacity to dramatize.
Dramatize:	Improvise a theme based on one of the above knots. Use everyone in the group all the time. (Transformation from one role to another is possible.) Work so that the drama has a clear beginning and end.
Share:	Dramas.
Reflect:	Share ideas that caused group to select a specific knot.
	Which ideas were not chosen? Discuss why?
	Which knots were not chosen by any group?
	Which knots were most often chosen? Discuss why?
	Share associations people have with the word knot after watching the improvisations.

Text:	A STORM COMING
Focus:	The consequences of absence of forgiveness
Length:	50 minutes.
Write:	Any words which come to mind related to the word, Regret.
Write:	On separate cards 3 'if only' statements.
Collect:	Cards.

Select: One card.

Speak: Seated on a 'special' box or chair, speak about this 'if
                 only' statement as if it were your own, i.e. 'if only I'.

Response   Following each groupmember's statement, write one
task: reason why this 'if only' statement may never become a
                 reality, e.g. lack of talent, lack of persistence, and one
                 reason why it might well become a reality, e.g. ability to
                 think ahead, ability to wait.

Tell: A storm coming.

Share: In pairs. Talk with your partner about your statements,
                 the general theme. Precede every sentence you speak with
                 the words: "Please, listen to me."

Reflect: On entire session. Include a reflection on self-
                 forgiveness. Decide what to do with the unused 'if only'
                 cards.

Text: A STORM COMING
Focus: Associations with give and take
Length: 1 1/2 hours

Preparation: In a circle, group members throw an imaginary ball.
                 Throw it as if it were of different sizes, shapes and
                 weights.

                 Explore various ways of walking in pairs, trios and larger
                 groups.

Move: Find a place on the floor and sit down. Think of
                 something you want to give to someone. Move toward the
                 person (people) and, using no language, try to give your
                 gift.

Now think of something you would like to receive. Express your wish nonverbally to another group member. Try to have your wish fulfilled.

Move: In pairs. Explore how a one-legged person can be supported in order to walk. Change partners at least once and continue the exploration.

Write: On a large sheet of paper the group collectively write words associated with give and take.

Share: Thoughts, feelings and ideas connected with the previous exercises.

Tell: "A Storm Coming."

Write: Nephew's reflection on the episode many years later.

Share: Writings.

**Response-
task:**   Simple gifts for Nephew to be given to each storyteller.

Note: All gifts are to be left unopened until each participant has told his/her "Nephew's reflection".

Reflect: Upon entire session.

Text: A STORM COMING
Focus: Justification of greed
Length: 1 1/2 hours

Paint: An image of greed.

Write: A few lines beginning with: "I am the voice of greed. I...."

Share: Images and writings.

Write: About a real life situation where someone describeş using
                greed. Consider the following questions:
                - Who is the character?
                - What is the character greedy for?
                - How does he/she get hold of what is wanted?
                - How come he/she continues to be greedy?

Read/write: Collect the writings and redistribute them to group
                members. Each participant reads a "What I'm greedy for
                and how I got it" story. Then each group member creates
                a genuine defense for the greediness in the story as writ-
                ten by a person in authority. Use several arguments to
                justify the greed. Return response and original story to
                story's originator.

Share: Both writings with the group until everyone has read
                his/her story and justification.

Response-   While listening to the stories and justifications, each par-
task: ticipant makes a list of the various arguments used (pover-
                ty, need, etc).

Select: One argument from the complete list which you dislike
                most.

Share: With the group why the particular argument is disliked.
                For example, "I do not like the plea of weakness. When I
                am weak...."

Note: Make sure group members are committed to their choice
                before talking begins. Encourage participants to make
                notes about their choices.

Tell: "A Storm Coming."

Discuss: In small groups talk about Nephew's way of punishing
              Uncle Wolf.

Share: In the large group exchange ideas, feelings and thoughts
              regarding alternative solutions, bearing in mind how
              social pressures affect choice.

Reflect: On entire session.

Text: HOW DIFFERENT PEOPLE CAME TO EARTH
Focus: Imaginary environment
Length: 50 minutes

Vocal   Each person warms up voice through use of yawns, sighs
warmup: and easy sounds.

Write: Take pen and paper and find a place in the room in which
              to sit. Imagine an environment and write down all the
              sounds you might hear there.

Note: This exercise is done in total silence.

Sound-   Create the sounds on your list and then start walking
making: around the room. Find a partner and share some of the
              sounds on your list, each listening in turn, to the other.
              Find another partner and share more sounds. Continue
              until you meet 2 or 3 people whose sounds you ap-
              preciate. Form a small group.

Create: A sound "picture" of your environment and the way you
              as a group live. The sound picture needs to be made up of
              both individual and collective components.

Share: Sound "pictures".

Respond/ write:	What the sounds evoked within you.
Tell:	"How Different People Came to Earth."
Write:	Gibberish explanations uttered by the people when they arrive on earth.
Teach:	The other group members your gibberish and accompanying movement.
Share/reflect:	Upon entire session.

Text:	HOW DIFFERENT PEOPLE CAME TO EARTH
Focus:	Encounters in a strange land
Length:	1 1/2 hours
Paint:	An image of "peculiar" and an image of "normal".
Write:	Words that come to mind for each image.
Share:	Images and words.
Tell:	"How Different People Came to Earth"…up to "He met all sorts of strange people and animals, the likes of which he had never seen."
Paint:	A series of pictures of who and what Rairou encounters on his journey.
Write:	About the aspect of the journey which has the greatest impact on Rairou.
Tell:	Rest of myth.
Paint:	Image of how Rairou feels at end of myth and an image of how Sacaibou feels at end of myth.

Share:	Paintings.
Reflect:	Upon entire session.

Text:	HOW DIFFERENT PEOPLE CAME TO EARTH
Focus:	Obedience and disobedience
Length:	1 1/2 hours
Tell:	"How Different People Came to Earth"…up to "So he decided to punish Rairou."
Dramatize:	In pairs, one partner acting as Rairou, the other as Sacaibou, improvise: - The nature of the punishment; - Rairou's and Sacaibou's feelings during the punishment and possible retribution; - Ways peace might be made between them.
Share:	Essence of dramatization.
Tell:	Rest of myth.
Reflect:	On issues of obedience and disobedience.
Note:	If people rely too heavily on writing out scripts, suggest group members work nonverbally in the beginning. Explore a number of possibilities before choosing what to share.

Text:	MAUI MURI CATCHES THE SUN
Focus:	Problem solving
Length:	50 minutes
Paint:	An image of "day" and an image of "night".

Write:	About an experience when you felt the day to be too short.
Share:	Images and writings.
Tell:	"Maui Muri Catches the Sun"…up to "to make Ra, the Sun-god move more slowly."
Write:	About how you would succeed in doing this if you were Maui muri.
Paint:	Images to illustrate your solution.
Share:	Writings and images.
Tell:	The end of "Maui Muri Catches the Sun."
Reflect:	Upon the entire session.

Text: MAUI MURI CATCHES THE SUN
Focus: Urgency
Length: 1 1/2 hours

Move:	The group stands in a circle. One group member initiates a very slow movement. The next person imitates the movement sequence but slightly increases the speed with which it is done. Each person, in turn, does the movement, increasing the tempo until the movement cannot be done any faster. Then group members pass the movement on with decreasing speed and intensity until the movement reaches its original form.
Note:	The exercise can be repeated with different movement sequences.
Sound:	Group sits in a circle. One group member starts a slow

rhythm. The group repeats the rhythm, gradually increasing the tempo until the climax is reached. Reverse the process, reducing the tempo until original rhythm is achieved. Repeat with different rhythmic patterns and sequences.

Paint: Image evoked by the word, Hurry.

Write: Word associations around the word, Hurry.

Drama: In pairs, create a brief scene with ends with the word, hurry. You have 10 minutes to make a 1 minute scene.

Share: Improvisations.

Response-task: While watching the improvisations, notice common themes. Make a note of how you might feel in each situation.

Tell: How Maui muri catches the sun.

Write: A list of what you believe you never have enough time to do.

Share/reflect: Lists with partner and suggest one personal change for partner, to create more time.

Reflect: On improvisations, common themes, emotional responses.

Text: MAUI MURI CATCHES THE SUN
Focus: Challenging great power
Length: 1 1/2 hours

Paint: An image of power.

Move: In a circle. Each person in turn adopts a posture of great power.

Sound:	Create hand and body sounds of power beginning with the softest possible sounds, gradually increasing their intensity and volume.
Write:	On a large sheet of paper, as a group, words associated with power.
Reflect:	On paintings, movement and sound experiences in relation to the word associations.
Tell:	"Maui Muri Catches the Sun."
Move:	In pairs, for 10 minutes, explore the movement patterns of interaction between Maui Muri and Ra. Exchange roles.
Write:	Describe in one word the characteristic Maui Muri and Ra needed most of all.
Paint/clay:	Create a symbol for the two characteristics.
Share:	Movement experiences and symbols.
Reflect:	Upon entire session.

Text:	THE SPIRIT WHO COULDN'T MAKE UP ITS MIND
Focus:	Ambivalence
Length:	50 minutes
Paint:	Image evoked by the word, ambivalence.
Move:	Each group member finds space in which to move. In turn, every group member calls out an action such as walk, crawl, hide. Each member does these activities ambivalently.
Write:	Take paper and write whatever comes to mind.

Response-task:	During sharing, create a collective doodle on a large piece of paper.
Share:	Images, writing and experiences.
Reflect:	On the collective doodles.
Tell:	The spirit who couldn't make up its mind.
Write:	A 2 line tribute to the wise shaman on the occasion of his anniversary. (Participant decides what kind and number.)
Share:	Tributes.
Reflect:	Upon entire session.

Text:	THE SPIRIT WHO COULDN'T MAKE UP ITS MIND
Focus:	"Good" and "bad" behavior
Length:	1 1/2 hours
Paint:	Image evoked by word, Chaos.
Share:	Images.
Write:	On one side of a piece of paper the word, good. On the opposite side write the word, bad.
List:	5 things (topics, actions, feelings etc.) which you consider to be good and 5 which you consider to be bad.
Share/discuss:	Lists.
Tell:	"The Spirit Who Couldn't Make up its Mind."
Response-task:	As participants listen they write down behavior considered to be good or bad.

Select: From list, one example of good behavior and one of bad regardless of which character in story behaves like this.

Speak: The examples using words to express ideas in a feeling mode.

Note: Facilitator may need to instruct participants to use "I" when presenting their behavior examples, "I am feeling destructive." or "I am feeling as if I need to hide my distress."
Participants may close their eyes while doing this part of the exercise.

Move: Choose a posture which is representative of each of the two examples chosen.

Reflect: What could get you out of this way of being from another way of being. What is needed?

Write: What you have decided is needed and how it could be provided.

Share: Postures and writing.

Connect: Make connections between your daily life and your images and writings.

Share/reflect: Experiences and insights.

Text: THE SPIRIT WHO COULDN'T MAKE UP ITS MIND
Focus: Connections between opposites
Length: 1 1/2 hours

Write: On a sheet of paper two words which represent to you a pair of opposites equivalent to YES and NO.

Paint: Image of each of these two words.

Note: Facilitator note the pairs of word opposites on separate pieces of paper. Redistribute the papers.

Link/write: The words you have just received with a real life experience. Write down the experience.

Share: The life experience.

Response-task: After hearing the pair of opposite words to which the life experience is related, write down one word which, to you, forms a connection between the two words.

Give: This word to the one who told the life experience. No one looks at words received until all group members have shared their written life experience.

Read: The words given to you to detect a common denominator or trend. If none seem right, select one word out of those received which you like best as the interlinking word between the pair of opposites with which you have been working.

                Example: If you have been working with good/bad and no trend is discernible but you notice and like the word, accept, then this is the word you select.

Share: Selected words and word chosen to describe common denominator or trend.

Write: Word associations around your selected word. List all words which come to mind.

Paint: Image of how you feel following the word association task.

Share:	Images.
Tell:	"The Spirit Who Couldn't Make up its Mind."
Reflect:	On connections between life experiences, images and the story. Share issues evoked.

Text:	WHY IMBOTO IS ALONE IN HEAVEN
Focus:	Leadership
Length:	50 minutes
Write:	On one end of a sheet of paper the words, to lead. At the opposite end of the paper write the verb you consider to be the opposite of, to lead. In between, list all words which you believe to interconnect these two verbs.
Move:	In pairs, blindfold partner and take him/her on a 1 minute blind-walk. Exchange roles.
Share:	Experiences with each other.
Paint:	A suitable symbol for a leader.
Share:	Symbols.
Write:	About an experience where you were the recognized leader.
Response-task:	Collectively make a list of all the disadvantages and advantages leadership seems to engender.
Share:	Experiences.
Tell:	"Why Imboto is Alone in Heaven."

Response-task:	Collectively make a list of words of comfort for Imboto.
Reflect:	On issues arising from being a leader.

Text:	WHY IMBOTO IS ALONE IN HEAVEN
Focus:	Feelings associated with being left behind
Length:	1 1/2 hours
Paint:	Image of what is evoked inside you by the words, being left behind.
Write:	On your paper a word which expresses or is evoked by your image.
Write:	Make a connection between your image and word and write about a personal experience evoked by them.
Share:	Images, words and experiences.
Tell:	"Why Imboto is Alone in Heaven."
Write:	Imagine that you are a member of the tribe of Chief Imboto. You have just arrived on earth and realize the cord is broken. Write Chief Imboto a letter.
Write:	Remind yourself of your personal experience of "being left behind". Write a letter to yourself based on the letter you wrote to Chief Imboto.
Share:	Letters written to Chief Imboto and yourself.
Response-task:	Collectively make a list of useful gifts for the one left behind.
Reflect:	Upon entire session.

Text:	WHY IMBOTO IS ALONE IN HEAVEN
Focus:	Solitude and togetherness
Length:	1 1/2 hours

Move: Stand in a circle. As a group, slowly find a position which expresses optimum togetherness. Freeze when the position is reached. Very slowly, disconnect and move toward a position which is an expression of complete solitude. Freeze when this position is reached. Very slowly, abandon this position and return to circle.

Move: In groups of 3, explore the themes of solitude and togetherness for 5 minutes, keeping the movement continuous. Use sound and eye contact when appropriate.

Paint/write: An image of the feelings evoked in you by this experience. Put a word to your image and write the word on your painting.

Share: Images, words and experiences.

Tell: "Why Imboto is Alone in Heaven."

Drama: Each group member, in turn, will become Chief Imboto in a continuous improvisation. Sitting on a chair, the actor or actress playing Imboto has 1 minute to talk about the situation he/she is experiencing.

Reflect: Upon feelings evoked by improvisation and by the entire session.

Text:	THE STORY BAG
Focus:	Containment in a crowded space
Length:	50 minutes

Preparation: Group members should stretch and warm up their bodies.

Move: Create a human container using 1/3 of the group. When the container is made, the remaining 2/3 enter it one at a time. Each person enters and finds a space (sitting, lying etc.) and settles into stillness.

                              This stillness is the signal for the next person to enter the container. The container will become crowded but the exercise continues until all 2/3 are inside the container.

Sound: Each participant (one at a time) makes a sound which reflects how he/she feels. When the sound stops, the next person begins. Continue until each person has had a chance.

Move: Slowly empty and dissolve the container. Each person gets pen and paper and finds a private space.

Write: Whatever comes to mind.

Share/reflect: Writings.

Tell: "The Story Bag."

Note: Group members can draw/doodle as they listen.

Reflect: Upon entire session.

Text: THE STORY BAG
Focus: Hidden qualities and origins
Length: 1 1/2 hours

Write: A list of words associated with the word, Origin.

Tell: "The Story Bag"...up to "The spirits inside were miserable."

152

Paint:	A picture of the story bag.
Write:	Answers to the following questions using no more than 2 or 3 words: - Where does the bag hang? - Is this where the bag belongs? If not, where does the bag belong? - How did it get there? - Who owns the bag? - How did the bag come into her/his possession? - What will he/she do with it? - What is the real function of the bag?
Write:	The story bag's own story using ALL the above information. Use as many senses as possible.
Share:	Stories.
Response-task:	After listening to each story, write on a piece of paper, a quality which this particular story has yet which does not seem apparent because nothing is said about it in the story. Fold the paper and give it to the storyteller. Do not read qualities until all group members have told their stories and received their folded papers.
Read:	Hidden qualities.
Reflect:	On what has been written. Share responses.
Tell:	The rest of "The Story Bag."
Reflect:	On entire session.

Text:	THE STORY BAG
Focus:	Storymaking and reasons for storytelling
Length:	1 1/2 hours
Tell:	"The Story Bag"…up to "The stories inside were miserable."

Paint:	Image of inside of story bag.
Write:	On the outside of the bag there is an inscription. Write the inscription on your paper.
Share:	Images and inscriptions.
Write:	Answer the following questions in a few words: - What is the theme of the last story that went into the bag? - Who is (are) the main character (s)? - There is a problem. What is the problem? - Why has it occurred? - The problem is solved. Who solves it? - How is it solved?
Write:	The story using ALL the above information.
Share:	Stories in small groups.
Response-task:	After hearing each story, each group member writes down on a piece of paper why this particular story has to be allowed out of the bag and why it needs to be retold. Fold your paper and give it to the storyteller but no one looks at "reasons for retelling" until all stories have been told and "reasons" received.
Read:	In large group reasons for retelling.
Reflect:	Upon the connections between reasons for re-telling stories from the story bag and telling the stories of your life.
Tell:	The rest of "The Story Bag."
Paint:	An image of the way you are feeling right now.
Reflect:	Upon entire session.

Questions focusing on knots

1. What images come to mind when you think of the word, knot?

2. What expressions do you use which reflect the experience of knots?
   What occasions evoke the use of these expressions?

3. Think of words which are synonymous with the word, knot. How are they similar? How do they differ?

4. What is your most memorable experience with a knot?

5. How is the process of being knotted reflected in your body?

6. How do you feel you knot yourself?
   What do you do to unknot yourself?

7. How are you tied to other people?
   How do you feel about this connection?
   What do you do to reinforce it?
   What do you do to break it or change it?
   What evokes a particular response?

8. What stories about knots come to mind?
   How did you first hear them?
   What makes them memorable?

9. Were you ever tied up as a child when playing?
   How were you released?
   How did you feel about the experience after it occurred?
   Has time changed your feelings?

10. What do you do with "loose ends"?
    How do you feel about them?
    What part do they play in your life?

11. Have you ever felt badly out of breath?
    How did you regain your breath?
    What did you learn from your experience?

12. What kind of knots do you prefer?
    On what occasion(s) do you use them?
    What do you do when you don't know how to tie the necessary
    knot required by the situation?

13. How are knots metaphors in your life?
    How do you use them to communicate your feelings to others?
    What kind of knot describes your relationship to yourself?
    How do the knots in your life change?
    What creates the new knot?

CHAPTER SIX

THE TREE

The tree stands.

Whatsoever stands has strength. Strength to be erect, supported by a base, with energies soaring in all directions. Standing marks an end to enfoldment. The seed stretches toward manifestation.

When we stand we relate to our environment in a way which is essentially different from when we crawl. Acquiring bipedal locomotion fundamentally changes our relationship to and with the outside world. We stand on our own two feet.

Once we stand we learn to move and to stand still. Without stillness and rest, we cannot continue to go forth. Each phrase needs to find its own ending, each movement its rest though this may be no more than a temporary halting place. For when standing we may find rest, but it is a resting within the constraint of the innately active.

When we stand we can watch attentively; the stillness serving heightened awareness. We wish to hear distinctly, see clearly, smell and sense accurately what goes on around us. We are able to stand guard, ready to notice and decide, defend or attack, depart or stay.

Sometimes we enter where our movement is not welcome. We may then take refuge in stillness. Movement always signals presence, life with its inherent dangers. What stands and does not move inspires both fear and trust. The standing indicates life and purpose; the protective guard, the expecting parent, the musing farmer or the watchful child. All are images of ambiguous potency.

Thus the first gesture or sound emerging from a frozen creature never fails to startle us, to call us back into a moving reality where we need to adjust in order to relate. Interaction begins where stillness ends. The journey, our story, continues when standing leads to walking. Trees stand.

The tree grows.

When we grow we become enlarged by degrees; slowly and gradually. The passage of time is enfolded within this process of continuous change, leaving marks of impact and interaction. The energy activating a particular phase of development will complete itself. Then a transformation to a new form, a different matter, occurs. A new journey begins.

Growth is guided by principles and limitations of nature and nurture. We do not know whether processes of birth and growth are identical or even similar. Is growth more than the continuation of energy and identity which are present "in the beginning"?

The mystery of growth cannot be adequately explained by means of visual and verbal representations of process and product. For they are one, manifest yet unfolding, constant yet ephemeral. What "is" equals "what is, what has been and what shall be" simultaneously and sequentially.

Wherever the simultaneous and the sequential meet, growth occurs. Whenever they separate, change ceases. The continuous encounters the discontinuous. This rupture of the connection between the simultaneous and the sequential marks the end of life. Death is the absence of growth. Thus growth is the outcome of the interaction between the constant and the changing, the seed and the twig. Trees grow.

The tree has roots.

Roots provide support. They supply the emergent structure with a nourishing, sustaining base. Most roots are hidden by the earth as it envelops the tree as our past embraces the present of our life. When we are rooted we have a sense of belonging and a profound connection with our source of inspiration, with that which gives strength to our being.

Whatever has roots needs to be transplanted carefully for the process of connecting with a new environment is fraught with difficulty. As connections dwindle reality becomes precarious. The entire structure trembles at the slightest impact, affected by even the most gentle touch. The provision of nourishment is fragile and easily threatened.

Our roots allow us to bend and to be steady, to extend and to receive. Without them we are lost, unable to produce or reproduce. We must find a way to nurture and develop inner strength, to compensate, initially, for the absence of access to external nourishment. When we become uprooted we need to take great care until we reassume the mutually enhancing relationship between rootedness and environment. Trees have roots.

The tree is available.

We demonstrate our preparedness to be of use whenever we are available; willing to perform a function, to respond to a demand. Availability implies approachability and thereby vulnerability. But what can be used is open to abuse. The defenseless one is at the mercy of the one who demands.

The respectful approach to what is available does not depend upon the anticipation of potential usefulness or scarcity of resources. Protection against maltreatment dwells within the relationship, between user and supplier. The quality of their interaction determines the outcome. The more unaware and passive the supplier is, the greater the responsibility resting upon the user. For the permission to exhaust is not implicit in the permission to use.

Whenever we are in need, and therefore demanding, we have to guard against acting blindly. Though we make ourselves available we need to try to prevent the depletion of our resources and to protect the user from the illusion of limitless plenitude. Whatever is used has to be replenished. This requires time, effort and energy. Availability enables use. Use necessitates nourishment. Trees are available.

The tree shelters.

When we seek shelter we need protection, safeguarding against the impact of weather, roving animals or people. We need a home away from home. We become refuges upon the shores of other people's well being. We are the unexpected guest.

A shelter can never be more than an temporary abode which allows us to regain our breath, to recover our strength. In this place of resting we are suspended between the old and the new. The circumstances which made us seek shelter are assessed. We reflect upon the outside from inside; we consider the inside in relation to the outside. We may have to abandon our journey, reroute our path. For if nothing changes we may once again feel a need to seek shelter.

Meanwhile, the shelter exists, providing us with a sense of safety. No questions are asked; a process is facilitated. We do not have to examine the place as a potential dwelling for permanent residence. We have no responsibility regarding its continuing presence. Our task is not to abuse but to use what is offered so that we may continue our respective journeys with an increased chance of arriving at the chosen destination. When we bid farewell, the shelter stays where it is; witness to defeat and resurrection, a symbol of duration. Trees shelter.

The tree belongs.

When we belong we are entitled to be present. We need not expect questions about the reasons behind our stay nor persistent examination of our commitment. It is self-evident that we are in the land that is home, where we have an undisputed right to be; if not through birthright then because time has passed. Once upon a time each one of us became incorporated in the organism of a group.

Sometimes we have to bid farewell to the place on earth which was ours for identification, the niche intimately interwoven with the essence and fabric of our being; the container of our history, supreme witness to the events of our life. Then we are assured that we shall be missed for we belong. Just as an uprooted tree creates a gaping hole in the darkened soil, so our going leaves a gap within the circle of our companions. The newly completed form merely betrays the inside hole which testifies to our departure. Our absence is felt and recognized. We are mourned for we were wanted.

Slowly and gradually the emptiness is filled, with memories and events until one day, nobody will know why, the wound has turned imperceptibly into a scar. There is new growth and the cycle is completed, the circle renewed.

Thus we sow and we reap. We are born and we die. The ground we knew as children is the land we till as adults. The seed of birth becomes the tree of our being. Trees belong.

The Stories

The three eggs
The Tree/Burma

There was once a poor woodcutter who spent his days cutting and selling wood. Although he worked long hours, he earned little money and was barely able to feed and clothe his family.

One night, the woodcutter dreamed he saw a beautiful fairy smiling and waving to him from the hole of a huge tree. The next morning he went into the forest to cut wood, hoping to find the tree he had seen in his dreams, wishing that it housed the tree-spirit he had dreamt about. Just before dusk he found a large tree with a hole in its trunk and decided that this must be the tree which housed the tree-fairy.

From then on, every time he worked in the forest he left a small present for the fairy. Often he talked to the tree-spirit telling it about his life and family. Unbeknownst to him, the tree-fairy grew fond of him and decided to give him a present in return for all his care.

The next day, when the woodcutter came to place his present at the foot of the tree, he found a bird's nest which contained three golden eggs. The woodcutter was astounded and knelt beneath the tree in gratitude. He knew his days of poverty were ended, that his family would no longer have to worry about money.

As he ran home to show the eggs to his family, a bird swooped down and snatched one of the eggs in its beak as it flew up into the air, quickly disappearing out of sight. The woodcutter was upset but knew that even two golden eggs would be of great help to his family. Thirsty, he knelt down to scoop some water from a stream. As he drank, one of the eggs fell into the water and was swallowed by a hungry fish.

The woodcutter mourned the loss of the second egg yet he knew that even one egg would be of aid to his family. Carefully holding the remaining egg close to him, the woodcutter hurried home. As his family gathered round, their cries of joy attracted the attention of a greedy neighbor. Watching through the window, he saw the woodcutter place the egg in a jar of grains for safekeeping. When the woodcutter and his family were asleep, the neighbor crept into the house and stole the last of the three eggs.

When the woodcutter woke up and found the third egg missing, he felt sad and ashamed. He went to the tree-fairy to apologize for his carelessness. All day he chopped wood with a heavy heart. At dusk, he slowly began to make his way home.

While he was carrying his load of wood he looked up and saw a tree full of ripe fruit and decided to take some home for his family. As he picked, his hand touched a bird's nest and when he looked into it, he saw the first golden egg. With a heart full of happiness, he shouted his thanks to the tree-fairy.

When he arrived home, a surprise awaited him. His son had gone fishing and when the woodcutter's wife opened the fish to clean it for dinner, there lay the second golden egg.

The greedy neighbor, hearing the shouts of joy, came to the house to hear what had happened. Their good news filled him with terror. How was all this possible? That night, when all were asleep, he crept into the woodcutter's house and returned the third golden egg to its place of safekeeping in the jar of grains.

The woodcutter sold the three golden eggs for enough money to keep him and. his family comfortable for the rest of their lives. But the woodcutter never forgot the source of his good fortune and continued to bring presents and to talk with the tree-fairy each day for as long as he lived.

Willow wife   *The Tree/Japan*

Close to the hut of a poor man named Heitaro grew a beautiful, tall, willow tree. In the winter, ice crystals on the bare branches sparkled in the sun. In spring, the new green shoots provided a source of hope. In summer, the tree shaded him from the heat and in the autumn, the brightly colored leaves were a sight to behold.

Heitaro loved the willow more than anything else in his life. When some of the villagers wanted to cut down the tree to use its wood, Heitaro convinced them to use wood which he gave them. He could not imagine life without his lovely willow tree.

One night, when Heitaro was praying under the tree, a beautiful young woman appeared. She looked as if she wanted to speak with him but was too shy to do so.

"Honorable lady, I see you are waiting for someone. I will leave."

She spoke softly, "There is no need. No one will come."

"Does he not love you any more.?" asked Heitaro.

"He will not come because he is already here." With these words she smiled and disappeared.

Each evening as Heitaro came to pray beneath the graceful willow boughs, the woman appeared. One night, Heitaro asked, "Will you be my wife, you who come to me from this willow?" The woman agreed to marry him and in time, a child was born. Heitaro knew more happiness than he could ever have imagined.

Years passed. Word came that the Emperor needed fine wood to build a temple to honor the Goddess of Mercy. The villagers decided to offer the wood of the willow because it was the best tree to be found anywhere. Heitaro said to his wife, "Before I met you I could not have endured the loss of the willow but now I have you and the child. We will comfort each other."

The villagers arrived and started to cut down the tree. With no warning Willow wife cried out in anguish, "Husband, It is growing very dark. The room is full of whispers. I am being cut to pieces." Suddenly, the willow fell with a loud crash. Willow wife was no more.

Coyote steals fire *The Tree/Crow/N. Amer. Indian*

In the beginning man lived happily, eating berries, enjoying the warmth of the sun, swimming in the cool water. But when winter came and nights grew cool, man became afraid. Children died from the cold; old people shivered, too cold to move; and food froze. Coyote, like the rest of the Early People did not think about the cold until he came to the place of humans and saw them mourning their dead, starving because their food was frozen.

The next summer, when Coyote was traveling, he came to a village. People spoke to him, "Look how the sun warms us. Feel how hot these stones are. If only we could have this warmth in our tepees when it is winter." Coyote listened and thought about the FireKeepers who lived on a distant mountain. He knew they never gave anyone any of their fire so he decided to steal some of it.

Coyote went to the top of the mountain and watched how the FireKeepers guarded their fire. As he crept around he broke a small branch. The FireKeepers heard the noise and cried out, "Who is there? Who comes to steal our fire?" But, when they looked around they saw only a grey coyote asleep.

All day and night Coyote watched the FireKeepers. He noticed that between the second and third watchers there was a short period of time when no one guarded the fire. The third watcher was too sleepy to move quickly in the early morning.

Coyote ran down the mountain and asked some of the Early People to help him steal fire for the humans who were starving and dying because of the cold. After the Early People agreed to help, Coyote ran back, up to the top of the mountain. Once more a FireKeeper shouted, "Who is there? Who comes to steal our fire?" Once again, when they looked, they saw only a grey coyote asleep in the sun.

All day and night Coyote waited. Then just as the second FireKeeper called to the third to keep watch, Coyote stole a small glowing coal of fire and ran down the mountain. The three FireKeepers ran after him screeching, "Stop thief." They caught Coyote by the tip of his tail. As Coyote felt the FireKeepers' hands, he threw the coal into the air. Chipmunk caught it and began to run but she could not outrun the FireKeepers. She threw the coal to squirrel who in turn threw it to frog. Unable to hold on to it, Frog threw the coal into Wood who swallowed it whole and just stood there, as always.

The FireKeepers gathered around Wood and begged, yelled, pleaded and screamed, "Give us back our fire." They chopped and hacked at Wood but Wood continued to stand. Wood did not give up their fire. At last, the Firekeepers left.

Coyote knew how to take the fire from Wood. He went to the village and showed the humans how to rub two sticks together and how to spin a pointed stick into a hole made of Wood in order to get the fire out. From that time on, humans have known how to stay warm and eat well, during the coldest of winters.

Trees *The Tree/Bible/Middle East*

Yahweh's Tree...(from the prophecy of Ezekiel)
I shall take a seed and plant it upon a high and lofty mountain. It will grow
and become a noble tree and bear much fruit. You and the beasts will live
in its shade and all the birds will nest in its branches. I, Yahweh God, will
plant this tree.

> A tree by a river... (Psalm 1)
>
> Happy the man who delights
> in the law of the Lord.
> He is like a tree
> planted near the flowing water,
> that yields its fruit in due season
> and whose leaves never fade.
>
> Wisdom is a tree of life...(from the book of Proverbs)
>
> Wisdom is a tree of life
> for those who hold her fast;
> those who cling to her, live happy lives.
> Blessed is the man
> who meditates on wisdom and understanding,
> who builds his nest in her foliage
> and spends the night in her branches,
> who sets his family in her shade
> and lives in her shelter.
> In her glory he makes his home.

The spirit in the tree *The Tree/Central and South Africa*

Once upon a time there was a young girl who lived with her father and stepmother, a woman who was very cruel to her. One day, while crying on her
mother's grave, the earth opened up and a bit of green began to sprout. It
became a small sapling and then grew into a strong young tree. The wind
moved the tree's leaves, turning into a voice which told her to eat of the tree's
fruits. As soon as she ate them the girl felt better and stronger.

Her stepmother, noticing the changes in her stepdaughter, became curious and followed the girl to the tree where she saw her eat its fruit. That night, she insisted her husband cut down the tree.

As the tree lay dying, the young girl wept until she saw a small round shape pushing out from the trunk. It grew into a fine pumpkin, out of which trickled a delicate flow of juice. As soon as the girl sipped the juice she felt better and stronger; once more there was a change in her.

Her stepmother, observing this, followed her and threw the pumpkin into a pile of manure. When the girl went back she found a tiny stream gurgling out from the dead trunk. But once again her stepmother found out about the stream and made her husband cover it up with sand.

The next day as the girl lay weeping, a young man approached. He saw the dead tree and decided that its wood would make a fine bow and very good arrows. The girl told him that the tree had once grown from her mother's grave. The two young people took a liking to one another. Together they went to her home so that he could ask her father for her hand in marriage.

Her father agreed on one condition, that the young man shoot twelve buffalo for the wedding feast. Although the hunter had never shot more than one buffalo at a time, he loved the girl and agreed to do it. Taking his new bow and arrow, he set out to find the buffalo.

He had not been out very long when he spied a huge herd. He strung his bow and shot the arrow into the closest buffalo. Much to his surprise the first buffalo fell dead, followed soon after by eleven more animals. The young hunter hurried back to tell the father to send many men so that they could bring the buffalo to the village. The hunter married the girl amidst great feasting and the two lived happily ever after.

The return of the flowers   *The Tree/Aborigines/Australia*

When the creator, Baiame, no longer walked the earth the flowers and trees all died except for three trees which he marked as his own. Only here could the bees make honey. Only here could parents show their children how the earth used to look when flowers and trees graced the earth. Parents and children looked at the honey, longing to taste its sweetness yet they dared not touch the sacred trees. In time, the scent and sight became a fading memory which only the oldest people could remember.

After many years, the All-seeing spirit told Baiame how the people revered his trees, touching no part of the honey made by the bees. As a reward for their respect, Baiame sent them goonbeams and manna though the drought continued and the earth remained bare. The children were delighted with their new found food but the older people mourned the absence of life as it had been, when trees and flowers grew everywhere.

One day, a group of wise elders decided to journey to Baiame to plead with him to return trees and flowers to the earth. Quietly, just before dawn, they slipped away, traveling to the foot of the great mountain. Patiently, they searched for a way up the heights until they found a path of stone steps, cut by the spirits of Baiame.

They climbed for four days and four nights, unwilling to rest before reaching the summit. At the top, too exhausted to go any further, they rested near a bubbling spring of fresh water. To their surprise, the water not only quenched their thirst but also revived their spirits. They stood up, looked around, and saw in the distance, stones piled in the shape of a circle. No longer tired, they made their way to the center of one of the stone circles.

Here they heard the voice of Baiame's spirit messenger who asked the elders why they had come. They told the spirit how all the trees and flowers died when Baiame no longer walked the earth. They spoke of how the bees disappeared. Then, they asked how the trees and flowers and bees could be returned to earth.

The spirit messenger ordered the attendant spirits to lift the elders to the place of Baiame, where flowers and trees bloomed eternally. Tears streamed down their faces as they gasped in awe at the sight of so much beauty. They listened carefully as Baiame told them how they might return trees and flowers and bees to the earth.

Following his instructions, the wise elders gathered as many different trees and flowers as they could hold in their hands. Then the spirits carried the elders down into the stone circle. Here, the elders received further instruction. When the voice of the spirit messenger ceased, the elders climbed down the path of stone steps carefully cradling the tiny plants.

The people of the earth welcomed their elders. They looked with astonishment at the brilliant colors. They smelled the sweet fragrance of the tiny shoots and welcomed the busy sounds of the bees gathering nectar.

Once more trees and flowers graced the earth filling the hearts of the people with hope and joy.

As the spirits foretold, there are still times of drought when the goonbeams and manna take the place of honey but the trees and flowers thrive, sheltering the bees who return with the new rains.

The Tree - The Structures

Theme: THE TREE
Focus: The tree as symbol of myself
Length: 50 minutes

List:
    On board or paper which whole group can see, all of the qualities associated with tree. Do not try to categorize responses. Whatever comes to mind is spoken and written down with no questions asked or comments made.

Paint:
    Image of myself as tree.

List:
    Words or phrases which come to mind.

Divide:
    Into groups of 3-5.

Select:
    Each person selects one quality from the list on board with which he/she wants to work.

Improvise:
    A movement that begins and ends using the chosen word as the accompaniment.

Order:
    The movement phrases so that each person knows when to go. The group may choose to have everyone move at the same time, two or any combination as long as everyone does his/ her sound and movement phrase.

Improvise:
    A beginning and ending for the movement phrases so that everyone in the group knows when to start and finish and how the whole piece begins and ends. Plan what people who are not moving, if any, will do while others are moving.

Share:
    Movement pieces with entire group.
Reflect:
    Upon "how tree is symbol of myself".

Theme:	THE TREE
Focus:	The mystery within a tree
Length:	50 minutes

Bring:	Group members bring in photographs of trees that affect them strongly. (Magazine pictures may also be used as long as they have no writing on them.)

Place:	Photographs in center of room.

Look:	Group members look at all the photos and then select the one with which they choose to work. If several people want to use the same photograph they can gather around it.

Paint:	An image which comes to mind after looking at the photograph.

Write:	A story which begins…"There was once a tree" and which ends with "And that is why….".

Paint:	Image that comes to mind after writing the story.

Share:	Images and stories.

Reflect:	Upon the tree as resource.

Text:	THE THREE EGGS
Focus:	The willingness to serve
Length:	50 minutes

Mime:	In a circle, group members pass an imaginary object around from one to the other in the following ways:
	1. the same imaginary object;
	2. the same imaginary object which is then given a new way to use it each time it is received;
	3. an imaginary object is received, used, changed and passed on.

Move: Group members sit opposite each other, hold hands and establish eye contact.

Recall: A time when I received a gift.

Speak: One says, "I have received a gift. It was...
Each in turn repeats this until all have spoken.

Move: Group members let go of hand and eye contact. Each stands up and takes a brief walk through and around the room, then all return to group circle.

Tell: "The Three Eggs."

Write: For 2 minutes any thoughts which come to mind.

Paint: Image evoked by the words "to receive".

Share: Something about the writing and paintings.

Reflect: Upon entire session.

Text: THE THREE EGGS
Focus: Dreams of beauty
Length: 1 1/2 hours

Imagine: If you could have a beautiful dream, what would it be?
(Do not share or write it.)

Recall: A beautiful dream you have had. (Do not share or write.)

Write: Half a page around the theme, "My beautiful dream".

Sit: As far away from other group members as possible.

Read: Writings one by one as if you were speaking to a **group of** guardian-angels, who dwell near you.

Share: In pairs, with your partner, a memorably beautiful dream (or fantasy):
A   tells dream;
B   listens without speaking;
B   talks (caringly) about ways in which A might be able to make the dream come true in real life;
A   listens although A can stop B at any point.
Reverse roles.

Tell: "The Three Eggs."

Reflect: Upon connections between your own experiences and those contained within the story.

Text: THE THREE EGGS
Focus: Poverty and the sharing of troubles
Length: 1 1/2 hours

Write: Word associations around the words: emptiness, fullness, three.

Recall: An experience of poverty.

Write: About your experience.

Share: With a partner, your word associations and writings.

Discuss: When, and with what kind of person, you are prepared to share your troubles.

Write: Some of the characteristics of this person.

Tell: The whole group the story of "The Three Eggs" up to "He went to the tree fairy to tell her what had happened".

Write: What the woodcutter tells the fairy, how the fairy responds and what the final outcome is.

**Response-
task:**   Create as many spaces on a piece of paper as there are
group members (including self). After a group member
has shared a story ending write in each space which gift
of character/quality this particular woodcutter embodies
such as honesty, endurance, sense of humor... Share this
quality which you have written down with the storyteller.

Tell: Original story ending.

Reflect: Upon session making connections between experience of
poverty and the traits shared by the listeners to the story
endings.

Text: WILLOW WIFE
Focus: Containing a gift
Length: 50 minutes

Recall: A place on earth that is precious to you.

Write: - What makes this particular place precious?
- How often do you go there?.
- What originally made you go there?
- What gift does this place give to you?

*Create: Out of available materials, a small symbolic container for
your gift. Do not complete it.

Write: On a small card, a brief declaration about the container
and its contents.

Tell: "Willow Wife."

Create: Work with container and card for a little longer.

Share: Something about the special place in the containers bearing in mind something which might be learned from
Heitaro's experience.

Reflect: Upon entire session.

*Suggested materials include: twigs, newspaper, string, glue, feathers, scissors, paint, clay, string and colored paper.

Text: WILLOW WIFE
Focus: Taking risks and losing
Length: 1 1/2 hours

Walk: Around room.

Improvise: Speak words, "I lost" in as many different ways as possible. Experiment with various strengths of vocal and physical expression.

               Continue to walk but instead of saying words mostly to self, imagine you are addressing one or several people. Again explore a variety of approaches.

Freeze: On the spot when you remind yourself of whom (in your imagination) you are addressing.

Sit: In place.

Speak: Stand up and briefly speak. Address the ones you were talking to in your imagination. Explain, if necessary defend, your loss. When finished, sit down.

Move: Into large circle when all have spoken.

Tell: "Willow Wife."

Move: Back to place where you were sitting.

Imagine: It is now 2 years after the death of Heitaro's wife.

Speak:	Stand up and briefly speak as if you were Heitaro. Tell about your loss if a few sentences.
Return:	To circle.
Write:	Briefly about what ever comes to mind.
Reflect:	Upon the session.

Text:	WILLOW WIFE
Focus:	Feelings surrounding loss
Length:	1 1/2 hours
Recall:	An object you were once given and then lost.
Response-task:	While listening, record on a sheet of paper how you might have felt had it been you who lost the object.
Describe:	The object to group.
Share:	A few of these responses.
Write:	On a sheet of paper, 3 numbers below 25. Keep the paper.
Move:	To a partner. Stand opposite each other. Establish eye contact and really look at one another. From time to time close your eyes and discontinue contact.
	A slowly walks away in different ways while B stays in place.
	Reverse roles.
Write:	On one side of a sheet of paper, everything that comes to mind related to being left behind. On the other side of the paper write down what enables you to cope with this experience.
Tell:	"Willow Wife."
Look:	At paper with 3 numbers below 25.

Write:	Each number is a year which Heitaro has lived since the death of his wife. He keeps a detailed diary. Make a diary entry for a specific day in each of the 3 years.

Response-task: When listening to the diary entries ask yourself how or where this Heitaro might also find comfort. Make a small painting of this comfort. Give painting to group member who shared diary entry.

Share: Diary entries.

Reflect: Upon entire session.

Text: COYOTE STEALS FIRE
Focus: Seeking fire
Length: 50 minutes

Write: Word associations around warm and cold.

Imagine: A situation in which you are cold.

Improvise: Movement which reflects/expresses your experience.

Move: Huddle together in small groups. Encourage one another to move in order to keep warm.

Recall: For each other, times when it was warm.

Improvise: Build an imaginary fire. Let yourselves be warmed by it. Move accordingly. Extinguish fire and return to large group circle.

Tell: "Coyote Steals Fire."

Drama: Group members cast themselves in the various roles required by the story. It is possible for several people to choose and play the same role.

Group recalls different scenes as the story is developed.

Group locates the improvisation in space and reaches agreement regarding use of language and sound.

Group enacts the story.

De-role: All group members reflect upon links between themselves in role and their other life experiences.

Reflect: Upon entire session.

Text: COYOTE STEALS FIRE
Focus: Jealously guarded possessions
Length: 1 1/2 hours

Paint: On one half of a sheet of paper an image of jealousy. On the other half paint an image of sharing.

Im-provisation: Divide the group into 2 halves. One group is the "have's", the other group is the "have not's".

The "have's" decide on something rare which they guard. The "have not's" wish to obtain what the "have's" possess and devise a system using only wit and words (no physical force) in order to get it. The "have's" do not want to lose what they have. The group has 5 minutes to explore various tactics. Reverse roles.

Look: At your jealousy and sharing paintings.

Write: Down any feelings/thoughts you have on this same sheet of paper.

Write: Take a new sheet of paper and write about a memory which springs to mind whether or not there appears to be an obvious connection to the ideas of jealousy and sharing.

Tell:	"Coyote Steals Fire."
Com-memorate:	Using a piece of card, create a memorial placque to celebrate Coyote's successful mission to steal the fire.
Talk:	Choose a partner. Take your paintings, writings and memorial placque with you. You have 10 minutes each to share your work and to discern some links and make connections.
Reflect:	In large circle upon entire session.

Text:	COYOTE STEALS FIRE
Focus:	Obtaining warmth
Length:	1 1/2 hours
Write:	Word associations around warmth.
Select:	One word.
Write:	Down one word which is, to you, the opposite of this word. Now write a word which, for you, connects these two words.
Paint:	An image evoked by this third (connecting) word.
Paint:	A small image of a landscape.
Write:	Quickly answer the following questions: - What is the landscape called? - Where in the landscape is all the warmth kept hidden? - Why do no people or animals have access to it? - Who decides to try to obtain the warmth? - Which difficulty has to be overcome? - Who or what enables a promising or successful outcome? - How is the warmth continued? - Who or what assures that this will continue to be so?
Write:	Your story.

Response-task:	While listening to each story, distill one sentence which resonates within you. Write this sentence down.
Share:	Images and stories.
Tell:	"Coyote Steals Fire."
Write:	Connect sentences together into a meaningful whole for you.
Reflect:	Upon session, sharing writings if desired.

Text:	TREES
Focus:	Exploring what is evoked by a text
Length:	50 minutes
Distribute:	To all participants, a card containing the text: Yahweh's Tree.
Paint:	An image which represents what these words evoke in you.
List:	5 words related to the image. Write each word on a separate piece of paper.
Collect:	These pieces of paper. Shuffle.
Re-distribute:	Papers. It doesn't matter if participants choose their own word.
Read:	The 5 new words you have picked.
Write:	One sentence for each word which represents whatever the image evokes within you.
Share:	Your words and decide on a sequence.

Read:	Your sentences related to the words in the sequence you have chosen.
Adapt:	Sequence and sentences where necessary to create smooth and flowing continuity.
Read:	The entire sequence of sentences once more.
Reflect:	On whatever feelings and thoughts have arisen during this experience. Make connections with life experiences.

Text:	TREES
Focus:	The tree of life
Length:	1 1/2 hours
Recall:	A tree image which has caught your attention.
Draw/paint:	A representation of this tree.
Write:	List the qualities of trees/this tree which come to mind.
Share:	Some of these qualities and the qualities of your particular tree.
Distribute:	The text of "A Tree by a River."
Paint/write/ move/reflect:	Group members have 30 minutes to copy the text and perhaps to draw/paint/move or reflect. The text is there to be with and to allow it to evoke thoughts, memories and possibilities.
Talk:	Choose a partner and talk for 10 minutes each about what you have just done.
Reflect:	Return to circle and reflect upon entire session.

Text:	TREES
Focus:	The wisdom of wisdom
Length:	1 1/2 hours

Imagine: A human being sitting, standing or perhaps doing something. Hold on to your image.

Imagine: Another human being, this time someone who is wise, in a similar way. Remember this image.

Write: About the various differences between the two images.

Response-task: As you listen to each member's writings describe in one sentence what this person's definition of wisdom might be.

Share: Writings with group.

Give: Each person their possible definitions without discussion.

Talk: In groups of 3 talk for no more than 10 minutes about situations in your life where wisdom has been needed.

Talk: Change to a new group of 3. Talk for 10 minutes about the full consequences of the absence of wisdom.

Return: To circle.

Paint: An image incorporating wisdom and the absence of wisdom.

Distribute: Text of "Wisdom is a Tree of Life."

Write: Each group member writes a story which will enable a young child to learn the difference between wisdom and the absence of wisdom. If group members need help, consider the following:

- Who is expecting trouble?
- What is the nature of the trouble?
- What would be a wise attitude to take?
- Who comes and offers bad guidance?
- What is the bad guidance?

- Who comes and offers good guidance?
- What is the good guidance?
- What is the final outcome?

Read: The stories.

Discuss: Compare the possible definitions of wisdom with the
                 stories and evolve a generally acceptable definition of
                 wisdom and how it differs from deviousness, intelligence
                 and acceptance.

Reflect: Upon entire session.

Text: THE SPIRIT IN THE TREE
Focus: Doubting and keeping faith
Length: 50 minutes

Sit: In groups of 3. Quietly, sit near one another and hold
                 hands for 3 minutes.. Then disengage hands.

Walk: In pairs. One person closes her/his eyes, the other guides
                 partner on a walk; first by firmly holding the partner,
                 then through just the use of voice. Change roles.

Paint: An image of doubt and an image of faith.

Tell: Text while members are painting.

Reflect: Upon session. Connect between the need to doubt and the
                 need to have faith.

Text: THE SPIRIT IN THE TREE
Focus: Receiving and remembering
Length: 1 1/2 hours

Recall: Your earliest or your most vivid memory of a tree or
                 trees.

Write:	Briefly write this down.
Response-task:	Draw a mnemonic image of each group member's story as you listen to them.
Share:	Tree memories.
Share:	Images with storyteller.
List:	Everything you have ever received from a tree or trees.
Choose:	Select one gift which you would like to receive again in the very near future without explanation.
Tell:	"The Spirit in the Tree."
Write/paint:	The story in your own words. At crucial moments (at least 4) on same paper as story, paint illustrative images. Although you use your own words and imagery do not change the basic outline of the story.
Share:	The retellings.
Reflect:	Upon the connections between vivid memories, what has been received from trees and the retellings.

Text:	THE SPIRIT IN THE TREE
Focus:	Longing and giving
Length:	1 1/2 hours

Paint:	A picture of a tree you would love to live close to. Place the image behind you.
List:	The names of all the possible parts of a tree (limbs, trunk etc.).

Share: The words.

Select: 7 of these words.

Paint: 7 images on one sheet of paper which represent the feeling evoked within you by each of these words.

Share: Your 7 paintings and what they represent to you.

List: Various ways in which you experience a tree to be useful.

Share: The lists.

Select: 1 or 2 of these useful characteristics.

Look: At your first painting (the tree you would love to live close to), your 7 feeling paintings and 1 or 2 of the useful characteristics and see whether there is anything you would like to add to your first painting as you listen to the story.

Tell: "The Spirit in the Tree."

Choose: One sentence from the story which resonates within you.

Write: This sentence on your first painting.

Move: In groups of 3 or 4, using your tree image sentence, create a brief movement improvisation which takes as its starting point, the tree's willingness to give.

Share: Your improvisation with the whole group.

Reflect: Upon entire session.

Text: THE RETURN OF THE FLOWERS
Focus: A world without flowers
Length: 50 minutes

Group
painting: On a large sheet of paper (at least 1 × 2 meters) paint an image of a flower garden in bloom. Finish painting in 10 minutes.

Paint: On a small sheet of paper your image of a world without flowers.

Tell: "The Return of the Flowers."

Write: One sentence at the top of a sheet of paper. Repeat this same sentence at the bottom of the paper. In 3 minutes write down all the other sentences which belong in between.

Read: In turn, the writings.

Paint: Return to the group painting of flowers in bloom and complete it.

Reflect: Upon the entire session.

Text: THE RETURN OF THE FLOWERS
Focus: The recovery of joy
Length: 1 1/2 hours

Remind: Yourself of something you noticed this morning after you got up and before you left your home.

Share: Recollection with other group members.

Select: 1 of the images a group member has shared and allow your mind to travel back through the past to a time when you noticed something similar.

Write: About the memory.

Recall: One of your grandparents. If you never met any of them imagine what they might have been like.

Write: Something which they particularly enjoyed (or might have enjoyed).

Imagine: Yourself as a grandparent. Think about something you particularly enjoy. Do you want your grandchild to know about this?

Write: What you enjoy.

Tell: "The Return of the Flowers."

Write: What the elders decided to say to the people of the earth including why they needed to go on this journey, what it had been like and what it feels to return with arms full of flowers. Include in the speech some words of advice for the people of the earth.

Response-   After each speech write 1 sentence which begins with, "I
task: want…"

Tell: Speeches.

Talk: With a partner about the "I want" sentences and the memories.

Reflect: Upon the entire session.

Text:	THE RETURN OF THE FLOWERS
Focus:	Becoming
Length:	1 1/2 hours

Paint: An image of yourself as flower.

Write: If a flower gave you a gift, which gift would this be?
             Write this on your flower painting.

Write: On a small piece of paper (which can later be identified
             as your's) answers to the following:
             - the name and age of a character;
             - the dwelling-place where he/she lives;
             - the gift which you have just written down.

Collect: These sheets of paper.

Re-distribute: Sheets of paper.

Write: A brief story under the title: How... received ....(gift
             from the flower). Include in the story some why's and
             wherefore's as well as some consequences of the receipt
             of this gift.

Read: The stories.

Collect: The stories. Each group member retrieves the story
             which was based upon his/her beginning.

Tell: "The Return of the Flowers."

Connect: Make connections between your image of "myself as
             flower", your gift story and your response to The return
             of the flowers.

Reflect: Upon the entire session.

Questions focusing on trees

1. What is your earliest tree memory?
   Has time affected the way you look at it now?

2. What is your most powerful tree memory?
   How were you influenced by your experience?
   What words come to mind when you think about it?
   Does this memory still have power? If so, what and how?

3. What part, if any, do trees play in your life currently?

4. Do you participate in any ceremonies or rituals involving trees?
   If so, what? How do you feel about them?
   What is their importance to you personally?

5. What qualities come to mind when you think of the word, tree?
   Which one quality is most important to you?

6. What tree might symbolize you?
   How do you come to make this choice?
   Would this choice have been appropriate five years ago?
   Do you think you will choose another tree in five years time?
   What might make this new choice come about?

7. What image comes to mind when you consider The Tree of Life?
   How does it relate to you? If not, why not?

8. What image comes to mind when you consider The Tree of
   Knowledge? How does it relate to you? If not, why not?

9. Have you or anyone in your family made a family tree?
   What was the impulse for doing this?
   How far back can you trace your family roots?
   What stories of your ancestors remain most memorable?
   Who told them to you? Under what circumstances?

10. Have you ever planted a tree? Under what circumstances?

11. Have you ever saved a tree? If so, how?

12. Have you ever watched a tree being cut down?
    How did you feel watching this?
    What images come to mind when you think about this memory?

13. Does the presence of trees play a part in your selection of where to live or work?

14. What images come to mind when you think of forest, treeless plain, or city? How do you feel when you consider these images?

CHAPTER SEVEN

TRICKSTER

Trickster is the eternal paradox, for the moment. Paradoxes are felt immediately and talked about forever. Whenever the paradox crosses our path we are likely to be affected. More often than not, the encounter is followed by a strong release of emotion. We laugh. We cry. We explode in anger. Suddenly a channel for expression has been opened. Although the way we choose to use this channel remains our responsibility, the creation occurred despite us, because of the impact of the paradox. Embracing all opposites, the paradox appears to be no solution. Yet it resolves everything even though nothing seems to happen. Although it resolves nothing, our perceptions are irrevocably changed.

The "ever-changing constant one" becomes manifest in times of stuckness when all known solutions lead to a growing awareness of limited sameness, when our energy cannot find an unblocked channel. The paradox is then born, out of the many forces which meet, within the contradictions and complexities of life. Whenever a collection of seemingly irreconcilable, opposite forces meet, there, in the everlasting flash of inspiration, Trickster, the paradox appears. We are lifted beyond the actual situation to continue on another plain until a further paradox is needed to overcome a difficulty.

Trickster is inherently present yet continuously absent; imminent and immanent. The one who dwells within us is the one we encounter without in a time of danger. The combination of events and circumstances which leads to its appearance eludes us. We are not in control of the manifestation, and because we are not in control and do not understand the processes which activate the trickster within to appear outside, we rarely appreciate the uninvited visitor who acts as if she/he is the true ruler of the castle.

How can it be that one so alien behaves as if we are intimately connected? We are affronted, perhaps angry. Our boundaries have been transgressed. The more the one who appeared out of nowhere suggests that presence is an undisputed right, the more we will demonstrate how much we wish him/her to disappear. We do not like to see our precious belongings taken out of the cupboards and handled as if the visitor has an unalienable right to do so. We certainly do not appreciate the puzzlement which dwells within us, as if we vaguely recognize the intruder and discern a deep but dim awareness of familiarity.

If only we could welcome the stranger and recognize the shadow as the reflection of our essence, our regrets as the ultimate stronghold of our dreams, then we might grow to live more comfortably with the visitor who sits in our favorite chair and chuckles while reading the most private passages in our carefully hidden diary. Infinitely superior yet completely indifferent; an impossible, enviable position. It is our position.

When Trickster manifests his/her innate presence we change shape. We can no longer be trusted to do as we promised. We surprise ourselves and behave in unexpected ways; shout at an old person, jump out of a moving train, refuse favorite food or laugh at jokes we previously did not find funny. Our behavior is unpredictable and why should we care? We move with cunning agility and we believe we hold the world in our hands.

We do. For we are inhabited by the grandiose power which spins a web of make-believe. We whirl. We stun. We attract. And people come; helplessly, hopelessly moving toward the source of the dynamic, vital energy, the beckoning light. They come and they crash upon the moment of the encounter for the light is hard, cold and uninhabitable. There is no space or room for anything else, anyone else, save the inner glow which radiates so fatally. The light shines and disappears. We present ourselves; mask upon mask, identified with no one and therefore, the owner of all. For the one who changes the masks is the one who is absent and ever present, the inner Trickster.

When we are elusive we refuse to take on form. We do not wish to be held responsible or identified; we do not want to be known. We evade, delude, avoid. The direction of our gaze is unsteady, the expression on our face shifts. Our whole body suggests that given a chance, we will disappear. Therefore, we come as close to absence as we can. We vacate ourselves as much as possible. Front stage is played by a group of characters, all of whom are us, but none of whom are we prepared to own. Is not the whole more than the sum of the parts? Trickster runs the show only by the grace of the self who withdraws.

When nothing matters we have either achieved a state of great enlightenment or one of total indifference, or both. We are no longer actively connected to the people around us. Although we are not reduced to inaction, what we do has become irrelevant. The choice is unimportant, the outcome does not matter. Trickster acts this way out of a profound awareness of the ultimate constraint of thought-limited choice and because of the undeniable reality of finite knowledge and final ignorance.

Trickster is absolute and therefore, innocent. We are only guilty when operating and acting within an awareness of a moral code. Trickster is beyond such knowledge. His/her actions are inspired by untempered desire, the simple impulse to act. The unity of beginning and outcome makes Trickster no more than a mediating midwife who witnesses the birth of beauty and beast without causing the conception of either.

Do not ask Trickster for commitment; it will not be forthcoming. Trickster cannot be committed to anything or anyone nor will explanations be offered. If it so happens that Trickster's actions coincides with other peoples' wishes, that is their good and accidental fortune. Nothing is promised or given by Trickster for to give implies acknowledgement of the existence of others. Trickster would rather not go quite so far.

Trickster generates space by crowding us out and confronting us with how we sullenly clutch to known patterns. Trickster fearlessly treads where most are reluctant to go; without love and without hate, acting and dreaming the wildest dreams in order to realize them all. There is no choosing. For does not choice depend on preference which in turn depends on memory and reflection? Reflection paralyses Trickster by reducing the lively, spontaneous one to inaction. Yet, our survival depends upon our capacity to make reflection and action meet. The struggle continues because the confrontation can be only partially successful. For Trickster action and reflection are reluctant soulmates even though they share the same inner world.

Our inner Trickster does not suffer fools lightly. We will be pushed, pulled and challenged until the subject of our interference wakes up and recognizes the true face of the one who approached, pestered, tortured and raped. Only then is the universal Trickster freed to continue wandering. As long as the victim fails to recognize who is encountered, the one whose task it is to awaken dutifully stays around. The pressure is increased until the original source of the difficulties is identified.

We have to know what is bothering us in order to free ourselves from it. As long as we fail to see, the difficulty is likely to stay around. Then our apparent solutions are merely temporary avoidances which eventually become our problems. Trickster, however, has infinite patience. Presence is guaranteed until the day that he/she is recognized, named and declared unwanted. Then, when the front stage is cleared, and the individual behind the scene is prepared to come out front, Trickster is liberated to go and perform in someone else's show.

When we cease to wonder we have lost our inner Trickster and we are deprived of a vital source of energy, a potent inner enemy as well as a passionate inner lover. Trickster is our bounce; the return of energy after we have had to bend our head in defeat. We may have lost, but only temporarily, is Trickster's message. We may have been sent away but Trickster assures us that we are not homeless. Life's energy will continue to flow through us and out of us as long as we allow Trickster to be. It may be difficult to accept that Trickster is; that the force which cannot be named or described is ever changing in its presence. Although we can, in fear, attempt to suppress his/her appearance on the surface of our existence so that we may appear to be reliable, this inherent strength is not to be played with. It needs an exit, which, if not provided willingly, will manifest itself by force.

Do not deny Trickster access to the world. They need one another badly. Without their continuing mutual encounter we shall all suffer for Trickster embraces all opposites. Whenever people inhabit a one sided house Trickster will appear in order to redress the balance, patiently staying around until multidimensionality is acknowledged and achieved, until the eternal paradox is accepted. Only when this happens can Trickster depart, returning periodically in order to ensure a continuing balance.

Therefore, Trickster is the great healer, the destroyer and the builder; the one who brings about change and opens up new vistas. We do not always like the view.

The Stories

The Caterpillar and the Wild Animals   *Trickster/Masai/Africa*

Once upon a time, Caterpillar visited Hare's house in the forest while Hare was away. When Hare returned and noticed tracks on the floor he shouted, "Who is here?"

Caterpillar answered in a loud and menacing voice. "I am all powerful. I am the great warrior who can crush elephants and turn rhinoceroses to dust. I am invincible." Hare ran out wondering what a small animal like himself could do against one who was so powerful.

As he ran he met Jackal who agreed to come back to Hare's house to help get rid of the mighty creature. Jackal called out, "Who is here in my friend Hare's house?"

Caterpillar answered, "I am all powerful. I am the great warrior who can crush elephants and turn rhinoceroses to dust. I am invincible." Jackal turned and left saying he could do nothing against one so powerful.

Once more Hare ran out looking for someone to help. But after hearing the fearsome words of the powerful stranger, Leopard, Elephant and Rhinoceros all agreed that whoever was in Hare's house was too strong for them.

Totally discouraged, Hare met Frog and told him of his troubles. Frog agreed to come and see what he could do. Frog shouted, "Who is here in Hare's house?

Caterpillar roared, "I am all powerful. I am the great warrior who can crush elephants and turn rhinoceroses into dust. I am invincible."

Frog gulped, took a deep breath and shouted back, even more loudly, "I am the strongest of all living creatures. I leap over mountains. I fly over rivers. I fear no one. Whosoever arouses my wrath lives to regret his foolish action."

When Caterpillar heard Frog's ferocious voice, Caterpillar came out and said, "Do not hurt me. I am only a caterpillar." The other animals who had been listening from outside dragged Caterpillar out. They all had a good laugh at the trick he had played.

The Harvest

Fox and Wolf harvested the field of barley which they had planted, cut the grain and carried the sheaves to the barn where they spread them out to dry in preparation for threshing. Then they asked Bear to help them thresh.

Wolf suggested they divide the work. Fox immediately climbed up to the rafters and said he would support the beams while the other two worked. As Bear and Wolf prepared the grain, Fox occasionally dropped a piece of wood on them to let them know he was working hard to keep the rafters from falling down. When Bear and Wolf complained, Fox told them they were lucky to have the easy work, that he was almost dead from working so hard to protect them.

When Bear and Wolf finally finished, Fox leaped down from the rafters and pretended to be totally exhausted. Wolf asked, "How shall we divide the harvest?"

Fox looked as if he were thinking and then said, "There are already three piles on the floor. The biggest shall go to Bear, for he is the biggest. The middle-sized pile shall go to Wolf for he is not the biggest and not the smallest. The smallest pile shall go to me for I am the smallest of the three of us." Bear and Wolf agreed and Bear got a heap of straw, Wolf got a heap of chaff and Fox took the little pile of clean grain.

They took their piles to the mill for grinding. Fox's pile made a rough sound as it was ground in contrast to the smooth sound made when Bear and Wolf's piles were ground. "Why is this?" asked Bear, "Fox's grain does not sound like our's".

Fox said, "Do not worry. Mix some sand with your grain and it will sound just like mine." Bear and Wolf mixed some sand with their straw and their chaff and when they started grinding, the sound was just the same as that made by Fox's grain. This ended their worry and they went home thinking they had the same supply of food for winter as did Fox.

Hermes and Apollo

Maia looked at her newborn babe snuggling happily against her warmth. She sang him one more song before calling to a nymph to watch him while he slept. As Maia walked away she thought she heard the tinkling of laughter but shook her head. No newly born infant could make such a sound.

High above her the sun-god Apollo drove his chariot in the sky. Each morning, as he made his way, he looked with contentment on his herd of cattle; this morning was no different. He smiled as he thought of them but his smile soon disappeared. This morning, though he looked everywhere, he saw no cattle. He stared, then called, then shouted to them but his only answer was silence. Consumed with rage, Apollo left his chariot in the sky and went to look for his cattle. Despite careful searching he could find no trace of them, not even a hoofprint.

The people of the earth sweated from the heat of the sun which did not set. Apollo paid no attention. He looked everywhere and finding nothing, promised a great reward to any satyr who could discover where his cattle were. The satyrs combed the mountains and found nothing but a lovely nymph tending a newborn babe who was making strange music. "What is the instrument the infant plays?" they asked of the nymph.

"I do not know. But this marvelous babe made it himself, out of a tortoise, and then strung it with some cowgut," responded the nymph.

"Cowgut?" roared the satyrs. "Where did he get cowgut? They quickly sped to Apollo who took the babe and the instrument and strode off to see his father, Zeus.

'This is the babe who has stolen my cattle," said Apollo in a fearsome voice. "He is the thief. He must be punished." The infant cried piteous tears, hoping to soften Apollo's wrath and ease the judgment of his father Zeus. The babe peered out from under his hand to see if he had reached Apollo's heart. He had not long to wait. "My cattle's skins have been found in this babe's cave." He held up the infant's hand. "See, his fingers are still stained with the blood of my cattle."

Zeus looked unhappily at the guilty infant and his furious halfbrother. The babe crooned with feigned innocence, "Mighty Apollo, you have great skill. No other could have found me out. Listen, I will play a song for you." The babe played sweetly on the instrument. "I made this just for you. Here, take it. We will make some music together."

Reluctantly, Apollo took the instrument and played as the babe took out another of his creations, a pipe cut from reeds. For a time their music filled the air and pushed away all discord. Then the babe overstepped himself and said, "I will give you this instrument as well if you will tell me how to read the future."

Apollo felt his rage rising again and looked at Zeus for help. Zeus said to

Apollo, "He has given you a gift, have you no birth gift for him?

Apollo observed the tiny child, Hermes, and said to him, "I will give you my golden staff with which I used to herd my cattle. If you wish to learn to read the future you must go to the muses on Mount Parnassus." He turned to his father and said, "It is time to leave. I must drive my chariot across the sky."

Zeus, noticing the smile of triumph on the face of his newborn son said, "I will not ask you what you wish to have as your birthright. I fear it would be more than I would give. I will make you god of thieves, of cunning and of make-believe. In addition, I will have you as my messenger but you must promise never to tell me lies."

Hermes said, "Father, I will always tell you the truth as long as you do not require that I tell you the whole truth. There must be room for fantasy." Zeus shook his head with laughter, pride and wonder at this new child of his.

Fox and Wolf   *Trickster/Tibet*

While traveling through the forest Fox felt himself grow very hungry. When he came to Wolf's house he stopped and peeked in. Wolf was out; only his two little children were home. Immediately Fox ran in, killed the children and took them home for his dinner. From the top of the mountain Mother Wolf saw her children being attacked by Fox and rushed home. By the time she arrived, Fox and her children were gone.

Father Wolf returned home and became enraged when he heard what happened. He vowed to kill Fox. Meanwhile, Fox was sitting on the edge of a mountain thinking. "Wolf will be furious when he finds out what I have done and will try to kill me. I must think of a plan." He sat down on a large stone and boiled up a big pot of glue.

When Wolf found him he asked, "Hey Fox, are you the one who killed my children."

Fox answered, "Not me brother. I sit on the edge of the mountain boiling glue."

Wolf asked, "What will you do with the glue you have boiled?"

"If you take the boiled glue and smear it on your eyes you will be able to see the countries of both gods and men! And, it also has an exceptionally fine taste," replied Fox.

Wolf believed that Fox was telling him the truth so he said, "Please Fox, smear some of your glue on my eyes." Fox pretended to give the matter some thought and then agreed. He took the boiling glue and smeared it all over Wolf's eyes.

Wolf cried, "Oh Fox, I can't see anything."

Fox said, "Close your eyes and look at the sun. That will help you to see all the wonders I have recounted." Wolf closed his eyes until they were firmly sealed. Gleefully, Fox crept away. Wolf, blinded from the glue, painfully made his way down the steep mountain slopes. He scratched the glue from his eyes and on the second day, both his eyes began to open.

Trickster Tales 15 and 16   *Trickster/Winnebago/N. Amer. Indian*

On Trickster proceeded. As he walked along, he came to a lovely piece of land. There he sat down and soon fell asleep. After awhile he woke up and found himself lying on his back without a blanket. He looked up above him and saw to his astonishment something floating there. "Aha, aha! The chiefs have unfurled their banner! The people must be having a great feast for this is always the case when the chief's banner is unfurled." With this he sat up and then first realized that his blanket was gone. It was his blanket he saw floating above. His penis had become stiff and the blanket had been forced up. "That is always happening to me," he said. "My younger brother, you will lose the blanket, so bring it back." Thus he spoke to his penis. Then he took hold of it and, as he handled it, it got softer and the blanket finally fell down. Then he coiled up his penis and put it in a box. And only when he came to the end of his penis did he find his blanket. The box with the penis he carried on his back.

After that he walked down a slope and finally came to a lake. On the opposite side he saw a number of women swimming, the chief's daughter and her friends. "Now," exclaimed Trickster, "is the opportune time: now I am going to have intercourse." Thereupon he took his penis out of the box and addressed it, "My younger brother, you are going after the chief's daughter. Pass her friends, but see that you lodge squarely in her, the chief's daughter." Thus speaking he dispatched it. It went sliding on the surface of the water. "Younger brother, come back, come back! You will scare them away if you approach in that manner!" So he pulled the penis back, tied a stone around its neck, and sent it out again. This time it dropped to the bottom of the lake. Again he pulled it back, took another stone, smaller in size, and attached it to its neck. Soon he sent it forth again. It slid along the water, creating waves as it passed along. "Brother, come back, come back! You will drive the women away if you create waves like that!" So he tried a forth time. This time he got a stone, just the right size and just the right weight, and attached it to its neck. When he dispatched it, this time it went directly toward the designated place. It passed and just barely touched the friends of the chief's daughter.

They saw it and cried out, "Come out of the water, quick!" The chief's daughter was the last one on the bank and could not get away so the penis lodged squarely in her. Her friends came back and tried to pull it out, but all to no avail. They could do absolutely nothing. Then the men who had the reputation for being strong were called and tried it but they, too, could not move it. Finally they all gave up.

Then one of them said, "There is an old woman around here who knows many things. Let us go and get her." So they went and got her and brought her to the place where this was happening. When she came there she recognized immediately what was taking place.

"Why this is First-born, Trickster. The chief's daughter is having intercourse and you are all just annoying her." Thereupon she went out, got an awl and straddling the penis, worked the awl into it a number of times, singing as she did so:

"First-born, if it is you, pull it out! Pull it out!"

Thus she sang. Suddenly in the midst of her singing, the penis was jerked out and the old woman was thrown a great distance. As she stood there bewildered, Trickster, from across the lake, laughed loudly at her. "That old naughty woman! Why is she doing this when I am trying to have intercourse? Now she has spoiled all the pleasure."

Loki and Baldur   *Trickster/ Scandanavia*

Loki was jealous of Baldur. He grew more furious as he watched people give love and attention to Baldur while he, Loki, received nothing but suspicion and dislike. One day he heard that Baldur had dreamed of his own death. He saw Frigg, Baldur's mother rush about getting promises from all the animals, vegetables, elements and minerals, that none would harm her son. Loki watched as the protected Baldur received the blows of stones and branches from the village youth without harm. Loki seethed with jealousy and vowed to find a way to kill Baldur.

Changing himself into an old lady, Loki waited to talk to Frigg when she was alone. By cunning conversation, he learned that she had not thought to ask the help of the tiny mistletoe which grows out of the oak. Out of Frigg's view, Loki changed back to himself and ran into the forest, searching everywhere for the small plant. When he found it, he stripped its leaves and berries and fashioned the mistletoe branch into an arrow.

He ran back into the village where Baldur stood and noticed Hod, Baldur's blind brother. "Why do you not throw stones or sticks as the others do?" asked Loki.

"I have nothing to throw and could not see where to aim it even if I had a branch or stone," explained Hod.

"You should have a chance to join the fun," said Loki. "I will help you." Loki put the arrow of mistletoe into Hod's hand and helped him to throw it at Baldur. The mistletoe arrow struck Baldur through the heart and he fell down, dead. People gasped and moaned and looked about to see how this had happened. When they saw the look on Loki's face they knew it was he who had murdered Baldur. They swore to get revenge.

Trickster - The Structures

Theme:	TRICKSTER
Focus:	Exploring trickster
Length:	50 minutes

Paint: A picture of trickster.

Locate: Your trickster in a landscape.

Share: Paintings and talk briefly about who and where.

Write: Brief answers to the following questions:
- What is the time of day?
- Whom does he/she/it encounter?
- What do they talk about?
- Which challenge is set?
- How are the problems overcome?
- What is the outcome?

Write: Story using all the answers to the questions.

Share: Stories.

Talk: About characteristics of trickster. Think about trickster as the embodiment of paradox for the moment. Recall "tricksters" you have known and been.

Reflect: Upon the entire session.

Theme:	TRICKSTER
Focus:	Creating a trickster
Length:	50 minutes

Reflect: On trickster as being....*and*...rather than this...*or*...that.

*Create: A mask from materials on hand which reflects aspects of an inner trickster. Work without judgment or censorship. Make sure you can breathe, speak and move comfortably while wearing your mask.

Convene: A council of tricksters.

**Improvise: With all group members wearing their masks, each in turn introduce him/herself as trickster giving name, most important traits and particular abilities. (Maximum 10 minutes.)

Reflect: Without masks, talk about trickster characters and connect to real life experiences.

*Bring in paper plates, cardboard, yarn, scissors, glue, stapler, bits of material, sparkles, etc.

** Facilitator remains outside "council". Does not wear or make a mask. Any groupmembers who are uncomfortable with the exercise, should be encouraged to watch.

Text: THE CATERPILLAR AND THE WILD ANIMALS
Focus: "Help!"......"No! Not from me."
Length: 50 minutes

Write: A predicament (easily noticed by anyone with a degree of sensitivity) on a piece of paper.

Collect: Papers and redistribute them.

Read: The predicament.

Write: A story about someone *not* offering help. Explain the motives at length.

Tell: "The caterpillar and the wild animals."

Im-provisation:	In groups of 4 (as jackal, leopard, elephant or rhinoceros) briefly develop your explanation/version of what happened outside the house.
Share:	These versions and explore how it is that the most fantastic explanations can be used in order to avoid acknowledgment of having been intimidated.
Reflect:	Upon the entire session.

Text:	THE CATERPILLAR AND THE WILD ANIMALS
Focus:	Keeping at bay
Length:	1 1/2 hours
Think:	About an effective, strongly worded sentence which will definitely keep other people away from you for awhile.
Write:	These words on a role or sheet of paper as if they were graffiti on a wall. Each group member writes something.
Improvise:	In groups of 3, choose one sentence from those written and create a brief improvisation which will end once this sentence is used.
Share:	Improvisations.
Tell:	"The caterpillar and the wild animals" up to: Frog shouted: "Who is here in Hare's house?"
Improvise:	In groups of 3, create a short scene which answers this question and ends the story.
Present:	The scenes.
Tell:	The rest of "The caterpillar and the wild animals".
Reflect:	Upon the entire session.

Text:	THE CATERPILLAR AND THE WILD ANIMALS
Focus:	Intimidation and transformation
Length:	1 1/2 hours

Paint: Image evoked by "intimidation".

Look: At the paintings.

Response-task: Leave a note near every painting stating which feeling this painting evokes in you.

Read: These notes.

Share: The notes and explore how (if necessary) the group could transform these feelings into those which are more comfortable.

Move: Embody the uncomfortable feelings. Develop a way of moving from the uncomfortable feelings to comfortable/enjoyable experiences.

Return: To circle.

Tell: "The caterpillar and the wild animals" up to: Frog shouted: "Who is here in Hare's house?"

Write: Your own ending.

Read: The various endings including the original.

Paint: The image evoked by "Transformation".

Share: The paintings.

Connect: Make connections between the paintings, the feelings and the story endings.

Reflect: Upon the entire session.

Text:	THE HARVEST
Focus:	Allowing someone to fool you
Length:	50 minutes

Recall: A memory of seeing a magician at work.

Response-task: Listen to memory and encapsulate this person's experience in one word. Write this word down.

Share: Memories.

Select: One word from those you have written down.

Stand: In circle.

Clap: A rhythm as a group.

Move: One by one, each group member will enter the circle in a brief movement improvisation or dance which embodies something evoked by the selected word. The selected word may be used as vocal accompaniment by group member. When the group member is finished, he/she will return to the circle and the next person will begin.

Tell: "The harvest."

Move/dance: Imagine that one evening there is a gathering of foxes, all like the one in the tale. They too stand in a circle and enter it one by one boasting in movement of their audacious tricks. Knowing that foxes must not boast for too long by themselves, each has developed a system whereby the other foxes copy and learn the boaster's movements. Thus, one by one they share their deeds. All dance the boasters' dances.

Talk:	About the conditions between being fooled and fooling.
Reflect:	Upon the entire session.

Text: THE HARVEST
Focus: Friendship
Length: 1 1/2 hours

Paint:	6 images on one piece of paper evoked by the idea of friendship.
Share:	Talk about the images and what they represent.
Tell:	"The harvest."
Write:	As Fox, Bear or Wolf, write a letter to an animal friend describing the recent events and whatever else comes to mind. The friend, someone you have known and been close to for years, is aware that this friendship of the three of you is important to you.
Collect:	The letters and redistribute them.
Write:	An answer to the letter you have just received bearing in mind the importance of the friendship of Fox, Bear and Wolf.
Return:	Both letters to sender.
Response-task:	On a big sheet of paper create as many spaces as there are members in the group. After each set of letters has been read, write/draw something in one space which relates to the concept of what friendship involves according to what is said in the letters.

Read:	The letters.
Discuss:	The ideas and feelings in some of the letters.
Reflect:	Upon the entire session.

Text:	THE HARVEST
Focus:	Conscience
Length:	1 1/2 hours

Paint:	An image evoked by conscience on half of one sheet of paper. On the other half paint an image evoked by absence of conscience.
Divide:	The group in half.
Discuss:	For 10 minutes one group talks about the contribution conscience makes to human well-being. The other half talks about the contribution absence of conscience makes to human well-being.
Return:	To circle.
Tell:	"The harvest."
Im-provisation:	In groups of 3 prepare an enactment of the story using all 3 group members who sooner or later play each of the 3 animals.
Present:	The dramas.
Discuss:	With first discussion group the other topic, (the one you did not talk about the first time) for 10 minutes.
Return:	To circle.

Place:	Paintings in the center.
Write:	Whatever you wish on your paintings.
Share:	Whatever is evoked by the material.
Reflect:	Upon entire session.

Text: HERMES AND APOLLO
Focus: Soft spots, teasing and the need for change
Length: 50 minutes

Write:	A list of possible soft spots (things, ideas, people) about which you do not like being teased.
Read:	The lists.
Select:	One soft spot you would enjoy working with.
Write:	A brief quasi-poetic tease for an *imaginary* person in 3 minutes.
Write:	Briefly about what you found difficult/easy when doing this task.
Paint:	An image of how you are feeling right now.
Tell:	"Hermes and Apollo."
Place:	Paintings in the circle.
Explore:	The relationship between the need for change, anger and teasing.
Reflect:	Upon the entire session.

Text:	HERMES AND APOLLO
Focus:	To charm, yearn, seduce
Length:	1 1/2 hours

Walk: Slowly around the room establishing eye contact occasionally. There is no reason to go out of your way to be friendly. Now, change your idea of your relationship to these people and make them important to you. Establish eye contact based on your new views of the importance of your relationships. Increase your use of charm.

Return: To circle.

Talk: Say something complimentary to the person next to you using all the charm you have. Having received a compliment, give one. Ask for something that is relatively small from the person next to you using all the yearning you have. Having listened to a request, make one.

Suggest something pleasurable for both of you to the person next to you using all the seductive powers you possess. Having listened to the suggestion, make one.

Tell: "Hermes and Apollo."

Create: A presentation using the 3 words, charm, yearn and seduce as your guidelines. All group members work individually. The presentation may include movement, drama or a visual representation.

Share: Your work with one another.

Talk: About the issues raised by the presentations.

Reflect: Upon entire session.

Text:	HERMES AND APOLLO
Focus:	White lies and half truths
Length:	1 1/2 hours

Tell: "Hermes and Apollo."

Recall: A favorite white lie.

Share: A white lie you have used recently.

Talk: With a partner. Decide upon an area of each other's lives about which you have little or no actual information. Interview your partner for a few minutes. Be aware that your partner will mingle truth with fantasy. Reverse roles.

Share: With partner how you felt not knowing what was or was not true.

Recall: A situation where you were not believed even though you told the whole truth. Remember your feelings but do not share this experience.

Prepare: In groups of 3, a presentation titled, "The face of half-truth". Use, sound, movement and/or drama.

Present: Your work.

Talk: About your experiences in this session, focusing upon your own need to protect privacy as well as your need to believe.

Reflect: Upon entire session.

Text:	FOX AND WOLF
Focus:	Morality as a way of coping
Length:	50 minutes

Paint: The image evoked by the word "danger".

Draw: With crayon or pen, and without lifting it off the paper, responses to the word danger.

Explore: With a partner all that is exciting and useful about danger; using movement, then sound and finally, words.

Write: List all these advantages.

Tell: "Fox and Wolf."

Write: In one sentence the moral of this story.

Collect: Papers and redistribute them.

Improvise: A brief-defense statement emphasizing why this particular moral advances mankind's well-being.

Discuss: Whether or not you believe these morals should guide our actions.

Reflect: Upon entire session.

Text:	FOX AND WOLF
Focus:	Triumph and retribution
Length:	1 1/2 hours

Recall: A situation in which you outwitted someone. If you cannot recall such a situation remember one in which you were outwitted.

Response-task:	While listening to the memories paint the image evoked by the word "triumphant".
Share:	Memories.
Play:	A few movement games such as tag.
Move:	Sit back to back with a partner. Try to push partner across the floor.
Tell:	"Fox and Wolf."
Write:	A letter to the animal community on behalf of Wolf asking that something be done about Fox.
Collect:	Letters and redistribute them.
Imagine:	You have been part of extensive deliberations with the other animal council members.
Write:	A letter to Wolf stating the decision the council members have come to and how the decision will be implemented.
Read:	Both the letter you received and the response you wrote.
Look:	At the paintings.
Talk:	About punishment, treatment, banishment and forgiveness.
Reflect:	Upon the entire session.

Text:	FOX AND WOLF
Focus:	Remorse and the longing for change
Length:	1 1/2 hours

Write: Words you associate with "remorse".

Remember: A time in your life related to "remorse".

Write: Briefly about that time.

Sit: Opposite a partner.

Move: Make some form of eye or physical contact while focusing your thoughts on "forgiveness". Do not speak.

Return: To circle.

Write: A little more for 3 minutes.

Share: Some of your writings with no discussion.

Tell: "Fox and Wolf."

Write: Rewrite the story (without retelling the tale) having everyone resist the particular bad deed which he/she committed. Each writer decides which bad deeds were committed.

Response-task: While listening, ask yourself which *new* temptations Fox, Wolf and others are now exposed to. Record these new temptations.

Read: The writings.

Discuss: The connections between remorse and the need for change.

Reflect: Upon the entire session.

Text:	TRICKSTER TALES #15 AND # 16
Focus:	Surprise, surprise
Length:	50 minutes

Recall: An occasion when you really felt surprised.

Describe: The experience.

Read: Winnebago tales #15 and #16 to group.

Decide: Which element in the stories surprises you the most.

Write: What this one element is.

Imagine: If you had the ability to use this surprise how might you use it? Where? When?

Write: A brief version of what might happen. Avoid censoring yourself.

Response-task: While listening to a story, work out a way in which this kind of fantastic happening could be reduced to size and made into a really good, actual surprise.

Read: Stories.

Write: Suggestion down on a piece of paper and give it to the reader.

Read: Responses.

Reflect: Upon entire session.

Text: TRICKSTER TALES #15 AND #16
Focus: An exploration of sexuality
Length: 1 1/2 hours

Write: On a piece of paper the word, "I". Leave some space and then write, "wander". Leave some more space and write, "aimlessly".
Following each word write a few words you associate with it.

Draw: Select a crayon or felt-tipped pen and allow it to wander aimlessly across the paper. If you lose your "aimlessness" try to recapture the feeling with which you began drawing.

Draw: Work with a partner. One draws a meaningless "squiggle", the other turns this into a representation of something. Play with this for awhile. Exchange roles frequently.

Tell: Tale #15.

Imagine: That you read/saw this story for the first time in a newspaper strip.

Draw/write: The story involving at least 6 different frames.

Place: Your strip near the others somewhere in the room.

Look: At the strips.

Choose: A particular phrase/moment/scene in one of the strips which gives you the most delight. Are you willing to share your choice with the other group members? If not, why not?

Discuss: The connection between this story and the way sex and sexuality are normally discussed with your family and friends.

Collect: Your strip.

Compare: The work you did around "I wander aimlessly" and the squiggles with the strip. Are there any relevant links?

Reflect: Upon the entire session.

Text: TRICKSTER TALES #15 AND #16
Focus: Permitted pleasures
Length: 1 1/2 hours

Talk: Group members sitting in a circle take turns mentioning as many things/experiences that give them pleasure.

Move: In pairs, stand opposite one another. Copy partner's movement faithfully. Through use of bodily expression aim to encourage partner to express great bodily pleasure.

Return: To circle.

Speak: The first person says in a tone of voice which inspires total disbelief, "I love…(and adds whatever he/she wishes to add). The next person increases the likelihood of being believed a tiny bit and says, "I love…(using same words). Continue until the last person nearly swoons at her/his own utterance. Repeat the sequence once again beginning with belief transforming into disbelief.

Write: One word which encapsulates the feeling derived from: "splashing about naked in the pleasantly warm water of a stunning forest pool".

Paint: Image evoked by this word.

Recall: A time when/where/with whom you last felt like this. Do
                    not share the memory.

Tell: Winnebago tales #15 and #16.

Write: A brief report of these events for your eccentric school
                    magazine, a woman's weekly or the local evening news-
                    paper.

Read: The reports.

Reflect: Upon issues raised by the work and upon the entire
                    session.

Text: LOKI AND BALDUR
Focus: If only....
Length: 50 minutes

Paint: An image evoked by destroy.

Clay: Sculpt an image evoked by destroy.

Read: "Loki and Baldur." Do not retell it.

Notice: The moments in the story where destruction and fear of
                    destruction or apparent triumph over destruction gain
                    hold.

Write: These moments down on a piece of paper.

Ask: Yourself what might, at each moment, have stopped these
                    events from developing in the way they did.

Write:	Which quality/characteristic would have been required. Formulate your statements and begin with, "If only...."
Share:	"If only..." statements with the group.
Place:	Paintings and clay work in the circle.
Select:	One of your "if only..." statements.
Change:	The "If only.." beginning into "I want.." (e.g. "If only Baldur could have been less frightened of death" to "I want to be less frightened of death.")
Reflect:	Whether this change in the statement feels personally relevant.
Talk:	About the implications of the change and your feelings around the issues raised.
Reflect:	Upon the entire session.

Text:	LOKI AND BALDUR
Focus:	Furious jealousy
Length:	1 1/2 hours
Tell:	The introduction of Loki and Baldur up to: "One day he heard that Baldur dreamed of his own death."
Paint:	A picture representing Baldur's dreams.
Tell:	"Loki and Baldur" up to:"Loki vowed to find a way to kill Baldur."
Paint:	A picture representing Loki's feelings.

Write:	Describe 3 incidents which occurred between Loki and Baldur at the ages of 6, 12 and 18 which help you to make sense of Loki's present feelings for Baldur.
Response-task:	Listen carefully to the stories and ask yourself what it is that this particular Loki needs to soften his heart and his jealousy. Write this on a piece of paper.
Read:	The stories.
Give:	What you have written to the reader. Do not read what you have been given right now.
Tell:	The rest of "Loki and Baldur".
Talk:	About the events in the story.
Look:	At your own writings and paintings.
Read:	The gifts (papers) you have been given.
Reflect:	Upon the entire session.

Text:	LOKI AND BALDUR
Focus:	Witnessing the unavoidable
Length:	1 1/2 hours
Paint:	An image of how you are feeling right now.
Tell:	"Loki and Baldur."
Paint:	An image of how you are feeling after you have heard the story.
Place:	Both paintings near one another somewhere in the room.

Write: An imaginary entry in a dairy kept by a wise person who witnessed the development of the situation between Loki and Baldur.
Describe in your diary entry, how this person feels, why he/she felt incapable of intervening and how this person responds to the swearing of revenge. Begin your writings by the words, "I am called....(name), the wise one."

Response-task: Listen to the entries and ask yourself what it is this "wise one" could learn. Also ask yourself what might comfort the "wise one" in these difficult times. Write responses down on paper.

Read: Your writings.

Give: Written responses to each reader.

Select: A written response that feels pertinent.

Share: This response with group.

Reflect: Upon entire session.

Questions focusing on Trickster

1. What image comes to mind when you think of Trickster?
    How would you describe Trickster?
    How would you describe people who have no access to their inner Trickster?

2. Do you know people who fit these descriptions?
    How do you feel about them?

3. What image do you have of the Trickster within you?
    How does your Trickster manifest itself?
    How do you feel about this aspect of yourself?

4. If you could choose to create a Trickster who would travel with you during your life, how would you create it?
    What would it look like?
    What part would it play in your life?

5. Trickster usually plays on the weaknesses or vulnerabilities of a person. What traits within you might make you vulnerable to a trickster?

6. What part does humor play in your life?
    Are you a person who tells jokes with enjoyment?
    Are you a person who laughs easily?
    Are you able to laugh out loud when you feel like it?

7. Under what circumstances do you feel uncomfortable when laughing?

8. Did you ever experience a time when laughter had a healing effect on you or anyone you know?
    What were the circumstances?
    How did the laughter heal?

9.   Do you know anyone considered to be a "practical joker"?
     Can this person take a joke as well as tell or make one?
     How do you feel about being around a "practical joker"?

10. Have you ever been around someone who seems very different in
     one circumstance than another.
     How do feel about this?
     What images come to mind when you think about this person?

11. What part does clothing and/or makeup contribute to the changing
     of a person?
     Do you ever do this? Under what circumstances? How do you
     feel when doing this?

12. Trickster is sometimes known as Shape-changer. If you could
     change your shape how would you change it?

CHAPTER EIGHT
HEALING

When we are seriously ill our capacity to receive is tested. Our relationships with people around us change. We now have to rely on them for help and support as we have previously learned to trust our inner nursing capacity when we suffer minor ailments. The way we treat ourselves is usually reflective of the way we hope and expect to be treated by those who become responsible for the facilitation of our recovery. The external process is similar to that which is internal.

During an illness we are set aside from the rest of the community who continue to go about their daily tasks. We can no longer perform our share of life's responsibilities or contribute our part to the collective celebrations. The hurting one is isolated and also withdraws. The energy which used to flow inwards and outwards is now focused on survival, maintenance and recovery. If the illness is chronic rather than acute, major changes in living have to be made which can require long term adjustments and have major impact on our lives.

When ill, we grow quiet. Our voice does not lift itself beyond the basic necessity of requesting, describing, complaining or advocating. Few are the utterances which reflect the normal connection with the outside world. When the ill person begins to show an interest in what is happening to others, those who are caring sigh with relief. Recovery has commenced.

Well people need to reach out to those who are ill, who have withdrawn, to offer support and sustenance. They have the opportunity to stretch themselves in order to gain hold of the attention of the one who is ill, who may be slipping into disconnected self-absorption. For if no connection is established, recovery is unlikely. We call back those who are dear to us, casting out our lifeline in the hope that the ill person will find the strength and spirit to re-establish a link, to hold on to life for his or her sake, and for our sake.

Yet in the process of withdrawal from communication and purposeful action there are gains as well as losses. We experience solitude and can con centrate on our self; we are offered an opportunity to meet the one who dwells within. We encounter in our feverish dreams the many faces and aspects of the one who is "I". During times of quiet, when resting, memories may present themselves with uncanny clarity. Whenever we have temporarily ceased to relate to the outside world in an active way, our inner life can find a voice with which to speak to us. Memories, dreams and reflections appear, asking to be heard, felt and considered. We are confronted with the contents of our inner storage areas, the undigested remnants of our previously active existence. The images may be of exquisite beauty or stunning in their perverse intensity, but within the whirlpool of inner activity, the energy and the will to recover are regenerated. The healing process begins, when within the profusion of sequential and scattered memories, the thread which is our life is once again seen, acknowledged, recognized and accepted. Recovery requires that we consent to take up the thread of our life. Without this consent, we die.

Healing then, is the process by which the one whose vitality is threatened is helped to reverse the processes of suffering, pain, and deterioration; to regain faith. By removing or mitigating the cause of disease we make healing possible. Ease can return. Always, the patient must consent to being helped. When the sufferer does not wish to be cured and wants, instead, to remain separate and centered on the self, then the lure to allow healing has to be made more attractive. The struggle with illness, however one perceives it, and to whatever cause we attribute its appearance in one individual yet not in another, is formidable. It may well be that the combined effort of the ill person and those who contribute to the recovery is not enough. When illness continues to attack and destroy then the will to live may surrender to the longing for the suffering to end. This is not the same as the wish to die, although death is the eventual result.

The helpers on the road toward recovery assume many forms and guises. Rarely do they appear in vague shapes, either in fantasy or reality. The ill one needs and looks for someone who will offer assistance, to bring relief and share the pain and worry. The purpose and the focus of the encounter are beyond doubt. One is ill, the other's help is required.

From the moment this implicitly explicit demand is made, the well person becomes mainly or only a healer. Alternatively, the request is not met because the one who is approached does not have the resources or knowledge with which to help heal. By removing themselves as did the priest and the Levite in the Parable of the Good Samaritan, they allow the ill person to see or be seen by the potential healer. When the healer arrives and asks, "How can I help you?" the possibility of healing begins.

The "I" of the healer is the "I" of the one who has the knowledge pertinent to the needs of the ill person. The healer is ready and willing to make his or her inner resources and wisdom available in order to promote well-being. The one asks, the other offers. Will the ill person accept this? When we are seriously ill, our capacity to receive is continually tested. Once begun, our capacity to differentiate, to choose which help we want is also continually tested.

We cannot receive unless we are aware and acknowledge the presence of the other. The spiral of centering on the self is temporarily interrupted to create space for the other who acts, pleads and intervenes. The demonstration of care signals to those who are ill that they are valued, that their community is neither willing nor ready to bid them farewell. Therefore, an effort is being made to ensure that their recovery will be complete, so that they will be restored and can grow from the experience. This possible growth exceeds merely returning to a previous position of health or even a renewed affirmation and consent to existence. It may well result in an awareness of the uniqueness of our being, a renewed valuing of the many connections by which our individual life is woven into the fabric of other people's existence. We matter to them and they matter to us. We are in relationship with one another through which a bond of intimacy is created which holds us all, ultimately, within the greater embrace of life itself.

How then does the caring manifest itself? How does a community ensure that the patient knows that her/his well-being is of importance to them? Above all, how does the person who possesses the knowledge and expertise which is relevant to the ill person become identified. Are we always able to recognize a healer when we are in need of one?

In times of danger there is little place for subtlety. The signs and signals of the healer need to be clear and unambivalent. The self-engrossed consciousness of the ill person must be able to distinguish between those offering assistance and those who know how to help. In this act and process of recognition, the bond to the outside world is strengthened. There is acknowledgement of the energy which flows toward the sick one, to help and eventually to heal, perhaps to cure.

The more often the one who now receives help has been a participant in healing events, the greater the chances that both helpers and help will trigger the patient's awareness of the actual situation, of the necessity to receive assistance from others. The realization that what is happening to one's self has happened to others, that there is a comparative predictability of sequence of events and interventions, is reassuring in a situation where the chaos of illness has disturbed the comparative security of daily life. Reassurance implies a renewal of inner security which means growing strength, then recovery.

The need for clear signals, for easy identification of the healer and predictability in the sequence of healing interventions, all lead to the ritualization of behavior, the ceremony which surrounds healing in most cultures. However a balance between ritualization and unobstructed spontaneity needs to be maintained. For whenever the ritualization becomes so extreme that the flow of energy is stultified, the interaction between helpers and patient loses its efficacy. The ritual is performed, not experienced. The patient becomes more and more lost, increasingly bewildered by the disconnected formality of the situation. When this happens the opposite of the intended occurs. The ill one withdraws further into the self in order to fight off the deadening impressions, to safeguard inner resources. The help offered is not received because it is no longer perceived and experienced as help. It becomes a destructive intrusion into an already painful and precarious private world.

Thus healers have the difficult task of assessing the necessary balance between the predictable and unexpected, the normal and specific which each particular patient needs. Occasionally, only the shock of the exceptional can jolt a particular patient into presence. Others may need to have their curiosity aroused in order to reconnect with their surroundings. The skill with which the healers are able to assess individual treatment needs reflects their ability to connect to a human being in need of help.

The encounter with illness brings us face to face with suffering. We struggle with our feelings about pain and loss. We face having to understand that being healed is not necessarily the same as being cured. Serious illness ultimately evokes questions about the purpose and meaning of life and death. To choose not to die is not necessarily to choose to live. The answers we evolve are relevant to our own healing philosophy and practice which reflects our knowledge about health, illness and the process of recovery. Above all, it bears witness to the belief system which supports and enhances our daily life.

This combination of knowledge and belief inspires and guides our healing practice, whoever and wherever we are. When the facts we have can no longer guide and justify our actions, we rely on beliefs to see us through, to meet the darkness of the dark night, to help us once more greet the light of day.

The Stories

The healing waters

Healing/N. Amer. Indian

The snows of winter lay as heavily on the ground as did the sorrow in the hearts of the people. Plague had struck the camp leaving many people dying and dead. Having lost his parents, brothers, sisters and children, Nekumonta now faced the death of his beloved wife, Shanewis. In despair he said to himself, "I must do something to help her or she will not see the light of one more morning. I will go and find the healing herbs planted by the Great Manitou."

Nekumonta made Shanewis as comfortable as he could, placing food and water near her. Then he covered her with a soft fur robe and said, "I must go to find some herbs to cure you. I will return very soon. Please, wait for me." Embracing her gently, he said goodbye and set off on his journey.

Wherever he went he saw only ice and snow. For three days and three nights he traveled along the frozen ground asking any animal who came in sight where the herbs might be but none answered. On the third night, weak from lack of food, Nekumonta caught his foot on an upturned branch and dropped into the snow. Too tired to free himself, he soon fell asleep right where he was. The animals of the forest came and saw him sleeping. They looked at his kind face and saw his loving heart. They prayed to the Great Manitou to help him find the healing herbs for his beloved Shanewis.

The Great Manitou heard the plea of the animals and sent a messenger to appear in the dreams of Nekumonta. In the dream he saw his beautiful Shanewis, alive and smiling, singing a song which sounded like the music of a waterfall. Then, suddenly, he saw a waterfall and heard a voice calling, "Look for us Nekumonta. When you find us Shanewis will live. We are the Healing Waters of the Great Manitou."

When Nekumonta awoke he searched all over for the Healing Waters but could not find them. Then he decided to look beneath the frozen ground. He was so weak he could barely dig; only his spirit kept him going but he continued and at last the hidden waters came into view. The Healing Waters streamed out carrying life and well-being wherever they went.

Nekumonta bathed in the waters and once more felt well and strong. He made a jar of clay and baked it in the fire until he knew it would hold the waters while he returned to Shanewis. He sped homeward as fast as he could go. His sorrow changed to joy as he thought of seeing Shanewis once more, alive and well.

When he arrived in the village and saw the sorrowing villagers he told them all about the Healing Waters and urged them to go and bring some water back. He found Shanewis very close to death and hoped he had not arrived too late.

Nekumonta brushed some of the Healing Waters on her parched lips and poured tiny drops of water down her throat. She fell into a gentle sleep. When she awoke, her fever was gone.

Nekumonta's heart was filled with great happiness. He and Shanewis lived together for many years. The Healing Waters helped to rid the village of the plague. Nekumonta was given the name of "Chief of the Healing Waters" so that everyone would know who had given them the gift from the Great Manitou.

How the hummingbird got its color   *Healing/South America*

Once upon a time the hummingbird was a small gray bird who longed to be brightly colored. Everytime she looked at the reds, yellows, greens and blues of the flowers, forest and sky, she sighed, wishing she could look as pretty. No matter who she asked, no one knew how to help her change the color of her feathers.

One day, while sipping nectar from a brilliant red flower, she heard a dreadful noise, so loud it shook the earth. She looked around and saw a panther roaring with rage. The hummingbird flew to the panther and asked him why he was making such a terrible fuss. The panther told her that he had stepped on a mouse nest one night and accidentally killed all the baby mice. Then, while he was asleep, the mouse-mother glued his eyes shut with gum and mud so he could not see. He did not even know whether it was day or night. The panther cried, "I wish I could see."

The hummingbird listened with care and then told the panther how she longed to be dressed in bright colors rather than in dull gray. She described all the ways she had tried to change her colors with no success. The panther listened to her tale and then said, "If you will peck out all the mud and gum from my eyes so that I can see, I will show you how to change the color of your feathers". Thus the bargain was made.

While the panther held his face as still as possible, the hummingbird pecked out all the mud and gum from the panther's eyes. This was no easy task as the hummingbird was very little and the mouse-mother had used a lot of mud and gum. But finally, the panther was able to see. True to his word, he took the hummingbird to the place where there were sands and clay of many different colors. The two mixed the colors of the earth, sun and stars into fine strands which the hummingbird wove into a beautiful dress. She used some of the spider's silk to make wings. When her new dress was finished, she took off the old gray one and put on the dress made of all the colors in the world. The panther looked at her and said, "Your new dress is very beautiful."

Now, all hummingbirds have beautiful, brightly colored feathers and shimmery, gossamer wings.

Grandmother spider   *Healing/Cherokee/N. Amer. Indian*

In the beginning all was dark. The animal people bumped into each other, stumbling as they moved. They all wished there could be light. One day, when the animals felt they could no longer stand the dark, they got together to talk. Woodpecker said, "I have heard that there are people on the other side of the world who have light." The animals cheered as Woodpecker continued. "Maybe they will share some of their light with us."

Fox spoke up, "If they have it, they probably won't give any to us. If we want light we'll have to steal it."

Everyone began arguing as to who should go. Each animal suggested someone who was strong, fast, intelligent or cunning. Possum spoke up, "I will go. I can hide the light under my fur." The animals agreed that he should go and off he went. As he traveled east the light grew so strong he had to screw up his eyes and even today, Possum's eyes are almost closed. When Possum arrived at the place of the light, he hid some of it in the fur of his bushy tail. It was so hot by the time he got home it had burned off all his fur which is why Possums have bare tails, even today. Possum arrived with no light.

The animals became discouraged when they saw Possum return empty-handed but Buzzard said, "I'll go. I will come back with the light." Buzzard flew so high the people of the light did not see him. He dove down, just as he does today, and caught a piece of the light and placed it on top of his head. The light was so hot it burned the top of his head and that is why, even today, buzzards are bald. Buzzard arrived with no light.

After two of the strongest, most responsible and determined animals failed, the others became even more upset. They sat around wondering what could be done. They moaned to each other, "Our brothers have done the best they could. Our finest have tried yet we are still in darkness. What shall we do now?"

Up piped a tiny voice, "Our men have done their best. Perhaps this is something a woman should try."

The animals looked around, trying to see the speaker. "Who is talking?" they asked.

"Grandmother Spider," she answered. "Although I am old, I have a plan. At least let me try. If I fail you will not lose much." The animals were sure she could not succeed but they agreed to give her a chance.

Grandmother Spider set to work. She fashioned a tiny clay bowl out of damp clay from the earth. She started east with her bowl, spinning her thread so that she could find her way home. When she got to the people of the light no one saw her because she was so small. She quickly took a tiny bit of the sun and put it into her bowl. Then she moved back along the thread she had spun. Even today, a spider's web looks like the rays of the sun.

When Grandmother Spider returned home with the light the animal people were amazed and overjoyed. "Thank you Grandmother Spider," they said. "We will always honor you. We will never forget that you rescued us from the darkness, that you brought us light."

The maiden with the wooden bowl   *Healing/Japan*

A long time ago there lived an old couple with their young daughter, a lovely, graceful child. After her husband died, his widow grew concerned about her daughter's future. She spoke to her child, "My beloved daughter, the world can be a cruel place. You are too fair to live alone so I am placing this bowl on your head. When I die, you must wear it always. The bowl will protect you against those who would do you harm."

Soon after, the old woman died. The maiden put the bowl on her head and went to work in the rice fields to earn her living. Those who saw her laughed at the strange sight of a maiden with a wooden bowl on her head but the young girl, remembering her mother's words, paid no attention. When young men tried to take the bowl from her head it would not move. After a time, they stopped trying, contenting themselves with calling her names.

A rich farmer noticed that she was a diligent worker and, paying no attention to the bowl on her head, invited the maiden to work in his rice fields. After the harvest, the farmer, even more impressed with the girl's bearing, invited her to stay with him and to take care of his ill wife. In time, the farmer and his wife grew fond of the maiden and treated her as if she were their own daughter.

One day the eldest son returned home from studying in the city. He was a wise young man who had grown tired of the parties and foolishness of his fellow students. When he saw the maiden with the bowl on her head he asked his father who she was. After being told, the young man began to watch her and soon came to love her. One day he asked her to marry him despite dire predictions from his friends that she might be ugly. However, the maiden refused to marry him saying, "I am but a servant in your father's house." That night she went to bed and cried herself to sleep for she loved the young man with all her heart.

In her sleep she dreamed that her mother stood before her with a smile on her face. "My child, you must marry this young man for he is good and kind and will love you well. Let your heart be light and without trouble."
In the morning, when the young man returned to ask her once more, the maiden answered yes.

When the plans were made for the wedding, the maiden tried to remove the wooden bowl but it stayed firmly on her head. No matter who tried to take it off, the bowl stayed fast. Finally the bridegroom said, "Enough. Let the bowl be. I love you as you are."

The wedding proceeded, followed by a great feast. As the maiden put the ceremonial glass of wine to her lips, the bowl on her head fell off with a great loud noise. As it fell, the pieces of it turned to gold, silver and precious jewels. Those watching were amazed at the riches that surrounded the maiden. Yet even greater was their surprise when they looked at her for the first time and saw that she was a beautiful woman.

Lo-Sun, the blind boy   *Healing/China*

Lo-Sun was a blind boy, thrown out of his home by his father who thought him useless. To earn a living, he and his loving dog, Fan, went to the city and stood on street corners doing a few tricks. With his blind man's staff, Lo-Sun was able to move around the city almost as quickly as if he could see. They slept where they could and people were often kind for the boy and his dog were friendly to all.

One night Lo-Sun dreamed that a voice called to him offering to cure his blindness. Lo-Sun spoke to the voice and asked, "What must I do to regain my sight?"

The voice replied, "Each time you do a good deed, no matter how small, a little bit of light will enter your eyes. If you continue to do this, eventually your sight will be restored. But, if you should one day do a bad deed, your eyes will shut tight and you will lose twice what you have gained with your kindness."

Lo-Sun woke up and felt Fan licking his face. The day was warm, the sun was shining in his face and he felt great happiness. All day he could think of nothing but his dream and the thought that one day, when he could see, he would go back to his father's house and show him what a mistake he had made. As he was walking he heard, "Give a coin to a man who is blind." Lo-Sun laughed and said, "I am also blind."

The poor man answered, "But I am crippled as well." Without thinking, Lo-Sun gave the man his only coin. All of a sudden, the blackness he had always known grew less dense. Lo-Sun knew his dream was true.

That night, as they lay in a tumbled down building, an old woman, weak from lack of food asked Lo-Sun for a crust of bread. After giving it to her, Lo-Sun noticed that the blackness in his eyes grew lighter. By morning, he and Fan were very hungry and set about to find some food. Fan captured a fat hen and, not finding anyone around, Lo-Sun took it to the market to sell for a good price. As soon as the money was in his hand, he felt some of the darkness return. What he had gained by his two good deeds was lost.

Refusing to be discouraged, Lo-Sun made his way back to where Fan had caught the hen. He asked all those who passed by if anyone had lost a hen. Although no one knew whose hen it was, Lo-Sun and Fan went to bed hungry. In the morning he was rewarded by a slight improvement in his eyesight. Within a few weeks Lo-Sun's eyesight had improved so much he could actually see shapes. He even imagined he could see the sunset. He determined to save every cent he made in order to buy a pair of glasses which he heard would further improve his vision.

While thinking about what it would be like to see, the same beggar who had asked him for coins once more asked for his help. Lo-Sun replied, "I have nothing to give you. I am starving too." In an instant all his vision left him and he was once more in total darkness. Angry at himself and the world, he sat down beside the banks of a turbulent stream. The sound of the water matched his feelings. Fan, sensing his misery, licked his face. Lo-Sun hugged his dog, grateful for her attention.

Suddenly he heard some men scream, "A man is drowning. Help, a man is drowning." None of the bystanders dared jump into the furiously moving water.

Lo-Sun said, "I will do it. I will save the man and show you that a blind boy is not useless."

People on the bank tried to stop him, "Don't waste your energy, he is only a worthless beggar."

Lo-Sun answered, "That is who I am as well. Go Fan, go!" Lo-Sun brought his dog to the edge of the bank and pushed her into the water. The dog swam to the drowning man and bravely struggled to bring him to shore but the current was so strong the little dog could hardly keep up. One of the bystanders brought a rope with a hook and threw it to the man, catching his clothing. Fan, thinking her work was over, released her hold and started to swim toward the shore. But she was too weak and when a powerful undercurrent grabbed her, Fan was dragged down and drowned.

Lo-Sun heard what happened from the cries of grief of those standing near him. He walked away, too full of sorrow to hear anything more. Tired, cold and hungry, he fell into a comfortless sleep.

When he woke, without Fan, he was full of despair. Then, much to his amazement, his eyes grew dazzled by the great light of the morning sun. He was able to see much of the world around him. He realized that asking Fan to save the life of a drowning man had given him his vision but he felt it was too great a price to pay.

As he got up to leave, a strange man came up to him. "I wish to thank you for saving my life yesterday." Lo-Sun heard the voice and gasped. The man he had helped to save was none other than his father who had thrown him out of his home.

As Lo-Sun was about to curse the man who had caused him so much grief, a soft voice from deep inside him said instead, "I forgive you."

The man hugged the boy and held him close, thanking the gods for their mercy. When Lo-Sun looked up and saw his father's tears, he hugged him back. The two embraced, letting the past flow away. As they stood looking at each other, the last bit of darkness left Lo-Sun's eyes.

Ulu and the breadfruit tree   *Healing/Polynesia*

Ulu knew his son would soon die if help were not found quickly. He went to the temple to pray for guidance from the great Mo'o. Upon his return, Ulu told his wife what must be done to save the life of their son. When Ulu was satisfied that she would do as he had asked, Ulu lay down and died.

Heartsick and griefstricken, his wife planted Ulu's head near their spring of clear running water. She buried his heart, entrails, feet, legs and arms near the door of their house. Then she went inside and lay down on the couch where they had slept together, waiting for the sun to redden the morning sky. When she heard the rustling of falling leaves and flowers, followed by the thumps of fruit dropping on the ground, she knew Ulu's prayers had been answered.

In the morning she went to the place where she had buried her husband's heart. There stood a tall, beautiful tree, its bright green leaves shimmering in the sun. She gathered the ripe fruit that had fallen from its branches and gave some to her ailing son. With the first taste of fruit the boy regained his strength. He grew to be a great warrior known throughout the island for his deeds of strength and wisdom.

Healing - The Structures

Theme: HEALING
Focus: A circle of blessings
Length: 50 minutes

Sit: In circle

Reflect: On the lives of the people in the group and on what is happening in your own life.

Paint: Image of how you are feeling right now.

Give: Each person 3 sheets of paper of equal size.

Paint: On first sheet, a blessing for one's self. On the second sheet paint a blessing for the person on your right. On the third sheet paint a blessing for someone in the room. Do not put this person's name on the paper.

Collect: The blessing for someone in the room.

Place: Blessings in center of circle.

Share: Each person in turn shares blessing given to self and then gives blessing to neighbor.

Paint: Image of how you are feeling right now.

Look: At 2 paintings.

Write: A few sentences evoked by the 2 paintings.

Pick: Blessing from center of circle.

Share: Blessings received.

Reflect: Upon entire session.

Theme: HEALING
Focus: A healing place and person
Length: 50 minutes

Divide: Into groups of 4 or 5.

Tape: As many sheets of paper together as there are members in group.

Paint: A place of healing as a group. Each member must paint. Each sheet of paper is a part of the whole and needs to have a single wholeness about it which satisfies the painter. Do not discuss ideas about healing places before painting. Paint until everyone is satisfied with group's notion of a healing place.

List: On a separate piece of paper the qualities of a healer (one who heals). Choose 3 which seem the most important.

Devise: In same small groups, a story which utilizes the place of healing and the 3 most important qualities necessary for a healer to possess.

Share: Paintings and stories.

Reflect: Upon entire session.

Text: THE HEALING WATERS
Focus: The courage to continue
Length: 50 minutes

Walk: Slowly around and through the room. Do not establish eye contact but do notice where you are going. Stop. Take note of where you are and decide to walk to another spot. Unexpectedly people will be in your way but make sure you reach your destination.

Having arrived, once more decide where to go next. This time walk with your eyes closed. Keep them closed. Upon arrival, open your eyes.

With your eyes closed, walk through and around the room again. When you become tired, crawl around the room but keep moving with your eyes closed.

Lie: Down keeping eyes closed.

Tell: "The healing waters."

Return: To circle.

Select: Any number below 20.

Write: About an important experience which Nekumonta had at the age this number represents. This memory is what keeps Nekumonta going during his difficult journey.

Share: These memory writings.

Paint: An image evoked by the word, "motivation".

Reflect: Upon entire session.

Text: THE HEALING WATERS
Focus: Solutions from the heart
Length: 1 1/2 hours

Decide: What kind of forest animal you want to be.

Write: On one side of a sheet of paper write the word health; on the other side, sickness.

List: Quickly, all the associated words which come to mind.

Paint:	Create 2 separate spaces on a sheet of paper. On one paint your image of sickness; on the other side, health.
Write:	In the space around/between these 2 spaces write about sickness and health.
Imagine:	A friend comes to visit you who complains of not feeling well. You are both aware that it is nothing serious. What are you most likely to suggest as a remedy.
Share:	Your responses with a partner.
Tell:	"The healing waters"...up to where the animals prayed to Manitou.
Write:	Your animal's prayer including a reason why this animal cares about Nekumonta.
Read:	The prayers in the following way:

Storyteller: "Thus the animals watched over Nekumonta and one by one, a prayer grew in their hearts. Then the first one spoke and said:..." First group member reads his/her prayer.

Storyteller: "Thus ..(name of animal) added her (his) voice. The next animal spoke,..."

In this manner all "prayers" are joined together within the frame of the story.

Paint/write:	Return to your sickness/health painting. Add whatever else feels right.
Reflect:	Upon the entire session.

Text:	THE HEALING WATERS
Focus:	Encouragement in a time of unwellness
Length:	1 1/2 hours

Recall: A day when things continued to go wrong.

Write: About that day.

Describe: How you felt in one word.

Paint: An image of this word.

Place: Paintings where everyone can see them.

Look: At paintings.

Response-task: Ponder what you would need most if you had made such a painting.
Write this on a piece of paper and leave this near the paintings. Do not read what has been written right now.

Tell: "The healing waters."

Write: In one word, the characteristic which Nekumonta possessed that allowed him to go on the journey.

Read: The responses to your painting.

Select: One response that feels particularly relevant to you right now.

Create: Using paint, clay, song and/or words, make something to encourage a sick person to take the journey towards health. Use your own word and the word from the painting response as part of your creation.

Share: Your encouragements.

Reflect: Make any connections that arise from the work and
              reflect upon the entire session.

Text: HOW THE HUMMINGBIRD GOT ITS COLOR
Focus: The color of boredom
Length: 50 minutes

Paint: Use as many different colors as you can to create a really
              messy muddle.

Improvise: In groups of 3 create a brief drama or movement piece in
              which the word, boring, is used at least 3 times.

Share: Improvisations.

Tell: "How the hummingbird got its color."

Collage: The whole group works together using painting and
              writing around the theme, "Longing for color". The work
              is finished when everyone in the group feels a sense of
              completion.

Talk: About your contribution.

Reflect: Upon the entire session.

Text: HOW THE HUMMINGBIRD GOT ITS COLOR
Focus: Needing something badly
Length: 1 1/2 hours

Paint: A picture which represents what it feels like to have a
              little need, a slightly bigger need, etc. Use at least 5
              different needs.

Recall:	A time when you needed something badly. Identify your need.
Write:	About your experience.
Share:	Your paintings and writings with the group.
Tell:	"How the hummingbird got its color."
Recall:	A time when you felt pretty gray and low.
Paint:	An image of what this period felt like.
Response-task:	Into this time of feeling think of something which is cheerful and uplifting. Paint /write what this is on a small piece of paper and give your gift to the one who has shared the "gray and low" painting.
Share:	Paintings with the group.
Receive:	Gifts.
Select:	One which feels pertinent to your life now, paying attention to how you feel inside.
Reflect:	Upon the entire session.

Text:	HOW THE HUMMINGBIRD GOT ITS COLOR
Focus:	Color within and without
Length:	1 1/2 hours
Paint:	Or draw an image of your favorite childhood outfit.
Write:	How old you were when you wore these clothes on the painting.

Write: A few sentences under the heading "color" on your painting.

Tell: "How the hummingbird got its color" up to, "She described all the ways she had tried to change her colors with no success."

Write: The ways in which the hummingbird tried with no success.

Tell: The story up to, "True to his word, he took her to the place where colors are."

Write: How the hummingbird succeeded in creating a colorful feather dress.

Share: Your paintings and writings with a partner. One person talks about color in her/his life while partner listens quietly, asking only an odd question or two. After 5 minutes reverse roles.

Return: To circle.

Share: One important aspect of your paintings and writings.

Reflect: Upon the entire session.

Text: GRANDMOTHER SPIDER
Focus: "Yes but..."
Length: 50 minutes

Create: In circle, each person speaks one brief sentence to convey a need or intention. (e.g. He wanted to buy some bread.) The next person begins his/her sentence with "But...."
The next person's sentence begins with, "However..."
Each person in turn uses but or however to begin the

sentence until it is the first person's turn again.
This person now completes the story by beginning his/her sentence with "And therefore...."

Talk:
2 group members publicly say something appreciative about you.
You react to their words by saying, "Yes but...." (Each group member has a turn.)

Paint:
An image of the feelings evoked within you by the words, "Yes but...."

Share:
Paintings.

Tell:
"Grandmother spider."

Write:
A short poem briefly praising the words, "Yes but..."

Read:
Poems.

Reflect:
Upon entire session.

Text: GRANDMOTHER SPIDER
Focus: Trying...failing...trying
Length: 1 1/2 hours

Paint:
An image of darkness and an image of light on the same sheet of paper using half for each image.

Write:
Describe the qualities of darkness and the qualities of light.

Draw:
On a sheet of paper create a path which you will call the path of "trying..failing.....trying". Indicate and name the obstacles which contribute to the failing.

Write: At the top of a sheet of paper, the words, "Trying mat-
              ters". At the bottom of the paper write, "That is why....".
              Now write whatever belongs in between.

Tell: "Grandmother Spider."

Share: Read your "Trying matters" writings and show your "try-
              ing...failing...trying" drawing.

Respond: Draw or write the inducements/encouragements which
              you have now received on your "trying.. failing...trying
              path.

Connect: Make connections between this work and your life ex-
              perience.

Reflect: Upon the entire session.

Text: GRANDMOTHER SPIDER
Focus: Hoping to fulfill a need
Length: 1 1/2 hours

Write: A sequential list of words that describe the different
              phases of the process which leads from need, to awareness
              of need to fulfillment of need (at least 7 words).

Draw: Symbolic pictures for each of the 7 words.

Select: Note, without sharing, one stage of the journey which you
              find most difficult.

Tell: "Grandmother Spider."

Choose: A phrase or moment in the story which resonates.

Write: This phrase or moment on a piece of paper in one
              sentence.

Devise: A compliment for each person in the group.

Write: Each compliment on a separate piece of paper and give it to the person for whom it is intended. Do not read the compliments yet.

Write/Draw: The story of Grandmother Spider using the 7 phases you wrote down earlier. As you do this, read your compliments.

Remember: The stage of the journey you found most difficult. Note which stage in the story corresponds to your stage.

Share: Work.

Reflect: Upon entire session.

Text: THE MAIDEN WITH THE WOODEN BOWL
Focus: After years of being teased
Length: 50 minutes

Tell: "The maiden with the wooden bowl"...up to the point where the young men and women in the rice fields tease her.

Write: A few sentences about the kind of teasing and unpleasant comments to which she has probably been subjected.

Collect: Papers and redistribute them.

Improvise: In groups of 3, explore the response to teasing such as those you have experienced on a playground, in a restaurant, at a bus stop. Experiment with the allegiance of the third person, befriending either the teaser or the teased. Reverse roles frequently.

Talk:	In your groups about your experience.
Tell:	The whole group the whole story of "The maiden with the wooden bowl."
Paint:	A picture of the wooden bowl and its contents after the bowl has come off.
Share:	Paintings.
Reflect:	Upon entire session.

Text:	THE MAIDEN WITH THE WOODEN BOWL
Focus:	The path of life's journey
Length:	1 1/2 hours
Paint:	An image evoked by the word, "difficulty".
Tell:	The maiden with the wooden bowl.
Draw:	The path which the maiden has had to go through life so far. Show the various difficult barriers which she has to overcome. Indicate which parts she may have found especially difficult. Convey where and how she may have found some comfort and solace.
Create:	One particular phrase/poem/song which kept her going and write it down.
Response-task:	When seeing/listening to a particular journey, think of what you can learn from this maiden. Write this down and share it with the maiden at a later time.
Share:	Your paintings, drawings and writings.
Share:	Some connections between the maiden's experiences and your own life experience.
Reflect:	Upon entire session.

Text:	THE MAIDEN WITH THE WOODEN BOWL
Focus:	The untold tale
Length:	1 1/2 hours

Paint: The image evoked by the word, "different".

Recall: An experience of knowing yourself alone (which is not the same as feeling lonely).

Write: About the memory.

Share: Your paintings and writings.

Response-task: As you listen to the story of "The maiden with the wooden bowl", the storyteller will stop at certain times. At this time, write about the thoughts/feelings/experiences which the maiden has though they are not mentioned in the story. As you write, visualize in your mind's eye, the image of a very pretty young girl.

Tell: "The maiden with the wooden bowl", stopping at the following suggested places:
- After the mother has died;
- During the work in the rice fields;
- Working for the farmer before son returns;
- Son comes home;
- After son has asked maiden to marry him;
- After maiden's dream about her mother;
- After the bowl breaks and riches revealed.

Write: Your commentary into a story.

Response-task: Paint a special gift for this maiden.

Share: Stories and receive gifts.

Choose:	One gift from those received which feels most pertinent to you at this stage in your life.
Share:	Feelings and experience.
Reflect:	Upon entire session.

Text:	LO-SUN THE BLIND BOY
Focus:	Forgiveness is a practice
Length:	50 minutes
Recall:	An experience of friendship with an animal. Focus on a particular moment in the relationship with this animal which gave you great pleasure.
Write:	One word to describe how you felt then.
Move:	Improvise a brief movement phrase which gives bodily expression to your feeling. The end of one person's movement becomes the beginning of the next person's movement.
Tell:	"Lo-Sun the blind boy" to the entire group.
Paint:	The image evoked by the word, forgiveness.
Write:	The word which you recorded earlier and use it to make a sentence. Write this sentence on several small pieces of paper.
Share:	Some of the feelings around your images of forgiveness.
Response-task:	Having listened to and looked at the material around forgiveness, choose some one(s) to give your sentence to.
Share:	Sentences received.
Reflect:	Upon entire session.

Text:	LO-SUN THE BLIND BOY
Focus:	The voice of doubt
Length:	1/12 hours

Walk: Around the room in a way that feels normal. Then change your walk and take 2 steps forward and 1 step backward. Explore a number of possibilities such as 3 forward, 2 back. Return to 2 forward, 1 back and walk this way for a while.

Draw: Use a pen or crayon, place it on your paper, and start moving forward. Do not hesitate or return. Only go forwards.

Using another color, with pen or crayon, place it on the paper and go forward. This time allow yourself to hesitate and to deviate but do not return or go backward.

In a third color place your pen or crayon on your paper. Feel free this time to go any way you choose, forward, backward, hesitating or not.

Tell: "Lo-Sun the blind boy."

Create: In groups of 3 or 4, a chant in which you say the words Lo-Sun's doubting voice might have spoken. Use an empty chair or cushion to represent Lo-Sun. Make a transition so when your group is finished, the next one will know to begin. Find a way to involve all the group members in your chant at some point.

Present: The chants.

Write: Lo-Sun's response in 3 sentences.

Share: The sentences.

Recall:	A memory related to light regardless of how tenuous the connection appears to be.
Share:	Memories.
Reflect:	Upon the entire session.

Text: LO-SUN THE BLIND BOY
Focus: When courage fails
Length: 1 1/2 hours

Recall:	An experience when you last felt determined to do something and actually did it.
Paint:	An image of how, in your determination, you then felt.
Write:	Responses to the following questions: - What is the landscape/location? - Who is the main character? - What is the predicament?
Pass:	Your paper to the person sitting next to you.
Write:	How you try to resolve this predicament and fail to do so.
Pass:	The paper on.
Write:	About another attempt (on the same paper) which also fails.
Pass:	Paper on.
Write:	After 3 unsuccessful attempts have been made, solve the predicament and write it down.

Read: The writings.

Tell: "Lo-Sun the blind boy."

Paint: An image of how you feel after hearing the story.

Compare: This with your determination painting.

Share: What you find most difficult in both story, painting and shared stories.

Write: The words, "when courage fails", on a sheet of paper and write whatever comes to mind in a few sentences.

Collect: Papers and redistribute them.

Read: The writings.

Reflect: Upon entire session.

Text: ULU AND THE BREADFRUIT TREE
Focus: To be allowed to rescue
Length: 50 minutes

Recall: A time in your life when you rescued someone or something.

Share: Rescuing memories.

Improvise: In pairs, one person stands in a precarious position (on top of a chair or table, with back against the wall etc.). The person is frightened and knows him/herself to be in great danger. The partner's task is to first reassure person that though he/she is in danger, help will be forthcoming. Then, using only the voice, partner guides person to safety. Reverse roles.

Response-task:	Listen to the experiences bearing in mind your earlier memory. Write, using encouraging language, 3 notes of guidance for those who will rescue in the future, 3 notes for those who might need to be rescued in the future and write 1 note for those who witness the rescue.
Share:	What was helpful and what was not during the rescue experience.
Tell:	"Ulu and the breadfruit tree."
Reread:	Notes and make any changes you wish to make.
Share:	Notes.
Reflect:	Upon entire session.

Text:	ULU AND THE BREADFRUIT TREE
Focus:	Trust guidance...yes or no?
Length:	1 1/2 hours
Choose:	A partner. Partner holds a crayon in hand not normally used to write.
Place:	Your writing hand on partner's non-writing hand and hold it securely.
Ask:	Partner what he/she would like to draw.
Guide:	Partner's non-writing hand to draw this picture. Experiment with writing. End by writing your partner's name. Do not talk as you work. Reverse roles.
Share:	With partner a little about your experience.

Write:	Word associations around, "guidance".
Select:	One word which you are willing to talk about.
Share:	Your experiences/feelings/thoughts.
Tell:	"Ulu and the breadfruit tree" to the whole group.
Paint:	An image evoked by the word, trust.
Write:	The words which the non-trusting voice inside Ulu might have written after he received the guidance as to the need for his own death and the manner of his burial.
Collect:	Papers and redistribute them.
Write:	The words which the voice of trust might have spoken which finally left Ulu at peace with his knowledge and tasks.
Return:	Writings to original writer.
Read:	Mistrust and trust writings.
Look:	At paintings. Add whatever you wish to add.
Reflect:	Upon entire session.

Text:	ULU AND THE BREADFRUIT TREE
Focus:	The relationship between gain and loss
Length:	1 1/2 hours
Recall:	An occasion when you did *not* act in order to allow/make place for something to happen.
Write:	About this experience.

Response-task:	Listen to each experience. Take a sheet of paper and make as many spaces as there are members in the group. In each space paint a small image which represents the word that comes to mind when you describe the experience to yourself. Do not write the word.
Tell:	"Ulu and the breadfruit tree."
Paint:	An image evoked by, acceptance.
Recall:	An occasion when you were reluctant to accept a gift (of whatever kind).
Look:	At painting you created in response to earlier memories.
Write:	A sentence for every image.
Select:	A few or all of the sentences that feel to be connected and sequence them into a meaningful whole.
Share:	Your writings.
Reflect:	Upon entire session.

Questions focusing on healing

1. What stories were you told about healing when you were a child?
    Who told them to you?
    When were you told them?
    How were you told them?
    What effect, if any, did they have on you?

2. When you were ill or hurt as a child, to whom did you first go for help?
    Is this the person you really wanted to be helped by?
    If not, who would really have made you feel better?
    What gave you comfort?

3. What is your first memory of being ill or hurt?

4. What is your first memory of seeing a doctor?

5. When you think of illness, what words/images come to mind?

6. When you think of healing, what words/images come to mind?

7. When you think of doctor, what words/images come to mind?

8. How have your notions of healing changed, if they have, from when you were a child.

9. What is your most significant experience with illness?
    How were you healed?

10. How would you heal yourself now if you could redo the experience?

11. What do you do now to make yourself feel better when you are feeling slightly unwell?
    What do you do for others?
    Do you treat family members different from friends?
    If so, how?

12. How do you recognize symptoms of illness in yourself, in others?

13. How does illness fit into your philosophy of life?
     Is all illness totally a medical problem?
     Do you think of illness as a message from the mind/body?
     If so, how? What do you do about this?

14. How do you heal yourself, or find ways to be healed when your illness is of the psyche?

15. Describe a place of healing for you. Who and/or what helps?

CHAPTER NINE

RETURN

Whenever we return we shall be confronted with questions related to fulfillment and intention. No longer shall we be able to avoid our doubts, the remembrance of the roads not taken, our awareness of the inevitable consequences of the passage of time. We shall witness changes to places and to people. We will have all moved, but to where?

Once we arrive at the place of departure, the one whom we became will look us in the eye. Our dreams demand accounting. Outcome and intention will be placed next to one another. Then, in the moment of recognition, we shall know the constant and the new, the lasting as well as the changed. We can only hope our courage does not fail us, that we do not deny the knowledge to be gained.

We return to discover that we have truly been away. The reality of our absence rarely presents itself more vividly than at the time of our homecoming. It is now we know the price we paid for leaving. How do we find the strength to return? Though the possible gains are great, the cost might be dear.

To re-turn is to turn again. In turning the straight becomes bent. Angular or curved, sharp or gentle, the outcome of turning remains the same. What was once a predictable continuity of direct extension develops into an unpredictable course. Around the bend anything might happen. What do we encounter when we return?

To return is to walk backward into the future. We face the past while we attempt to make sense of what is, what was and what might be. Do we confront the collapse of time into duration, the creator knowing creation? If we choose to do so we can only hope that the essence of who we are survives this confrontation, that something of our hopes and dreams remains.

Whenever we are assailed by inner doubts about the purpose and contents of our life, we are likely to return once more to the place and people who mattered to us...once upon a time. Our return becomes framed by our expectations, the anticipation of outcome. We worry and wonder. Are we remembered? Will we be recognized? What is known about our exploits? Are we still welcome? The answers will be revealed when we return.

We can only return because we departed. Without a journey we cannot retrace our steps. Thus the end is the affirmation of beginning; completion is the confirmation of intention fulfilled. We return knowingly, perhaps willingly yet blindly. The next beginning is hidden.

When we journey back, along previously known roads, we may experience emotions long thought dead, relive events buried beneath the happenings of recent times. The healed scars may still ache. Past glories may shine too brightly through our present view. The energy which once inspired our departure is manifest. What will happen if we face the original intent without losing awareness of the current journey?

During each return we experience the future of our past in the present, a past safeguarded only by the protection of memory. We may run a great risk by returning to what we once had to leave. While we travel back we may be pulled forward by the clarity of the apparently known; drawn irresistibly toward what was, to the promise of remembered fruitfulness. Hastening homeward we forget that the journey home equals the journey away from home. Though we may recall the way, time plays tricks on distance traveled.

Then, suddenly, we might hold back without quite knowing why. Reluctantly, the face of discovery becomes real, we cease our journey toward the place of our beginning. We no longer wish to continue. We fear what will be lost when we arrive. A sense of foreboding arises within. Fear and courage intertwine, inseparable soulmates. We continue once again.

Dislocated between here and there, then and now, we travel onward, always in danger of losing ourselves amidst the complexity of our beginnings. Hesitating, we draw breath while we rehearse in our mind's eye the imminent encounter between what was and what will be. How can we learn to remember through forgetting? Under what pretenses and misguided beliefs do we continue our journey? Do we truly need to return anywhere?

Every return is born of hope and expectation. Repetition offers us a second chance, a new future. Through repetition we enhance our experience, knowledge and skills. We demonstrate our mastery and control, our ability to make the unpredictable predictable. Thus we extend the past and defeat the transitory quality of time. We enter into duration.

When we return we create an opportunity to redress our regrets, those generators of current dreams. The road back home is paved with good in tentions. Our search for reparation and completion inspires our return and reveals our aspiration to achieve the exemplary condition. Why are we surprised that each return generates the ultimate challenge, to begin again?

Each return gives birth to new beginnings.

Beginnings are difficult.

The Stories

The monkey's jump *Return/China*

Long ago, on the top of a mountain, nestled in some green grass, lay a strangely shaped stone egg. One day, it split and out came a monkey made of polished stone. Soon there were many monkeys laughing and chattering, running over the mountain with great delight. But all was not play and in time, the monkeys asked the stone monkey to be their king. This fit quite well with his own plans for himself and he readily accepted.

As king, he traveled in search of wisdom and new sights. While on his journey he persuaded a magician to teach him how to do many tricks, including how to jump miles at a single jump. When he had learned what he thought he needed to know he decided to make himself Lord of the Sky.

His exploits did not go unnoticed. In time, Dragon, prince to the Lord Buddha, called upon him to help rid the world of the stone monkey's mischief. The two went to the cloud palace of the Lord of the Sky and found the stone monkey causing trouble for anyone who challenged his supremacy.

Lord Buddha asked stone monkey, "What is it that you want?"

Stone monkey did not hesitate, "I want to be Lord of the Sky. I want to rule the universe. I am sure I can manage everything better than it is managed now." Then stone monkey began to tell Lord Budhha all that he could do. "I can jump higher than anyone. I can…"

Lord Buddha raised his hand as if to say, "No more." He smiled and said, "I will make a bargain with you. Let us go outside where you shall stand upon my hand. If you are able to jump out of my hand, you shall be Lord of the Sky. But, if you cannot, you will be returned to earth forever. You will never come up to the sky again."

Stone monkey laughed, slightly insulted by such an easy challenge. "Certainly I can jump out of your hand Lord Buddha." The bargain was struck. They went outside and stone monkey stepped onto Lord Buddha's hand. He jumped so high he passed by the five great red pillars standing on the edge of the great beyond. Just to prove he had jumped so far, he scratched a mark on the highest pillar and then returned to the Lord Buddha.

Pleased with himself, stone monkey strutted around the ground. Lord Buddha asked, "When are you going to jump?"

Insulted, stone monkey puffed himself up and sneered, "I have already jumped. I have been so far I scratched a mark on the tallest of the five red pillars standing at the edge of the great beyond. I have kept my part of the bargain, now you keep yours."

"If that is true stone monkey, how do you account for this?" Stone monkey looked. There, on one of the Lord Buddha's fingers was the very mark he had left on the tallest of the five red pillars standing on the edge of the great beyond. Stone monkey had never left Lord Buddha's hand. Still not ready to accept his defeat, stone monkey listened as Lord Buddha said, "I hold the whole world in my hand. When you jumped my hand was always under you. No one, not even stone monkey can go beyond my reach. Now return to earth and leave the sky forever."

The Lady of Stavoren   *Return/Netherlands*

In the harbor town of Stavoren there once lived a wealthy woman whose ships sailed far and wide, bringing her exotic treasures and costly gifts. She lived alone in a huge mansion, trusting no one, allowing no children to play on her grounds.

The arrival of her ships brought excitement to the small town with the fine harbor and the return of the Good Hope was no exception. On board, its captain was particularly pleased for he knew he had a cargo sure to be welcomed by the Lady of Stavoren. The townspeople gathered on the wharf dancing and singing, happy to greet the safe arrival of the ship and its sailors.

Suddenly, all was quiet. As if by magic, people moved, leaving a wide path down the wharf to the ship. The Lady of Stavoren walked down to the ship to see what the captain brought her. He showed her the gleaming, golden grains of wheat which filled the ship's hold. The Lady was not impressed.

"In on the far side, out on the near side," she said with disdain. People gasped. The captain's face turned white. Hoping he misunderstood he took some of the grains and put them in her hand.

"In on the far side, out on the near side," repeated the Lady, coldly.

The voice of an old fisherman broke the stunned silence. "What are you doing? The grain is a treasure beyond compare. It will feed our children, make our bread and keep the mills of Stavoren busy for a whole year. It has value more than gold." The Lady of Stavoren paid no attention and stood, waiting for the captain to carry out her orders. "My Lady," said the old man, "if you throw this grain into the sea, the sea will be revenged. There will come a time when you will gratefully beg for a few grains to eat. Mark my words."

"Do you think you can frighten me with your words, you poor, simple fisherman?" She held one of her hands up for everyone to see, using her other hand to take off a large jeweled ring. "Look at this ring! Before I beg for a single grain of wheat I'll have my ring back from the sea." She threw her ring into the sea and walked back to her mansion as the captain gave the order to dump the grain into the sea.

One night in spring, after the cold and hard winter passed, a fisherman knocked on the Lady's door. "Who knocks on my door at this hour? Do you bring me news of my ships?"

"No great Lady," said the fisherman. "I bring you a fish from the sea so big only you can afford to buy it."

"How dare you bring such a thing to my front door!" said the Lady. "Take it to the kitchen. Give it to my cook. She will pay you for your efforts."

The Lady, curious about such a large fish, went to the kitchen and watched the fish being slit open. She gasped with fear as she saw her jeweled ring drop from the belly of the fish. Unable to control herself, she ran out of the house where she was stopped by the old man who tried to save the grain.

"Your ships sank just outside the harbor. There was no reason; the sky was clear, the sea was calm. It was as I told you it would be. The sea would not let your ships pass the harbor where you spilled the grain."

No longer do the people throng down to the harbor to watch the arrival of the Lady's ships. The town of Stavoren is deserted. People have gone to harbor towns where ships can enter, where there is work for those who make their living from the sea. No one lives in Stavoren now, except for an ancient fisherman and an old woman dressed in the remnants of once fine clothes who walks the empty streets looking for a small bit of grain with which to feed herself.

The ending of the dream   *Return/Bushman/S. Africa*

Porcupine spoke to all the people of the Early Race. "We must pack our bags and pots and skins and shells. The new people who are coming will live where once we dwelt. This shall become their place. We have been the dream people and now the dream is complete. We must go now. When we return, we shall be only creatures and the Real People who come shall be only people."

"What will these new people be like old Grandfather?" asked the young mongoose.

"The Real People will be like us for we have cast our shadow. They shall be ugly and beautiful, hurtful and loving, stupid and cunning, just as we have been for we have learned these things for them," answered Mantis.

Young Mantis asked, "Will the Real People who come have your power?" When Mantis did not answer, Young Mantis asked, "How shall they survive without your magic?"

Mantis grew quiet, thinking how to answer. "They will not need my magic. Just as I found the strength to sit in the face of danger and Porcupine saved us from the All-Devourer and you found the wisdom to act wisely when you were frightened, so will they. The Real People will find the courage to face what they must. They will not need my magic"

Then the people of the Early Race did what needed to be done. They found the courage to pack their food bags, gather their children and leave their old life behind. They walked slowly, not without tears, back toward the beginning of life.

Maui and death   *Return/Polynesia*

Maui and his wife Hina lived peacefully with his mother, Huahega. One morning when Huahega was still sleeping Maui noticed that although he and his wife still had only black hair, his mother's hair was black and gray. Puzzled, he woke his mother up and asked why this was so. Huahega told him that this was a sign of her becoming an old woman, that she would soon die. Maui grieved and asked his mother, "Is there nothing I can do to prevent death from visiting you?"

"Yes my son," answered his mother. "You must take the stomach of Rori,

Sea-slug-of-the-deep-set-eyes. Then death will not visit us."

Maui searched the edge of the lagoon and found Rori living amidst the coral. "What brings you here?" asked Rori.

"I have come to give you my stomach in exchange for yours," said Maui. Rori protested, "If you take my stomach I will die."

Maui answered, "If you do not give it to me I will kill you." Rori continued to refuse but Maui furiously squeezed up the stomach of Sea-slug and was in the midst of swallowing it when Maui's brothers saw Maui. They ran to him and stopped him. Maui had to give Sea-slug back his stomach and took his own and put it inside himself. He shouted at his brothers, "Why have you stopped me from taking the stomach of Sea-slug-of-the-deep-set-eyes? Now, because of you, death will come to visit us."

Sadly he made his way back to Huahega and told her what had happened. Maui's mother listened and then said, "It is the way. In time you must follow me upon the path I now travel. You too will grow old and die." Maui sat quietly next to his mother and listened.

Persephone's return   *Return/Greece*

Demeter grieved when she found out her daughter Persephone had been kidnapped by Hades and taken to the Underworld. She refused to visit the earth to bestow her blessings. Forests died, streams dried up, only starvation and death visited. All of the Gods and Goddesses on Olympus pleaded with Demeter to return to her duties but the sorrowing mother refused. "Give my daughter back to me. Return my daughter. Give me back my child and I will give the earth its blessings. There is no other way."

The Gods and Goddesses sadly made their way to Zeus knowing he alone had the power to end the suffering of the earth's peoples. Zeus sent his messenger Hermes down to Hades but clever as he was, Hermes could not convince Hades to release Persephone for he loved her dearly. Hermes would not take no for an answer.

Using all his charm and skill, Hades finally relented. Hermes praised the sacrifice of Hades and then remembered that Persephone could only be returned to earth if she had eaten nothing of the food of the dead. Hermes asked Persephone, "What is it you have eaten here in Hades?"

"Nothing," answered Persephone, "except for six pomegranate seeds."

Hermes grew quiet, thinking of Demeter's grief. "You shall be returned to earth but not forever. You must spend one month in Hades for each seed you have eaten."

And so, each year, when Persephone returns to earth, Demeter gives thanks and blesses the earth causing trees to grow tall, flowers to appear and seeds to sprout. When Persephone returns to Hades, Demeter retires, grieving for her lost child. Winter ends the bountiful time. Yet now people know that winter will not last forever. Spring will return.

How Raven came to leave the earth   *Return/Indian/Canada*

When his work was finished and the world completed, Raven spent his days fishing and hunting with the people. One day when he was in a village, resting, Raven watched a young man with an evil face walk up to a woman drying fish for her large family. Much to Raven's horror, he heard the young man demand, "I want all your fish and the basket you have just made." The woman said nothing, filled the basket with the fish, and gave them to the stranger.

When the man left, Raven asked the woman, "Why did you give that man all your fish and the new basket you worked so many hours to make? Who is he?"

The woman answered, "That is Axsuq. He and his mother have been in this world as long as you have. Unlike you they create only pain and trouble. We are all are afraid of them because they hurt those who do not do their bidding."

"But why has no one told me of them?" asked Raven.

"We are ashamed of our fear. They have warned us that if we talk to you we will be punished and our families killed," replied the woman sadly.

Raven asked, "Has no one ever tried to kill Axsuq and his mother?"

"No," said the woman. "Not only do we fear Axsuq and his mother but also the giant bear of Axsuq who tortures and kills those who displease Axsuq. There is nothing to be done."

Raven disagreed, "This is terrible. I must do something to end your suffering." The young woman tried to dissuade him because she feared such a plan would cause more trouble but Raven would not listen.

He traveled to many villages looking for Axsuq and his bear but found no trace. Then, just as he was leaving a village, Raven saw Axsuq go up to an old man, demanding his fine skins. Before the old man could respond, Raven said, "No, you shall not take them." The villagers grew frightened and tried to warn Raven not to interfere but Raven said, " You shall not take what is not yours to have. If you want to challenge someone, fight with me." The villagers went to stop Raven but once again he stopped them and said, "Why do you hesitate? Do you fear me?"

Raven was answered by a huge black monster bear who spread his evil blackness as he sped toward Raven. Axsuq screamed, "Kill him. Kill him." The bear rushed at Raven, hot saliva dripping from its great mouth, the huge arms spread upward, ready to kill. Raven stood quietly. The beast raised up to strike and as he moved within an inch of Raven, Raven thrust his great spear into the bear's heart. The villagers watched with disbelief and growing fear as the huge creature slowly fell to the ground and died.

Raven said to Axsuq, "Now you are alone. It is your turn to fight with me." Axsuq took his bow from his shoulder, preparing to draw one of his arrows. Raven did not wait. Quickly, he let loose an arrow from his hunting bow, killing Axsuq in an instant.

Instead of thanking Raven, the villagers wept. "Now we will be punished. Axsuq's mother is more evil and more terrible than her son. She will take her revenge on us." Before more words could be said, a horrible stench filled the air. Darkness descended though it was early in the day. Raven looked and saw the most terrible looking creature he had ever seen. Motioning to the villagers to be still, he remained calm.

"You are Axsuq's mother. Why are you here?" asked Raven.

The creature, dripping blood and pus, smelling like rotted meat, laughed a mirthless laugh. "You have killed the bear of my son. You have killed my son. Now it is your turn to die."

Raven said, "I am mountain maker, creator of all life. Do you think it is nothing to kill me?"

Axsuq's mother laughed contemptuously and said, "How easy it is for you to stand before me, protected by your creator's mask and mantle. You would act differently if you were mortal like the villagers."

Raven remained calm. "You think you scare me with your words but you are wrong." With that, he flung off his creator's mask and mantle. The villagers yelled this was a trick, that he would surely die. Raven refused to listen. He picked up his spear and watched the creature turn into a huge and poisonous snake, covered with hard scales through which his spear could not penetrate.

As he looked at the snake Raven felt a new and strange sensation in his body. Sweat poured from his trembling limbs; he could barely move. He knew fear for the first time. Then, when he thought he could not continue, another feeling filled him, giving him the strength he needed to go on. "This must be what humans call courage," he thought to himself. Exulting in his new found energy he called to the snake, "I am ready for you. Let us see what you can do against a mere mortal you stench filled beast."

The snake attacked with vomit and spit but Raven jumped out of the way. Once more he taunted the snake. Once again she attacked with her open mouth spewing foul smelling steam, breathing hot upon Raven. When she came close, Raven saw his opportunity. As she flung herself upon him, Raven jammed his spear deep down into her mouth and out threw her eyes. The snake screamed in pain and died an agonizing death.

At first the villagers stood still, staring at the dead creature, unable to believe their eyes. Then they turned to Raven with words of gratitude. He looked at them, as if for the first time, and then said, "Say no more. I merely did what needed to be done. Now it is time for me to leave."

An old man said, "Of course, you are tired. You must rest."

Raven shook his head. "I do not leave to return. I must go to where I came from."

A young woman asked, "Have our fears offended you?"

"No," answered Raven. "I leave because my work here is ended. As long as evil was amongst you I was needed. Now, evil has been vanquished and it is I who must leave. You have what you need most to survive. You feel fear because you know death. You have courage because you know fear. You are strong enough to take care of yourselves."

The villagers began to weep quietly. Raven said, "Do not cry. It is time for me to go. But know that I shall watch you. If you really need me I will return". Then, as the villagers watched, Raven slowly flew away until he could be seen no more.

Now, Raven remains with us in the stories we tell. We know that some day, he may return. This is the way it is.

Return - The Structures

Theme:	RETURN
Focus:	Going and coming
Length:	50 minutes

Sculpt: A clay image of going.

Sculpt: A clay image of coming.

Place: Sculptures in relationship to each other.

Write: Briefly write answers to the following:
- Who is going? From where?
- What are the circumstances of her/his going?
- Why must he/she go now?
- How does she/he feel?
- What is she/he going to do?
- How will this be accomplished?
- What does it take for him/her to return?
- Who/what greets him/her upon return?
- How does she/he feel after returning?

Write: Story using information obtained from questions.

Share: Clay work and stories.

Reflect: Upon entire session.

Theme:	RETURN
Focus:	A journey's end
Length:	50 minutes

Recall: A time when you were about to begin an adventure of any kind.

Paint:	Divide paper into 3 parts. On the left side paint an image of feelings just before you began your adventure.
Write:	Some words that reflect those feelings near your image on the same side of the paper.
Recall:	Arrival back home after the end of the adventure.
Paint:	Image of feelings at this time on the right side of the paper leaving the center clear.
Write:	Words that come to mind which reflect your feelings upon return near the image just painted.
Create:	A path which took you from the beginning of your adventure back to your arrival at home.
Recall:	Events and feelings as you made your adventure.
Paint/draw:	Images on path which take you from departure to arrival and back to your starting place.
Recall:	What made the greatest impact upon you when you returned?
Write:	Memory.
Share:	Images and writings.
Reflect:	Upon entire session.

Text:	THE MONKEY'S JUMP
Focus:	Daring to respond
Length:	50 minutes

Recall: A dare or challenge to which you once responded.

Write: One word, on a small piece of paper, which describes the way you felt when you decided to respond.

Collect: These pieces of paper.

Tell: "The monkey's jump" up to, "I will make a bargain with you".

Re-distribute: Pieces of paper.

Write: Your own ending using the dynamics which arise from the word you have just chosen.

Response-task: As you listen to the endings, ask yourself what it is that you appreciate about this monkey's efforts. Write this on a small piece of paper and give it to the respective monkey storyteller after all endings have been shared.

Share: Endings.

Tell: Ending of "The monkey's jump."

Read: The appreciations.

Connect: Make connections between the story endings and your own life experiences.

Reflect: Upon the entire session.

Text:	THE MONKEY'S JUMP
Focus:	Jumping to reality
Length:	1 1/2 hours

Warmup: The body by gently stretching, taking small jumps and a brief easy run around room.

Move: Explore in many different ways, how, as a group you can transport a group member safely through the room without her/his feet ever touching the ground. Each group member will have a turn to carry and be carried.

Paint: Image evoked by the words, "jumping to the outer edge of the universe".

Tell: "The monkey's jump."

Write: At the top of a sheet of paper, the words, "in the palm of my hand". Write these same words at the bottom of the same paper.
Write what ever comes to mind in between.

Response-task: Cut some small shapes out of colored paper, one for each group member. Draw a representation evoked by the writing and give it to the respective group member after all writing has been shared.

Share: Writings and feelings evoked by stories.

Reflect: Upon entire session.

Text:	THE MONKEY'S JUMP
Focus:	This is what happened
Length:	1 1/2 hours

Draw: A picture of your hands on a piece of paper.

Move:	In groups of 3. One person gives one hand to first partner and other hand to second partner.
Talk:	First partner describes the hand with no interpretation. Second partner talks about the way the hand feels, what he/she senses about the hand's capabilities. Reverse roles so that each group member experiences each aspect of the activity.
Return:	To circle taking hand painting with you.
Share:	Feelings evoked by work for a few minutes.
Tell:	"The monkey's jump."
Write:	Upon his return, monkey wishes to share what he has experienced and gained with the other monkeys. Write what he will tell them.
Response-task:	A 2 sentence thank you speech to the monkey telling of his experience.
Read:	Stories.
Give:	Thank you speeches to respective monkeys.
Read:	Speeches.
Connect:	Make connections between stories and the earlier work.
Look:	At your hand picture.
Write/draw:	Anything you wish to add.
Reflect:	Upon the entire session.

Text: THE LADY OF STAVOREN
Focus: To recognize a gift
Length: 50 minutes

Write: Words associated with, valuable.

Draw: 7 valuables in your possession.

Move: In pairs, convey without using words, the meaning of your valuables to your partner. Reverse roles.

Tell: "The Lady of Stavoren."

Write: The words, "A gift ignored," on the top of a sheet of paper. Add whatever seems to follow including what, where, who, solution and outcome.

Response-
task: Create as many spaces on a sheet of paper as there are group members. In each space, as a group member shares his/her work, record in words or image which gift these writings and paintings offer you.

Share: Writings and images of valuables.

Share: Response images and words.

Reflect: Upon the entire session.

Text: THE LADY OF STAVOREN
Focus: A warning ignored
Length: 1 1/2 hours

Write: "I warn you" on a sheet of paper and add what ever else needs to follow.

Present: Your writings to the group as if they are the ones you are warning.

Share: Feelings evoked by this activity.

Tell: "The Lady of Stavoren."

Choose: To be one of the young or old people on the quay-side who have witnessed the scene and who later left Stavoren. Who are you?
            You have just heard that the Lady's ring came back to her and that shortly afterward her ships sank. You feel compelled to write a letter to her which includes an account of the effect her action has had upon you.

Write: This letter.

Place: 2 chairs near one another. One chair will be used by the letter writer, the other by the Lady of Stavoren.

Move: One by one, sit on the chair of the letter writer and address the chair where you "know" the Lady of Stavoren sits.

Read: Your letter to her.

Change: Chairs.

Improvise: As the Lady of Stavoren, respond to the letter you have just received. Continue until all group members have read their letters and responded as the Lady.

Paint: The image evoked by the word, reconciliation.

Reflect: Upon the entire session.

Text:	THE LADY OF STAVOREN
Focus:	Recovering from disappointment
Length:	1 1/2 hours

Walk: Around the room repeating the words, "I am disappointed. I am disappointed." Repeat the words many times. Other words will come to mind; let them be. Witness what they are and speak them.
Continue to intersperse your words from time to time with, "I am disappointed." Adapt your way of walking to the words you speak.

Freeze: Stay where you are and hold the position you now have. Focus on one sentence out of all those you have just spoken.

Unfreeze: Walk a little more around the room and then return to the circle.

Tell: "The Lady of Stavoren."

Sound: In groups of 3 explore the sound possibilities evoked by the following 3 words: force, permission, balance. Do not speak words.

Improvise: In these same groups of 3, retell the story. Take into account your work around the 3 words. Use as much sound and movement and as few words as you can during the retelling.

Present: Your retelling.

Share: Your response to the presentations and what they evoke within you.

Reflect: Upon the entire session.

Text:	THE ENDING OF THE DREAM
Focus:	In the beginning
Length:	50 minutes

Paint: The image evoked by the word, "renewal".

Tell: The ending of the dream.

Paint: The image evoked by the words, "in the beginning".

Recall: An experience which relates to both words.

Response-task: While listening to each memory, select a phrase or image which resonates within you. Briefly record this response in words or image.

Share: Memories.

Arrange: These resonant responses in a sequence which is meaningful to you.

Create: Something which uses the sequence and the elements within to encapsulate the fear and courage, the complex range of emotions, that the words, "in the beginning" inspire.

Present: Your work.

Reflect: Upon the entire session.

Text:	THE ENDING OF THE DREAM
Focus:	Before and after completion
Length:	1 1/2 hours

Paint: The image of, "completion".

Write: On a sheet of paper what is evoked by the word, "completion".
Before you begin be aware that your writings will, in themselves, require completion. Therefore, take the end into consideration as you begin.

Paint/draw: A symbol of completion.

Tell: "The ending of the dream."

Sculpt/paint/ The image of one of the Animal People who are in this
draw process of transition.

Share: All your work with one another.

Design: A brief ceremony of "Blessings" by sharing the blessings you know or those you design. Address your blessings to the people on either side of you as well as to those with whom you are connected. Make use of your paintings and writings in this ceremony.

Create: "Blessings" ceremony.

Reflect: Upon the entire session.

Text: THE ENDING OF THE DREAM
Focus: In order to make place
Length: 1 1/2 hours

Write: List of common courtesies.

Collect: Lists.

Reflect: On what being courteous requires of the person who is prepared to act in this manner.

Select: In pairs, 1 or 2 of these requirements.

Move: To an area in the room where you can work. Sit next to
               one another on the floor.
               Without words or signalling physically, sense when your
               partner is ready to work. Using nonverbal communi-
               cation, explore the possibilities of the characteristic(s)
               you have selected.

Return: To circle.

Paint: Image evoked by the word, "vision".

Tell: "The ending of the dream."

Write: An address to mankind where you speak about the im-
               plications of the animal peoples' preparedness to become
               "all together animals" in order to make place for the
               people of the human race.

Share: Writings and paintings.

Connect: Links between your work on courtesy characteristics,
               painting, writings and your life experiences.

Reflect: Upon entire session.

Text: MAUI AND DEATH
Focus: Being old
Length: 50 minutes

Recall: Your first/earliest awareness of the difference in ages be-
               tween people which might have been a realization of "be-
               ing old".

Write: About this awareness.

Write: Words associated with, old.

Recall: Something an "old" person has said to you which has left
              an impression on you.

Write: These words.

Tell: "Maui and death."

Paint/draw: Image evoked by an aspect of the text which resonates
              within you.

**Response-
task:**   On a sheet of paper create as many spaces as there are
              members in the group. In each space record something
              that you wish to be able to remember from what this
              group member has just shared.

Share: Writings and images.

Share: What you have recorded.

Reflect: Upon entire session.

Text: MAUI AND DEATH
Focus: I..death..dying..you
Length: 1 1/2 hours

Sit: On the floor with a piece of paper and felt pens or
              crayons.
              Close your eyes.

Draw: An image evoked by the word, "death" keeping your eyes
              closed.

Move:	After you finish your drawing, lie down.
Recall:	Images and feelings about death and dying. Open your eyes and continue your thoughts.
Look:	At your drawing evoked by, death.
Share:	In pairs, your paintings and some of your thoughts and feelings (3 minutes each).
Write:	The words, death and dying at least 3 times on a sheet of paper. Then write "I" 3 times and finally write, "you", 3 times. Create sentences around these words.
Return:	To circle.
Tell:	"Maui and death."
Response-task:	On a sheet of paper create as many spaces as there are group members. In each space make a small symbolic representation of what you believe you need/need to learn, in order to live with the awareness of life and death given your responses to each group member's writing.
Share:	Your writings.
Reflect:	Upon the entire session.

Text:	MAUI AND DEATH
Focus:	The 7 ages of man
Length:	1 1/2 hours
Write:	On 3 small pieces of paper, 2 good/1 bad things that can happen to people.

Collect: These papers and put them in a pile in the center of the circle.

Write: On a large sheet of paper, at varying intervals, 7 ages (possibly but not necessarily) ranging from very young to very old.

Draw: Near each ages, an image of something simple which is pleasant that someone of this age might experience. Then draw an image of something complicated for that same age.

Write: In a few words, describing something painful that some-one of that age might experience.

Look: At the work of other group members.

Take: 3 pieces of paper from the good/bad collection but do not look at what they are. Leave 1 or 2 near someone's drawing. No one can receive more than 3 pieces of paper.

Return: To your own drawing. Open a good/bad paper.

Decide: At which age you want to add this to your 7 ages work. Open each of the remaining papers and add them to your 7 ages work.

Draw/write: As necessary to complete your work.

Tell: "Maui and death."

Share: Your 7 ages work with a partner. Reflect on the good/bad things which you needed to incorporate. Explore Maui's response to the awareness of aging and death. Relate this to your own experience.

Reflect: Upon the entire session with the whole group.

Text:	PERSEPHONE'S RETURN
Focus:	Singing through the darkness
Length:	50 minutes

Write: Words associated with, cycle.

List: Examples of your own experiences of cyclicity.

Write: About one of these experiences beginning with the word, "I".

Paint: Image evoked by the word, "cycle".

Tell: "Persephone's return."

Response-task: As you listen to each group member's writings and see the paintings, remind yourself of a song.

Share: Your writings and paintings.

Recall: Painting/writing and mention the title of the song associated with the work.

Sing: A bit of this song with the group and invite the rest to join you for a verse or chorus.

Reflect: Upon the entire session.

Text:	PERSEPHONE'S RETURN
Focus:	Ways of waiting
Length:	1 1/2 hours

Paint: Image evoked by the word, "waiting".

Move: One by one take a posture which reflects your idea of waiting.

Speak: When everyone is in a posture of waiting, the first person to take a posture speaks, beginning with the words, "I wait and..." Each person in turn speaks until everyone has spoken.

Move: When the last person has spoken, each group member in turn returns to the circle.

Tell: "Persephone's return."

Paint: Your response to the story.

Place: Your paintings next to one another leaving space around them.

Move: Explore the emotional content of both paintings. Note differences and similarities. Find a way to resolve any difficulties evoked within you by the paintings. Allow the movement to end in a still-point and hold this position for a short time. Note what words come to mind during this time. Complete any unresolved movement work.

Return: To circle.

Share: Your experience.

Reflect: Upon the entire session.

Text: PERSEPHONE'S RETURN
Focus: The process of change
Length: 1 1/2 hours

Write: Words associated with, loss.

Select: One which feels relevant and about which you are prepared to talk a little.

Share:	Word. Talk about what it represents for you.
Draw/paint:	A picture of a fruit-bearing tree during at least 3 different stages of the year.
Place:	Your painting/drawing somewhere in the room.
Look:	At the different painting/drawings.
Select:	One which appeals to you, preferably not your own painting/drawing.
Write:	Something about the way in which the tree experiences each of the different stages. Let yourself be guided by the images. Personify the tree by beginning your writings with the word, "I". Write a brief thank you note to the imagemaker and leave this near the painting or drawing.
Move:	Take your writings with you and return to the circle.
Tell:	"Persephone's return."
Show:	A tree painting/drawing.
Read:	Thank you note left near it.
Connect:	Make connections with your earlier writings about loss and life experiences.
Reflect:	Upon the entire session.

Text:	HOW RAVEN CAME TO LEAVE THE EARTH
Focus:	A gift forever more
Length:	50 minutes

Put: A box of candles in center of circle.

Tell: "How Raven came to leave the earth."

Reflect: On the story. Think about which important gift Raven gave the people of the earth and at which moment this was given.

Write: The gift and when it was given.

Create: Using clay, paint, sound, movement or words, find a way to express and honor this moment.

Response-task: Take a candle from box in center of circle. As each person shares the work, the person sitting closest to the sharer will light the sharer's candle.

Share: Work with the group. When all work has been shared and all candles are lit, each person, in turn, will say some words before all candles are blown out at the same time. Candles can be taken home.

Reflect: Upon the entire session.

Text:	HOW RAVEN CAME TO LEAVE THE EARTH
Focus:	The courage to share fear
Length:	1 1/2 hours

Divide: Into groups of about 5.

Paint: Each person take paper and fold paper in half. On the left side paint an image of fear, on the other half paint an image of courage.

List: On paper, words evoked by fear and courage.

Write: One word that fills you with fear, and one word that gives you courage.

Share: Images and words in small groups.

Tell: To whole group, "How Raven came to leave the earth".

Select: One character in story of greatest interest.

Choose: Any 2 words which come to mind which you will use as your "script".

Move: Each person, one at a time, in small group, moves inside the small circle as chosen character using 2 words in different ways to express feelings. Choose movement which reflects activity of character (chopping wood, washing clothes, preparing food etc.)

Improvise: Each person, having chosen his/her character, using 2 words of "script", helps to create a retelling of the story using words and movement. Use whatever characters have been chosen even if this means some of the main characters are missing. Each group finds its own beginning and ending. Do not talk about improvisation until group has gone through 3 different retellings.

Note: Each person chooses own actions. No one tells anyone what to do or how to do it.

Talk: In small groups about the experience. Decide what will be presented to the larger group.

Response-task: Divide paper into as many spaces as there are groups. As you watch a presentation write down, in a few words, what enabled the fear to be shared. Paint a symbol of courage for each group.

Share: Improvisations.

Share: Response work.

Reflect: Upon the entire session.

Text: HOW RAVEN CAME TO LEAVE THE EARTH
Focus: "I am willing"
Length: 1 1/2 hours

Write: "I am willing...." on a sheet of paper in a way which is
            reflective of these words and complete the statement.

Place: These papers near to one another.

Write: Take a new sheet of paper and write on it a negative
            response to this collection of "I am willing" declarations.

Leave: This statement near one of the willing statements.

Reclaim: Your own willing statement and the negative statement
            closest to it.

Move: To a space within the room where you can be by yourself
            as much as possible.

Repeat: Both sentences to yourself until you have a sense of what
            feelings they evoke within you.
            Notice these feelings without trying to push them away or
            change them.

Tell: "How Raven came to leave the earth."

Paint: 5 paintings in 10 minutes.

Look: At the 2 sentences with which you worked.

Write: One sentence which contains a strong encouragement for
           you in a time of fear.

Stand: In circle taking sentence with you.

Chant: Each group member in turn chants his/her own sentence
           of encouragement in a time of fear. Group members
           repeat chant 3 times. Repeat until all group members have
           shared their "encouragement in a time of fear" chants.

Share: Paintings and any feelings evoked by the work.

Reflect: Upon the entire session.

Questions focusing on return

1. How old were you the first time you left home? Under what circumstances did you leave? How did you feel?

2. Did you ever return home after that for any substantial time? Under what circumstances? How did it feel to return home?

3. What do you think about Thomas Wolfe's line, "You can't go home again."?

4. How do you define home? When you think of home what images and feelings come to mind?

5. What images and feelings come to mind when you think of return?

6. To what or whom would you most like to return?

7. Have you unfinished business in your life? What would it take to finish it? What effect would this have on your thoughts and feelings?

8. If you have brothers and/or sisters, what notions do you each have about what it feels like to return to your home and/or your home town?

9. Have you ever attended a reunion? Under what circumstances? How did you feel? How did the occasion help you to reflect on your life? What of the experience remains meaningful? Would you attend another reunion? Of the same kind? Different? What kind of reunion would you definitely not attend? Why?

10. When you travel to a foreign country or a strange place how do you cope with all that is new and different?

11. How do you feel when you have to move. How does the reason for moving affect you? Where would you like to move?

12. How do you feel about being the person to whom others return?

13. How do you feel about being the one to "keep things going"?

14. Would you rather be the one who goes or the one who stays?

15. What memory of returning stands out when you think of all the times you have left someplace or someone and then returned to it or him/her?

PART 3
Notes for facilitators

CHAPTER TEN

ON MYTHMAKING STRUCTURES

A NOTE OF CAUTION

In this chapter we aim to introduce some of the thinking which underlies the design of mythmaking structures and the ways in which the structures are used in practice, whether this be in an educational, recreational or therapeutic setting. We take it as read that the intention behind the setting up of a mythmaking group profoundly influences the groupmembers' expectations as well as the nature of their contributions and the style of the facilitator's response/intervention. These issues will be explored later in greater detail. Suffice it to say now that we anticipate that the mythmaking structures in this book will be used by people who either have a developed interest in stories and who wish to explore these structures in order to nurture alternative ways of relating to the material, or by people who are secure in their professional skills and experienced in working with groups (educational, therapeutic, recreational). We expect such people to enjoy hearing and telling myths and tales and that they wish to use this material with their groups.

We feel substantial concern that people inexperienced in working with groups, and without the knowledge and wisdom gained from hearing and reading many stories, might be tempted to experiment with these structures. As long as care is taken to use the mythmaking structure IN ITS ENTIRETY (title included) without words being left out or changed, and as long as the tales are read, not told, chances are that the group will have a stimulating and enhancing experience. However, inexperience in itself might lead some people to feel an absence of caution and a desire to influence this apparently highly prescriptive method. Should this happen trouble will occur. Not may, but will. We are aware that this statement might cause some people to reconsider using this material. For others such a statement in and of itself equals the throwing down of the gauntlet, representing a challenge to which one needs to respond. We urge all readers to give the material a chance, as it is written, as it has been tested with many differing educational, therapeutic and recreational groups.

Despite frequent warnings to use the material as given, students in workshops have occasionally gone away and worked with their groups from memory, without the precise detail of a structure, doing "something like it". This has invariably led to difficulties which have at times been serious. Our concern about the likelihood of abuse of the structures has been such that we wondered whether or not to publish the book at all. However, after many years of using this material, with a wide range of groups having different abilities, in a variety of settings and in many countries, we trust that the structures provided are reliable and safe.

We therefore request that when you wish to develop your own ideas and insights in relation to the stories which we have included, that you design COMPLETELY NEW mythmaking structures, and that, where possible, you read as many different versions of these myths and tales as you can find. To this end we include a list of books and resources we have found helpful.

The development of a mythmaking structure

The mythmaking structures in this book have as their central core, a myth or traditional folk tale (collectively referred to as stories). The myths and tales are chosen for a variety of reasons, but above all, because we like them and because the many people with whom we have been able to share these stories preferred these to others. The stories are also representative within their own category of myth or tale. Another important consideration has been, however, that we wished to include stories from the various cultures and people whose traditional indigenous knowledge is endangered due to the pressure exercised by European/Western cultural dominance. We also selected stories which relate to a wide array of human preoccupations and predicaments. Each story addresses a particular human condition and offers us a wealth of experience and insight. Most human knowledge is gained on the crucible of human experience. The willingness to encapsulate this experience in a form which permits transmission to others requires generosity as well as wisdom. It is with the awareness of having received this gift that we aim to work with the stories.

Each mythmaking structure is developed on the basis of extensive comparison and detailed analysis of a series of myths and tales, similar to the one employed within a session. During the session the facilitator encourages the participants to embark upon either a structural and developmental journey, which parallels the one contained within the myth, or to explore a specific theme, which again lies at the center of the story. Through the completion of a series of tasks, which are purposefully sequential, the phases or aspects of development contained within the chosen story are recreated. Thus, the design of a mythmaking structure depends on more than the designer's ability to name and denote aspects of development contained within the story. Facilitators also need to notice and understand the relationship between these aspects. The characteristics of this relationship will ultimately determine the usefulness of a perceived and then recreated story structure. We say "perceived" structure because another person, who carefully compares a series of thematic myths and tales, may discern different inherent developmental journeys. Should this occur, then entirely NEW mythmaking structures must be designed which have their own intrinsic logic and which follow the developmental pattern in accordance with the individual's alternative perception of the material. We strongly discourage the temptation to alter the task sequentiality or task content as used in these mythmaking structures. Whatever benefits can result from mythmaking, profound confusion will be the inescapable outcome when tasks are no longer purposefully sequential and/or intimately connected to the perceived inner relevance and logic of the chosen myth or tale.

The mythmaking structures contained within this book follow the pattern of problem exposition, formulation of necessity, attempts at solution, resolution, acceptance/integration inherent in the story and reflection on the experience as a whole. The sequencing of the tasks provides a guided approach. This frees the participants to enjoy the liberty which results from the implementation of boundaries and enables them to feel the security needed in order to begin. Each mythmaking structure also contains implicit and explicit reorganizing properties which help to energize the participants. This energy will facilitate the completion of the various tasks within the prescribed time limits.

In summary

The mythmaking structures have been developed in the following way:
- A theme is chosen which the group will work around;
- A myth or tale is selected which represents this theme;
- The myth/tale is subjected to extensive comparison with other texts and content analysis.

The myth/tale is contextualized (cultural background, philosophical/ethical context);

- A series of tasks is created which paraphrase the chosen theme and the content/context analysis; (The tasks take account of the optimum use which can be made of intra-group and group-facilitator interaction possibilities and the various ways these can be utilized in the paraphrasing of the story construct.)

- The mythmaking structure is compared to other, already existing structures, to ensure that its design is consistent;

- The mythmaking structure is "tried out" with a group(s) who are willing to explore its possibilities and provide feedback to the facilitator;

- The structure is, where necessary, amended and tried out again;

- The structure is used with groups, where and when appropriate.

In order to create new structures, the designer needs knowledge and understanding of:

- The essential components of a mythmaking structure, i.e.

TEXT and TASK, which will constitute a theme and/or developmental pattern around which a group will work;

- The processes and patterns of interaction between the various tasks, the text, facilitator style and intervention, and context;

- The outcomes likely to result from the use of these processes and patterns with various participant groups of widely different cultural backgrounds.

The text

Although each myth and tale has a unique nature and quality, patterns and themes become clearly discernable after reading and studying tales from all over the world. We encounter, among others, myths of creation, of paradise and floods, saviors and rebirth, as well as tales about ill-treated and abandoned children, trickster-wanderers and animal sages. The more we read, the more we can increase our ability to notice and pay attention to detail. We learn to recognize story group and subgroup. For example, in the "myths of creation", we will see creation through the occurrence of a primordial sacrifice, or by one creator god, or two duelling twin brothers, through emergence from one world to the next, or the earth-diver motif where an animal (mostly) dives deep under the water in order to find some earth. Within the tales, in each group and subgroup, we will discover the common elements and unique twists. It becomes possible to discern inherent patterns of repetition, common approaches to solving difficulties and recurring sequences of events.

When we design a structure, full use is made of our knowledge of both the themes and the emerging patterns, the morphology of a tale. It is the particular way in which the usual and the unusual are combined within a story that will provide us with clues about its latent and manifest content. The point of deviation from the common pattern is of specific interest because it is precisely here that a unique way of approaching a difficulty begins. This turning point in a myth or tale often becomes the pivotal point to be simulated in the mythmaking structure and which is, above all,

designed to enable the participants to benefit from these traditional problem solving methods. Each structure is therefore closely matched to the
specific problem solving properties of the chosen text.

Each tale contains an answer to an implicitly or explicitly posed problem. It indicates the degree of necessity or motivation required in order to
begin the arduous task of problem resolution. It also contains within its
underlying structure the *method as well as the way* by and in which this
problem was first approached and understood, the errors which were
made, and the later solution is found. It therefore matters that the facilitator
makes an appropriate analysis and correctly paraphrases from contained
material to the mythmaking tasks to be completed.

When we wish to explain that $2+2=4$, we can decide to make use of four
apples to aid our explanation. We can also take two apples and two oranges
or three apples and one orange though the latter already complicates matters. We could not use three apples and two oranges. We suggest that the
basic structure of the myths and tales which we have included in this book
has an analogous, near mathematical clarity, to its construct and morphology. Although we stated earlier that this structure is "perceived" and
therefore relative, it is also true that our work is based upon extensive study
of these and other texts and it might well be that there are not too many or
even no perceived alternatives to the perceived structure we have identified. At this stage we are, however, hesitant to make this claim.

We have stated that in order to design a mythmaking structure we need to
come to grips with the actual content of a myth/tale. However, it is equally
important that we familiarize ourselves, as much as possible, with the way
in which the text was used amongst the people from whom it originated.
This context will provide us with further information regarding its ascribed
problem solving properties. We need to know whether this story was one
which could be told and retold by anyone under any circumstances and at
any time, or whether specific conditions and requirements were placed
upon those who recounted these stories. Where restrictions do apply they
often refer to location, time, audience and manner of recitation/telling.

Some tales could only be told as part of the celebration during a religious
festival to be held in a sacred place at a specific day and time during the year
(e.g. many myths of creation). Others can be shared any time and any place
but only when the purpose of the telling is clear to all who are present and
when this purpose remains unchanged (myths of healing). The audience

preparedness to listen and participate is an essential requirement which we tend to take for granted. The manner in which the audience prepares itself to become audience, and later to be an audience, can also be subject to stringent prescriptions and regulations ranging from fasting and purification rituals to simple (but extremely complex) attention focusing practices.

The placing of limitations upon the retelling safeguards the story's potency as well as its efficacy. The conditions under which the story may be recounted profoundly influences its content and construct. Therefore, in any analysis of a given tale, these need to be taken into careful consideration.

Lastly we shall need to take into account the relationship between a particular story and mankind's general development of patterns of thought and reflection (from historical, philosophical, socio-political and psychological perspectives). Each story needs to be understood, not only as part of the history of its people, embedded in a particular culture, but also in relation to stories of kindred kind from other peoples. At the same time, we need to study and be aware of the relationship between this text and the general ethical/socio-political roads on which all people travel.

We have often found it helpful to conceptualize a particular story in the broader theoretical frameworks offered by the study of comparative religion, political history, linguistics and developmental psychology. In one instance, while working with a group of academic scientists specializing in theoretical physics, we chose as our theme, beginnings. It was a most insightful experience and while it would be too much to suggest that a grasp of quantum physics facilitates the design of mythmaking structures, one could also say such is not far from the truth.

The extent to which we accept that the stories contain and safeguard crucial *problem solving methods*, and possess simultaneously inherent *problem solving properties*, determines how much importance we attach to:

- further research determining the extent to which this is so;

- the aim to understand and to describe how this might be so;

- the exploration of possible analogies in other fields of study which might explain this phenomenon.

Even if we do not embark upon these studies for any of the reasons stated above, the attempts to create an explanation for the many phenomena and experiences which are reflected in these stories and to formulate some meaning (however primitive or complex) out of feelings and events to which we are all exposed will probably lead, sooner or later, to the study of seminal works in the related fields of comparative religion, ethics, history and psychology. Such studies can only benefit the understanding and respect with which we approach these stories.

The themes

The stories in this book have been arranged in groups of six, united by a theme in seven thematic chapters. We begin each of these chapters with an introductory section where we explore the way in which these stories and the mythmaking structure work have resonated within us, what they evoke, which stage of the journey through and in our lives the theme might represent and which human predicaments and situations it encompasses. These sections also contain, in veiled form, some of the theory in the fields of mythology and psychology which we consider fundamental to the general understanding of the theme (not of the stories per se).

The stories within each theme, and especially the theme itself, provide material from which connections can be made across time (present, past and future) and across experience (knowledge, memories, fantasies). The establishment of these connections contributes to the change in group and individual levels of energy and the development of continuing access to inner/creative resources. Whether or not participants make regular use of the access gained will be influenced by the duration and circumstances of the program (the number and patterning of group sessions), the appropriateness of the selected stories within a given theme and the participant's sensed need for self-expression.

Although each facilitator will select the theme, story and the mythmaking structure best suited to the particular group, it is necessary to stress that it is usually best to begin with the least bewildering, the most easily accessible themes and mythmaking structures. All mythmaking structures contained in this book facilitate the participant's functioning and exploration at a level which is appropriate to them. However, someone else's disclosure or story can have an unsettling or disturbing effect upon a group member. This is more likely to occur with some themes rather than with others. Also, when a group works with a theme or story which is too complex, then the group and the process are liable to become unnecessarily frustrated. We suggest the following graded usage of material in this book:

1.	Beginnings	4.	Beginnings
	The Tree		Passages
	Healing		Knots
			The Tree
2.	Beginnings		Healing
	Passages		Return
	The Tree		
	Healing	5.	Beginnings
			Passages
3.	Beginnings		Knots
	Passages		The Tree
	Knots		Trickster
	The Tree		Healing
	Healing		Return and Beginnings

The tasks

Once a theme has been chosen, a myth or tale selected, and the process described under "Text" has been worked through, then the design of mythmaking tasks begins. When we look at the various tasks it becomes clear that many are based on the making of images, whether the medium or material used is the body, (for sound, movement, language imagery) or material (e.g. fingerpaint, clay or glue). The range of imagery tasks can be summarized under:

- the making of visual images;
- the making of movement/bodily images;
- the making of sound images;
- the making of language images (written and dramatic).

The tasks are always designed in such a way that they will generate a quick and spontaneous response in a prescribed mode. The immediacy of the required response aids in the making of the distinctly individual nature of the contributions. It is a personal response to a shared task.

> When a mythmaking structure is designed, we decide upon:
>
> - the construct of the task;
>
> - the sequence of the tasks;
>
> - the time allotted for the completion of a task;
>
> - the required nature and mode of response to the sharing of the work (e.g. mnemonic drawings, prescribed forms of writing or dramatic improvisations);
>
> - the closing process.

The purpose or reason behind a given task is never explained. Some participants can find this initially rather difficult but the instruction to do something has to be taken on trust. Remember what is prescribed is a specific form of exploration, and the direction a certain exploration might take. The content is NEVER prescribed. The task loses a great deal of its potency once why's and wherefore's are made explicit. For then, the participant will aim to work in accordance with these stated reasons and will anticipate a certain outcome. This is similar to the bud which has been opened in spring by a researcher curious to find out what kind of a flower the bud will become. A bud so opened is unlikely ever to flower.

We understand that a facilitator might be hesitant to accept the mythmaking structures in this book as they are. After all, the writers do not know their groups. We certainly encourage anyone who wishes to use these structures with a group to explore them by themselves or with friends. This experience will make clear what kind of personal material the structures generate within the future facilitator. We also suggest, in case of doubt, the structure simply not be used or that the facilitator aims to retrace our thinking behind the structure so that understanding of the tasks and their sequencing is enhanced.

The tasks are chosen to "paraphrase" the developmental and problem solving processes contained within the myth or tale. They are also designed to ease the creation of connections across time: our present and past, our present and future, and our past and future. We also wish to encourage the establishment of connections across experience, such as:

- memories and current knowledge;
- memories and anticipated reality;
- knowledge and anticipated reality;
- memories and longings/fantasies;
- knowledge and longings/fantasies.

Through the sequencing and structuring of the tasks, participants are encouraged and enabled to make links between what they apparently know about something, and what they have experienced, feel, sense and intuitively understand in relation to the theme or story with which the group is working.

All of us have predominant or habitual ways of approaching the experiences of our lives. Some of us think first and feel later. Others have hunches which might appear completely alien to those who relate to life primarily on the basis of their physical sensations. Thinking, feeling, sensation and intuition have been called functions of the human psyche. The tasks within a mythmaking structure encourage participants to explore various ways of relating to content. There is no one dominant or preferred mode; use is made and encouraged of all functions.

> In one session, for example, a group member, a chemist by profession, thought of fire as a process of chemical transformation. However his religious education taught him that fire was a symbol of the sacred. He found it difficult to talk about his feelings about fire and made no associations with fire as a source of comfort, light, heat or its consuming nature when out of control. In the course of the session he was helped to develop a differentiated self-awareness in relation to fire and to his understanding of a creation of fire myth.
>
> This differentiated awareness is profoundly influenced by the participant's current and past experience with fire: its absence or continuous availability,the trauma of being burned, the panic of being trapped by a fire raging out of control. All

experience and consequent associations are relevant to an individual's understanding of the role fire plays in his/her life. It will influence future personal relationships to fire and with a fire myth.

Ultimately, all tasks are sequenced purposefully in order to follow the mythical pattern and to generate: optimum accesses to the imagination; ease of expression in a variety of modes; insight and clarity regarding individual and group connection and contribution; and interest and desire to continue exploration and expression.

The nature of the group's participation — the facilitator's role

The facilitator's role varies, depending on the group's purpose and the content of the contract between facilitator, group and institution (educational, therapeutic, recreational). Regardless of these factors, all facilitator's share the following responsibilities:

- to set and keep definite boundaries regarding space and time;

- to ensure that the work is completed in accordance with the given structure;

- to introduce and instruct in ways that encourage group members to respond;

- to create an environment that is free from judgment;

- to encourage and support the development of each person's unique and authentic voice in all modes;

- to be able to help group members to connect across boundaries of time and experience;

- to know how to structure the process of reflection so that each session ends with a sense that a journey has been made and a safe arrival has been reached;

> - to ensure that each person's contribution is heard and acknowledged with respect to content and context.

It is not uncommon, particularly in the beginning, for group members to feel unable to respond to a given set of instructions. What many experience is a sense of blankness, an inability to think of or do anything. This feeling is in part, a response to panic, the fear of inner emptiness. In educational settings this is a particularly painful issue because academics (teachers and students) are expected to be articulate at least when speaking or writing. However the facilitator knows that beyond the blankness there is a voice, an image and/or an association. The inner controller (censor) holding the group members in this paralyzing embrace needs to be tempted to release its hold so the imagination can be allowed expression. To help overcome group members' fears and panic, the facilitator speaks words of encouragement, knowing that the first action is usually the most difficult. Enforced imprisonment within a critical self can be overcome to allow the expression of inner life to begin.

The process of "silencing" or "by-passing the censor within", thereby liberating the authentic inner voice, is then aided by a quick succession of various tasks. Group members are given little or no time to stand back and quietly assess or re-assess their commitment to expression. The flow of the imagination needs to be continually stimulated. The critical self has to be wooed, temporarily, into acquiesence, or better still, into momentary surrender in the full knowledge that whenever people do not want to participate they have a duty to refrain. Group members have a primary responsibility to themselves; they have to be trusted to know their own boundaries. However, it is the facilitator's responsibility and task to create a safe situation that stimulates, encourages and supports the extension of these boundaries.

The process of extending boundaries is complicated by a phenomenon having to do with balance. Not only does each person have a unique, inner balance, so does each group. Every facilitator can expect that if the task deals with success, someone in the group will fail in some way. If the problem is to make a journey and to achieve what is intended, someone will find something unintended. It is as if there is an anchoring process which roots the group to a whole response. Although this apparent "inability to do as the others do" may be difficult to appreciate and absorb, it must not be denied by the facilitator's wish to have completion in accordance with the tasks which have been set, nor must the person be left in isolation. Actually, the presence of this difference is often the sign of a healthy group response. Explanation of the phenomenon is one way of easing tension within the group caused by difference. In no case should the group member be forced into a corner from which there is no exit other than capitulation. When honest participation is welcomed and noted, the manner of participation can change and be changed without strain. Always, the facilitator needs to be aware and convinced of the importance of the continuation of the storymaking journey just as a guide knows that the chosen route is the appropriate path in order to arrive at the selected destination. Without this conviction, participants may give up at crucial moments on their journey and abandon their plan. On returning home from the session they will then face an inner sense of having failed to arrive. Because participants will probably not know why they feel as they do they may have difficulty making themselves feel better.

During the sessions, the group leader has to focus not only on the task at hand, but also on the specific purpose of the whole session. The extent to which each facilitator is prepared to exercise the authority needed to maintain the boundaries (especially that of time) equals the degree to which participants are enabled to give expression to their inner world. Once group members feel initially safe, the courage needed to face the unknown is born.

The way in which reflection will take place and the session brought to closure

Just as the facilitator's role varies in accordance with the group's purpose and the content of the contract between facilitator and group and institution, so does reflection and the way sessions are brought to closure. Regardless of the difference in purpose, all facilitators share the following tasks:

> - to insist that all intentional messages be "I" messages rather than "you" messages;

- to insist that group members differentiate between not completing a task by choice or not following instructions as a way of demonstrating their own personal disappointment or disapproval;

- to focus and maintain definite boundaries regarding space, time and task;

- to allow and encourage difference;

- to provide various modes of reflection for singular tasks and after a complete session or series of sessions;

- to resist pressures sometimes arising from groups who want to know the "right" answer or the "real" way;

- to know how to insure that each group reaches a safe arrival before the end of a session;

- to encourage connection across time and knowledge.

The essential purposes of reflection are to provide participants with the chance to absorb what has happened, to think about their contribution and to process the contributions of others. In one sense, reflection provides a way and time to empty or set aside previous experience to make room for that which is to come.

Connections and outcomes likely to result from mythmaking session

Although specific connections and outcomes are difficult to predict because participant groups and group leaders differ in their nature and purpose, group members always share the following human concerns:

- what to do with private dreams, wishes, fantasies and fears;

- how to overcome difficulties and setbacks;

- how to answer questions related to the meaning and purpose of life and death;

- how to deal with the stages and phases of one's life;

- how to cope with pain, loss and suffering;

- how to recognize and hear one's authentic voice;

- how to deal with difference and diversity.

Although it is easy to list skills that participants commonly achieve during mythmaking sessions, it is more difficult to give the reader sufficient information that will encourage continued exploration when the work becomes complex and the direction not immediately clear. The following case studies of real individuals (names and circumstances have been changed to protect their identity) offer insights into the process of fostering growth and change. The examples chosen exemplify the critical point from which new direction became possible. It is necessary to remember however, that every teacher, therapist and counselor, no matter how skilled, does not succeed with every person in every situation. Difficulties will occur but courage, patience and a clear sense of purpose and structure will eventually change the downward spiral into one that flows upward and outward. We have chosen to exemplify the following outcomes and connections:

- overcoming difficulty in taking a new direction;

- learning to tolerate ambivalence;

- improving access to creativity;

- learning to express ideas, wishes, and fantasies hitherto hidden and for group members to see individuals in the group in new ways;

- learning to reframe problems to find new solutions;

- increased awareness and appreciation of other peoples' history, traditions and value systems.

Overcoming difficulty in taking a new direction

Whether in education or therapy, participants need courage and determination to continue with the program on which they have embarked. It is always tempting to give up, to leave the dissertation unfinished, to find "perfectly good reasons" why a course should be dropped, or to discontinue the search for new ways. When we find ourselves at a crossroad, where past patterns and present possibilities collide, external events such as listening to a story can take on special significance. Through identification, the listener/participant, can receive encouragement to continue despite the inevitable difficulty we encounter in the midst of change. The key one young person found was located in an unlikely place, a hot concrete pavement in a Harlem, New York City (USA) playground where Alida Gersie was working with a group of teenage ex-drug addicts.

> "One afternoon I was sitting in the blazing sun at the edge of a basketball court while some of the young people were playing. I was tired, bored and far from home. It was not easy for a white Dutch woman to work in this setting. One of the group, a black girl named Deirdre, came and sat down next to me. We talked about the heat, the length of the game... Deirdre talked only about the present, never the past; she felt she had no future.
>
> I pondered on the name Deirdre. Given my love of stories, it was not surprising that the ancient Irish tale, DEIRDRE AND THE SONS OF USNACH came to mind. I had been fourteen and a lonely teenager when I first read the story.
>
> I heard myself telling her, 'I don't suppose you know the story of DEIRDRE AND THE SONS OF USNACH do you?' That afternoon on the hot pavement, while the others were playing ball, I told her the tale. Deirdre, who could not tolerate being touched, snuggled up to me. She listened to the sad life of the Irish Deirdre as tears filled her eyes.
>
> The next day in group therapy, the girl shared her own tragic tale. Between sobs she said, 'It hurts, that other Deirdre. I wanna make it better. I wanna live. I wanna make it better.'

The story of Irish Deirdre reflected her own life experience and inner world. Several weeks later she confided that on the afternoon of the storytelling she had made plans to run away from the treatment center. Hearing Irish Deirdre's story helped her to find the inner resources necessary for her to solve the problems she faced."

Learning to tolerate ambivalence

In times of uncertainty there is a tendency to try to make order from chaos by narrowing possibility and excluding paradox. Events and thoughts are labeled good or bad, right or wrong, possible or impossible. The resulting rigid ordering is experienced as reassuring and comforting. It can be rather unsettling then, especially when one is older and/or experienced, to realize that one feels very much of two minds about an issue and cannot or should not try to come down on one side or the other.

A middle-aged high school teacher of mathematics enrolled in a series of mythmaking sessions in order to accompany her husband who was enrolled in another adult education course. Her initial views indicated that she had a highly structured approach to life which did not allow for indecision or ambiguity. She had long ago developed ways of solving her problems and expected to continue doing so. She was extremely judgmental; all her work, and often that of her classmates, was criticized according to her standards of perfection.

During mythmaking sessions she wrote stories with a common theme, that of someone who wants to make a change but is too frightened to do so. If left to her own devices she would have torn up her stories or made everything all right through the use of deus ex machina (solution from heaven). However one of the rules of a mythmaking session is that all instructions have to be followed and all stories finished before the end of a session. During one class she could not finish her story no matter how she tried; her frustration and fear were evident. When faced with the request to share her story she very reluctantly read her unfinished tale, then slumped in despair, incredulous that she had failed to do what was required.

Although there are no comparative and external standards used in mythmaking work, the mathematics teacher was unable to shed her own definition of good student. Despite repeated assurances from the teacher, and encouragement from the class, she continued to make statements such as: "Usually I'm a very good student," or "This is the hardest class I've ever taken and I have a master's degree. I'm going to quit!" or (to the facilitator) "You expect too much. You should accept as fact that some stories can't be finished."

The class identified with her struggle to value herself as she was. Many of them were dealing with the same issue. One of her classmates, noting the woman's despair pointed out that the problem was not her inability to finish the story but in her refusal to allow her heroine to feel courageous and cowardly at the same time. After considering this, the mathematics teacher sat up and asked, "Can I really write about a fearful heroine?" With the assurance that this was not only possible but likely, she finished her story.

Her recognition and acceptance regarding the existence of am-bivalence and the need to tolerate paradox was a turning point for her. From that night she began to laugh more, judge less and understand how her previous notions of excellence had im-paired her ability to learn. Although her attitudes did not change immediately, she was willing to learn to reframe her old questions of: "Is my work good?" and "Am I ok?" into "What am I learning?" and "What can I contribute to the experience of the class?" Easing up on her performance standards enabled her to soften her rigid code of behavior making it possi-ble for her to experience life with more pleasure. She began to find the class exciting as well as frightening, learning to accept the occasional inevitability of paradox. Her changing perspective resulted in class participation that was good-humored, more open and less doctrinaire.

Improving access to creativity

When group members are asked to paint or write in response to a given task, many of them refuse, saying they cannot write or paint. They explain, patiently, they are not creative. When asked when it was they last painted or wrote they often reply, "At school." For them, their experience with writing or painting years ago resulted in the lifelong concept, "I am not a creative person." Judgments made by teachers, parents or other important persons continue to function as an internal frame of reference for the assessment of personal creativity. When this happens, the group's facilitator faces the participants' fears of evaluation with its anticipated rise or fall in social status and respectability, often disguised as hostility or cynicism.

Although it takes time and positive experience, participants usually learn that in these groups such a scale does not exist, that what matters is *a* contribution, and the only quality noted is that of authenticity. The group quickly discovers which statements and stories connect to "lived" experience and which are the result of distancing from reflection on this experience. The latter represents mainly external knowledge which is not knowingly connected to feeling. Although this type of story is generated in the course of a mythmaking procedure, it becomes less important and less common as attention and care are given to those expressions which are owned by the individual. For a painting or drama not only originates inside the person, it is also wholly the work of an individual. It is this sense of connection and ownership which becomes important to and for participants.

In a therapeutic mythmaking group a distressed old gentleman haltingly told his first tale. "I walked on the road and saw a bird." When his fellow group members asked him what happened next, he said he didn't know. When they continued to ask questions he promised he would tell them at the next meeting, that for now the story was finished. During the next session his tale included the exploration of a forest, the discovery of a hut full of treasures and a traveling companion in the shape of an old tomcat. The old man nearly lost himself in the forest but with the encouragement of his listeners who did not want to be abandoned in a darkening wood, he finally found the way home, remembering all that happened.

The old man's language had been restricted for many months. At times all he could say was yes or no in response to questions. His hands shook so badly he could not lift a cup to drink. Following the storytelling, he fingerpainted a picture of the treasure house in the forest with remarkable control of his limbs. He took his picture back to his room in order to (his words) "Cherish what is mine".

When a person's self-esteem is low and they think there is nothing they can create, the experience of creating a unique image, a new story, or an original drama can restore individual and group faith in personal imagination. The old man in the above example learned that he had a voice worth listening to. He was one of numerous people whose inner resources were given no expression from the day he left primary school until the present; a span of 65 years!

First paintings and stories have substantial significance for those who have been creatively or expressively mute but these are not the only people who benefit from mythmaking. Professional artists whose livelihood depends on continuous access to their creativity also find value in these sessions.

On a gray spring day, a woman entered the classroom of an adult education mythmaking class. She held a large portfolio under her arm, smiling tentatively as she introduced herself. She told the class she was on sabbatical leave from the college where she taught art and asked to join the group. After being informed that all the paintings and drawings in the class would be done with fingerpaints and felt-tipped pens, she still insisted on joining.

After several months a fellow student asked why she wanted to be part of the class when she was not only a professional artist but quite successful in having her work shown and sold in major galleries. They asked what it was she learned from these simple ways of working. She explained that the night she first appeared she had been exhausted, in urgent need of refreshment and replenishment. Her professional life felt as if it were at a standstill. She found that the unexpected, quick ways of working and the discipline imposed by the structures allowed her to bypass her habitual approaches to painting and the way she taught painting. The work in class enabled her to discover new ways to work and restored her faith in her ability to create from inner resources.

Remembering her first class she told the group, "When I first came here my portfolio was empty. You should see it now." She strongly disliked the word inspiration, preferring to talk instead in terms of energy and motivation. The mythmaking structures provided her with ways to regain access to her inner vitality thus making it possible for her to gain renewed enjoyment and purpose from her own work as an artist.

Learning to express ideas, wishes, fantasies hitherto hidden and for group members to see individuals in new ways

People who work together on a daily basis often stop seeing each other as human beings and begin relating to each other only on the basis of function. The loss of personal connection can lead not only to a sense of estrangement from self, but also to a reduction in the possibility of further growth within the institutional organization. Mythmaking sessions can provide an opportunity for group members to view each other with fresh perspective, allowing previously hidden or unsuspected qualities to be seen and noted. In each of the following two examples, both people had a fixed place within their groups and were trapped by this although neither they nor their co-workers realized this until the described experiences. The gentle ways in which their new thoughts and feelings were given voice allowed the groups involved, the time and ease necessary to support the revelation of hidden sides.

A group of workers in a day care center for deprived children were participating in a day of training which focused on the development of team cooperation. Following some introductory warmups and an explanation of boundaries, the group members were given a large sheet of paper. They were asked to consider their concept of the unknown and to then make a fingerpainting of whatever resonated inside them when thinking about what the unknown meant to them.

Although they worked primarily with children under five, many workers had never used fingerpaints. After some initial resistance, images of great intensity were painted. The workers were part of a therapeutic team and accustomed to high levels of interpersonal disclosure. Nonetheless it was still necessary to remind them of the boundaries of the work as they prepared to share their paintings. Some of the pictures of the unknown which the group members talked about showed fear and enclosure. Others were influenced by personal trauma, yet others reflected expressions of curiosity and confidence.

The team's secretary, a capable young woman, thought of herself as "only an ordinary housewife, mother and secretary". She had no realization of the important part she actually played in the efficient management of the center. She showed her picture with great pleasure, acknowledging that despite being "ordinary" she was curious about life and its possibilities. When asked to share her fantasy with the group she confessed she wanted to learn to parachute jump. The group, shocked, responded with cries of, "You don't mean it. Not you!" As she continued to talk, it became apparent that she longed for a degree of excitement and danger, two elements totally missing from her life.

Some weeks later the secretary told the staff that she had decided to go abroad to visit her sister, about to give birth to her first child. She planned to travel by herself, by plane, to a place she had never been. The center staff encouraged her trip, sending her off with presents for the journey, pleased to see she had found a way to bring some excitement and change into her life.

This particular woman had many skills and qualities which were under-utilized in her daily work. As she grew more confident, her co-workers took note. A school-leaver who needed beginning office experience was appointed to relieve the secretary of the bulk of her repetitive jobs. Freed to develop new skills, she employed her courage and curiosity to become a first rate personal assistant to the Director.

Another member of the team, a social worker, shared her painting, a very frightening image of the unknown. She talked about her fear of change and her fear of the beginning of the week. One of her colleagues responded, "I notice that you always keep your coat on for a long time every Monday morning." Others nodded their heads in agreement. The social worker, feeling the support of the group, admitted she felt very anxious when going on a first visit to a troubled family. She talked of how frightened she was when she could hear fighting going on inside a flat or house while she stood outside ringing the bell. "Yet," she added, "I do ring the bell."

The team began to understand the professional commitment it took for her to continue going out on these first visits in spite of her fears. They saw that keeping on her coat on Monday mornings was a kind of ritual, unconsciously expressing her fears, yet one not sufficiently clear to be understood. From then on the team made arrangements so that when the worker had to go out on a difficult first visit she would leave a message with the secretary. Other members of the therapeutic team were informed, ready to assist if necessary. No actual help was given unless the social worker raised the issue with the center's manager. The act of sharing her fears and the back-up support system enabled the social worker to stop huddling in her coat. With her fears contained and the spontaneous offer of help from other staff, she. was able to work with greater confidence.

Learning to reframe problems to find new solutions

Competence in one's professional life leads to the establishment of systems and procedures that work most of the time. Occasionally one is confronted with problems which cannot be solved using habitual approaches; new solutions are needed. Sometimes, however, it is the question which needs to be examined in order for the problem to be resolved. Reframing questions and exploring possible alternative answers is part of the learning in mythmaking sessions.

A lawyer in his early sixties was baffled by a client's inability to understand the necessity to write a new will after the death of her husband. All his arguments left her unmoved. After working with an African story about a woman who learns the hard way how her inflexibility hurt her family, he decided that he had been too direct with his client and perhaps not sensitive enough to her unexpressed fears. He was asked to make some fingerpaint images as he thought about himself followed by images of his client, as if he were his client.

The lawyer was startled to see how vivid and forceful his own images were and how pale and tentative were those he made as if he were his client. During their next appointment he began their session by offering her a cup of tea, inviting her to talk about how she was feeling. Within a few minutes his client made several practical suggestions about what she wanted to have happen to her assets after her death which were easily incorporated into a new will.

Increasing awareness and appreciation for other peoples' history, traditions and value systems

Participants often express surprise at the wealth of knowledge and depth of insight relating to questions of life and death reflected in myths and traditional tales of early peoples. Ethnocentricity and the general unavailability of myths and tales in adult sections of libraries and bookshops have contributed to the construction of unfounded opinions which enhance Western peoples' self image while denigrating the value of so-called primitive peoples. The discovery of mythical material, in all its beauty and complexity, can be initially quite overwhelming for participants whose concepts of the world do not allow for other points of view or explanations. Mythmaking allows participants not only to expand their notions of how many different myths explain natural phenomena, they also serve to show the limits of their understanding and knowledge of the history, traditions and value systems of people across time and culture. Majority peoples often have an interest in keeping minority cultures isolated and under-valued. Judgments are then made without awareness or real knowledge. The following two incidents illustrate the impact such awareness and knowledge had on some participants.

> In a group run for older adults who were exploring creation myths from around the world, one person became increasingly upset. Finally she blurted out, "All these stories are nonsense. Everyone knows the real creation story is told in Genesis." While most of the group agreed with her, they had also been caught by the magic and beauty of the myths as well as by nagging doubt expressed by a group member, "How can we be so sure we're the only ones who know?" A long discussion with heated exchanges among participants followed. Some time later, the woman who raised the issue said, "Well, I've been thinking. Genesis is *my* story of creation. I guess other people have their own stories."

> After working with a series of myths from various groups of North American Indians a participant said, "I didn't realize

that savages could write such beautiful stories." There was a long silence. The person was asked, "How do you know they are savages?" The answer was a shrug of shoulders.

The beauty and the power of the myths contrasted sharply with Hollywood induced concepts of Indians. Nothing more was said. No one can force anyone to change views. But as we continued to read and work with the North American Indian stories another person finally held up his hands as if to say, "No more." The group asked him what the matter was and he answered, in pain and anger, "My God, I didn't know what we destroyed."

Relating inner and outer struggles: Finishing what is started

We have cited various examples to illustrate some of the processes at work in a mythmaking session and the ways in which the structures influence the outcomes. Let us look at some of the connections between theory and practice and establish some links between statements made in the introductory paragraphs in this chapter and the selected examples.

In most of the illustrations participants were asked to perform a task which initially seemed bewildering. For example, several members of the team participating in the training day (ex.4) wondered why they had to paint an image of the unknown and to express whatever the word evoked in them. It was only after connections across time and experience had been made (secretary's fantasy of parachute jumping and social worker's current reality of fear of home visits to problematic families) that the purpose of the exercise became clear to participants. In conjunction with feeling bewildered, many participants in mythmaking groups initially experience difficulty completing the task set by the facilitator without either the purpose of the task being explained in advance, or it being implicitly obvious. However, when a task is explained *before* it has been executed, the normal selection and defense mechanisms become operative and the participants consciously or unconsciously select what they will allow themselves to present. When this happens, they return to known ways of expression and established patterns of approaches to new situations, losing the opportunity for fresh response.

The combination of being asked to do something without quite knowing where it will lead, and of being encouraged to continue a journey once embarked on, can be a considerable challenge to participants. This is exemplified (ex.2) in the description of the anxiety of the woman mathematician when she was enabled to continue her story until it finally emerged from an internal resolution. Most systems seek a reduction of intolerable levels of tension by finding ways to reduce it. Many participants initially attempt to resolve their uncertainties by creating a solution to their story construct which is external to the story. This occurs when participants introduce a sudden, unsatisfactory twist to the chain of events or magic which results in a character who can resolve all difficulties with the wave of a wand. Both storyteller and listeners know that they have been cheated out of an inherently logical solution and that the real task has not been completed. If anything, this completion has been hampered.

As the group gains experience in working with each other they will encourage a participant to return to the point in the story where the "fantasy stopped being real". Group members will help the storyteller to find a resolution of the experienced difficulties which will lead to a solution which is representative of the energy required in real life to get out of an equivalently difficult situation.

During one session dealing with the theme of Passages, the mathematician (ex.2) wrote a story, inspired by the tale of Li Chi the Serpent Slayer (see index). In her story, a heroic young woman unwillingly fights a fire-spewing dragon. The participant's story described how water appeared out of nowhere, pouring down onto the beast, quenching its fire, finally drowning the dragon. The heroine watched all these happenings from a safe distance and then made her way home. The group expressed their dissatisfaction with the ending of the story. They felt it was too unreal to be true in terms of the reality created within the story. The woman was asked to start the story again from the moment in which the young heroine faces the dragon. Although upset at having to deal with the dragon all over again, with the encouragement of the group, she retold the story in the following way:

"Once again she faced the dangerous beast. She looked around but saw no one. She called for help. A knight appeared. She asked if he would kill the dragon for her."

The group grew very still, almost as if it were holding its collective breath. Their stern faces gave the woman no support for running away. With a voice barely more than a whisper, the mathematician continued:

"The knight said, I cannot kill the dragon for you but I will help you to kill it by yourself. You must do exactly as I tell you."

The storyteller paused. The group continued to feel anxious. They wondered when and how she would find the internal strength to do what needed to be done. Still, they said nothing; silently waiting, quietly hoping.

"The knight gave the heroine a sword. Carefully following his advice, she struck the dragon between its eyes, the only soft place on its entire body. Blow by blow, the beast was finally killed. When she walked up to the knight to thank him he neither moved nor spoke. She came closer and when he continued to be still and silent, she lifted the visor of his helmet. Instead of the expected man's face, she saw a vision of herself."

The storyteller was shocked when she realized that the young heroine had seen a vision of herself. This realization led to an immediate release of tension followed by feelings of euphoria and triumph. "I did it. I really helped myself," she said, her voice full of amazement. The group's tension was also released. They were very satisfied with the new ending and pleased with the way their fellow participant gained access to her previously unused strength. This woman had used her competent professional profile to hide an extremely frightened little girl who took cover behind her husband's strength and presence. When she recognized herself inside the knight's costume she was shaken into realizing that she possessed enough knowledge, skill and strength to overcome difficulties whose magnitude initially caused her to shrink away and respond with utter passivity.

In the mythmaking structures careful consideration is given to the need to "realistically" complete all work, not only by the sequencing and phrasing of the task's instructions, but also by the inclusion of response-tasks (tasks done while work is shared to enhance reflection and response). One of the functions of response tasks is to awaken the group's potential for healing through their capacity to solve problems. If a group has just begun to work together and is unable to express its concern about an incomplete story, then either the facilitator can draw their attention to the "fantastic" nature of the employed solution leading to the ending, or the unreal solution may be noticed in the nature of the responses given by individual group members. For what cannot yet be expressed consciously will virtually always be worked out symbolically.

Had the group accepted the mathematician's initial solution to her heroine's predicament with the dragon, then "gifts" (one kind of response-task) would likely have included gifts of awareness of strength, protective devices (helmet, shield etc.), nourishment, friendship or weapons with which to defeat the dragon. This can be stated with certainty because we have seen this phenomenon at work repeatedly. The power and comfort derived from these gifts is substantial and the long range effect may not be underestimated.

The sensitivity and accuracy of the messages contained within the gifts (given as a response-task) may initially be cause for bewilderment on the part of participants. However, gradually they come to recognize that the metaphor and symbol possess greater accuracy and explicitness than does direct verbal response. This may be because our internal censors are thrown into confusion when a rapid production of symbols and images is demanded by an external authority figure (facilitator). It may also happen because the metaphor is only the first translation of pre-conscious content while direct language is the outcome of subsequent processes of selection and rephrasing in which a great deal of the original focus is bound to get lost.

Access to creativity

Gaining access to personal and group creativity is an important aspect of mythmaking work, and in itself can be experienced as stimulating and enhancing of self-respect. We consider it important that participants not only have an experience of expressive activities such as writing, painting or enacting, but also that their experience will transcend the immediacy of the mythmaking session to contribute to a lasting awareness of personal creative ability and to the continuing actualization of expressive potential. We were therefore pleased to receive a letter about a year after we ran a short series of mythmaking sessions with a church-based community group of elderly people. In the letter, the organizer wrote:

> "....Amazingly, in the past year, new ideas are more eagerly received and enjoyed; the talents of the less confident are openly acknowledged by everyone. Best of all, they articulate as individuals and as a group, the special role we play in each other's lives..... New learning became fun — nothing to be feared." (This in contrast to a time when)..."Any activity which they consider frivolous, or one they have never done before would be negatively received. Occasionally, under ideal circumstances, a decided talent for words, poetry, music, painting or design would appear in an individual like a secret sin, and in spite of encouragement, would quickly go back into hiding. Now it has a chance."

We learned that the group continued to use fingerpaints and had, among other activities, painted their own Christmas cards. They also started to write and illustrate stories for a nursery group which used the same building.

These long-term effects came as something of a surprise to the staff working with these elderly people because when we met with them a week after the end of the mythmaking program they expressed their bewilderment and confusion as to the purpose and usefulness of the sessions. They commented that the main change then seemed to be that people talked to each other more than usual. It took time for the other changes to become apparent. The nature of the change following mythmaking sessions is such, that unless a clear recall of the "old days" is available and accessible, the developments which subsequently take place will appear to be organic and integrated. The new access to creativity will be experienced as internal and not reliant on the continuing presence of the facilitator. We ascribe this to the structures we developed where the role of the facilitator is one of pre-scriber of method and focus, never of content. The extent to which the facilitator becomes a mediator of insight and an enabler of change processes depends on the nature of the setting (educational, therapeutic, recreational) and on the nature of the contract between facilitator and group.

When a group member is asked to paint an image of, for example, "what ever gives sustenance" she/he is given both focus, and method, "paint an image". The actual content is entirely reflective of the person, and is therefore a unique expression of one's inner self. After participating in several mythmaking sessions, participants acquire the ability to recognize patterns which underlie the structures. This becomes clear not by reading but only by the process of doing. The patterns are then internalized and provide the bases upon which participants safe-guard continuing access to their creativity as well as some of the methods by which their impulses and ideas can be expressed.

Whether or not the expression develops into artistry depends upon the persistence, skill and talent of the participant. We aim, initially, to create access to each person's inner world and then to enable members to give this inner material voice and form. The discovery of the "actuality of originali-ty" is a source of comfort, delight and strength to most participants. Many of the other effects and changes ascribed to mythmaking work are derived subsequently from this discovery.

Getting to know the other: Sharing

Although many of the likely outcomes of mythmaking are person centered, people work within the context of a group. Therefore, "sharing" tasks have been included as well as "response" tasks in order to make full use of a group's development potential. Sharing tasks encourages group members not only to produce (bring forward) but also to share. For it is one thing to paint an image, another to talk about the image created. In the process of talking about the painting (story, sound-making, movement or drama) the participant often discovers new insights and aspects that had up to that point remained unconscious. Through the talking, the other group members are given conscious access to the personal, symbolic material.

We believe it to be of great importance not only to give expression to personal content but also to allow other people to know something of what the person knows about the image (drama, story etc.). To recognize that one is a person of content is only the beginning of a process which finds its completion in the recognition that other people also perceive this. The symbolic utterance is no more and no less than the first step toward actualized communication. The process of sharing, especially in the beginning of mythmaking work, will have to be structured (in terms of focus and method, not content) so that participants learn there is time and space for everyone to talk and be listened to, as well as time and space to listen while one is being talked to. Participants learn that issues of judgment and assessment do not belong in mythmaking sessions; the only requirement is authenticity. Initially, the facilitator may have to work hard to enable a group to function non-judgmentally and yet be aware of and appreciate difference. However, unless a climate of "appreciation of utterance" is created, where authenticity and the creation of access are valued, the mythmaking work will not succeed.

We realize we place great value on mutual awareness and communication. We do this because we have experienced, both personally and professionally, that this awareness leads to clearer and more satisfying forms of communication. At the very least they result in a release of tension and reduction of friction; and at most, produce a greater sense of self and a differentiated awareness of others. Therefore, participants are encouraged to talk about their own work and other people's work in terms of what they notice and experience. What matters is their personal relationship to whatever is made, said or seen. Everyone can make personal statements such as, "When I listen to your words I feel anxious," or "When I look at your painting it reminds me of the time I saw a rainbow."

What is *not* permitted is a statement such as, "Your painting looks like a badly painted prison." Such a statement becomes acceptable only when changed into a statement such as, "When I look at your painting I see a prison but it doesn't look like my idea of a prison were I to paint it." We can bear in mind that what Peter says about Paul says more about Peter than it does about Paul. However, unless Peter is enabled to realize this, the projection will continue. The group facilitator functions as the guardian of a "personal statements only" group culture. The group soon learns to appreciate and enjoy collaborating and to accept the necessity for this explicit rule. In this climate, individual utterances and revelations of the past, present and future, dreams, experiences and knowledge will become more personal and of increasing depth. The concurrent development of mutual intimacy, respect and trust enhances access to personal and group imagination and creativity.

Learning to listen

Most participants in mythmaking sessions believe they have had years of experience in listening to others. Consequently few would consider themselves to be in need of learning to listen. They are, after all, used to hearing instructions related to the boundaries of the permissable and the unacceptable. They have heard friends, family and acquaintances relate experiences, emotions and longings. These will have been received, commented on and perhaps absorbed. Why then do we say there is a need to learn to listen, to take a look at the ways and patterns of listening?

The quality and style of listening most of us offer is closely related to the setting in which the listening takes place and is also dependent upon our relationship with the speaker. What we actually hear (receive) tends to be at variance from the words spoken (send). The greatest distortion occurs when the sender speaks about the receiver, i.e. when the one who does the listening is also the one about whom the speaker speaks. Then, when we add the nature of the relationship between sender-receiver and speaker-listener to this phenomenon, we understand one of the reasons behind our insistence upon "personalized statements only".

There is, however, another difficulty which occurs when people are listening in a group. Many participants spend much of their time quasi-listening while their thoughts freewheel around anxiety producing situations such as, "What do I say when it is my turn to speak (act, sing etc.)? Also, once the expression of self has been stimulated, it is difficult to release the preoccupation with personal utterances in order to create real space for listening, much less to liberate response on the basis of having received what has been said. If the focus on self is allowed to continue unchecked, the unavoidable association between "expression of the self" and "inability to relate" is likely to occur. When this happens, many group members will return to more basic needs such as "not feeling lonely" which will curb their imaginative expression. We have seen this phenomenon of withdrawal from expression in action many times following a session where a participant was not enabled to create listening and response space for fellow group members. Preoccupation with one's own product and its personal impact hindered ability to listen and thus feel part of the group.

Person-centered and person-expressive activity is not the only reason participants lack ability to create inner listening space. When encouraged to talk about habitual ways of listening in a group setting, group members make statements such as:

> "I heard every word she said;
> "I was thinking about what I was going to say;
> "I forgot;
> "I don't know;
> "I cut off and began to think about something else;
> "It reminded me of the time when....;
> "I didn't know what you wanted me to do;
> "I don't care about what we're doing.

We noticed that many participants don't even have a vocabulary related to listening. What they mostly do is to describe what *did not* happen. There is a marked inability to verbalize the inner listening process. This is why we say that participants may hear (perceive with their ears and may, if pushed, repeat verbatim the spoken words) but they do not take in what has been said. They do not offer their attention. Listening is related to allowing access to what you hear, to selecting, connecting or responding. When one listens, something resonates inside the individual. What one hears may be recorded for later contemplation and consequent resonance but it is equally possible that what is heard goes in one ear and out the other. In the latter case, the hearing occurred but no impact was made nor was resonance enabled. Hearing is merely the beginning of the listening process, the initiation of communication among persons.

Response tasks: Ways to foster resonance

In our discussion of listening we focused on the spoken word but in the course of a mythmaking program participants also acquire the ability to include their other senses as well. Group members become able to "listen" with their ears, eyes, skin, smell and taste, thus learning to resonate with the widest possible register. By asking the participants to focus on a particular way of responding (i.e. to listen with more than their ears) and to respond accordingly in a specific way, their "listening vocabulary" is expanded.

We may ask a group to listen to a story and then instruct group members to make a little sketch-like drawing which will enable them to recall the story in years to come. It is important to note that the participant selects the essential material which will serve as the hook or point of reconnection for the memory. These mnemonic drawings are then shared with the storyteller. The type of selections made are highly relevant in terms of the group and of the individuals within the group. If the group meets for therapeutic purposes, the therapist may well decide to enable the participants to work with the nature and content of the selected memory hooks because the why's and wherefore's are of importance. In an educational setting participants may be asked to volunteer comments about the chosen memory hooks and to relate them to personal life experience in order to deepen and extend their work. As long as participation is voluntary, the "wisdom of the psyche" prevails. This means that whatever is shared freely, without coercion, is appropriate and within the boundaries of the given contract. Some individuals, especially in an educational setting, feel that any disclosure is embarrassing or wrong. These feelings can only change with new experience, that sharing inner material brings benefits not only to the person but also to the group. The storyteller will also find that there will be patterns of selection in the mnemonic drawings and that these patterns can add new life to a story.

> When working with tree memories a woman recalled how as a young Jewish child she had envied the Christmas trees of non-Jewish children. Then, one year when she was six, she convinced her reluctant parents that she really wanted and needed a tree of her own. She was allowed to have a tiny little tree to keep in her room provided she put on it only homemade ornaments. The tiny tree was decorated with bits of cotton, paper chains and gold stars and treasured for months. Even after it had lost all its needles it was still loved and cherished by the little girl. One day her father appeared in the doorway when she was in her room playing with the tree. He pointed at the tree and said it was time for it to be thrown away, The little girl protested but shortly after, the tree disappeared.

The group members were instructed to make mnemonic drawings after they had listened to the individual memory and then to share with the storyteller, the part of the story which seemed most important to them. In this case, there were several group members who made drawings of the father pointing to the dead, decorated tree. The woman was noticeably shocked that the father was given so much prominence. She defended him saying, "All he did was tell me it was time for the tree to be thrown out."
The other group members felt quite differently about his role. For some time people shared their experiences of parental influence, care and control. The choices made by listeners highlighted a part of the story which the storyteller considered only a minor detail. Not only did she become aware of how her memory appeared to other people and the impact it had on them, her attention was drawn to an alternative way of looking at the experience which until then had been inaccessible to her.

The benefits of such an experience in a therapeutic setting are probably obvious yet even in an educational setting such a sharing can make it possible for an individual to reconsider and revalue personal relationships. Although the mnemonic drawings may stimulate participants to listen and select for future use, they are also used to become aware of the story's strongest impact in the here and now. Response-tasks allow the participants to be guided into paying attention to the impact the story has on different senses as well as to the way it relates to their own experiences, knowledge and/or fantasies. Regardless of the form the "listening" will take, the contribution is first shared and then voice and form is given to the resonance following the prescribed mythmaking structure in accordance with the general precepts of mythmaking.

In the example of the woman and the Christmas tree, the participants were instructed to use the mnemonic drawing technique in part, because it is one way of moving beyond preoccupation with personal thoughts in order to focus on the storyteller. By requiring the listener to respond in a particular way, the participant learns to focus not only on personal inner life but on the expression of another person's inner life as well. The implicit assumptions that the participant is someone who possesses a memory and is capable of remembering, and that the story being told is worth remembering, increases the value attached to the process of storytelling. It also enhances the sense and awareness of both the listener and the storyteller.

It is neither possible nor necessary to discuss in detail all the various response-tasks we have designed and used. Suffice it to say that where specific response-tasks have been included in a complete mythmaking structure, they have been selected because of their focus and method as well as the way in which they relate to the theme of the session. They should not be replaced by any other response-tasks because they are an integral part of the designed structure.

The rhythm and design of a mythmaking structure

In the course of a mythmaking session participants will work at different levels of intensity, the greatest of which occurs when they are exploring a theme in its essence. We create a spiralling movement in the mythmaking structures in which the warmups and introductory tasks are used as enablers of concentration and to help raise the group's level of energy. These also prepare the participants for the major work which then has to be undertaken, the exploration of the theme. During this part of the session, many participants experience a sense of being outside real time, inside an unknown world.

Like a diver who has gone down to the depths of the ocean and who has to surface slowly and carefully in order to decompress safely, participants in mythmaking work also have to be helped to surface from their journey into the unconscious. The sharing and response-tasks slow down the process of return to real time and actual space and help the participants adjust to the new direction and to make connections with the other group members. These tasks also enhance the process by which links are established between the theme, the individual expression of the theme, and their own and other group members daily reality.

The process of surfacing and preparation for ending is a vital phase of the work. Without it, participants would be left adrift somewhere between the world of metaphor and the world of experienced reality, without necessarily knowing which is which. In a Chinese text, a wise man has awakened from a dream in which he was a butterfly. He then asks:

> "Last night I dreamt that I was a butterfly.
> Am I a man who dreamt that he was a butterfly,
> or a butterfly who dreams that he is a man?"

When participants have been engrossed in mythmaking tasks during the core part of the session, they may be temporarily affected by the intensity of the experience and by the content and quality of their metaphors. This could result in a confusion of reality such as the one voiced by the Chinese man unless a substantial period of time is devoted to making connections between mythical material and the world as we know and have known it.

No piece of material produced during a session is ever completely resolved or integrated then and there. But, an awareness of the issues which are around differs from a pre-conscious and unformulated sense of uneasiness because the unnamed has been named and what was private has become personal and public. The sharing of confusion and/or insight resolves some of the disturbance it generates inside the individual and diffuses some of the tension built up by these issues either before or during the session.

The material with which we work in mythmaking is potent, charged with the essence of human experience, of life and death. This means that great suffering as well as great joy have contributed to their gradual formation. The myths evoke a similar resonance inside the individual who truly listens. The intensity of this resonance can be temporarily more than the individuals feel they can endure. To enable them to stay open, and to continue to be able to listen and respond, participants need to be helped to find ways of limiting the impact of the mythic material on them without this resulting in their shutting down or closing off. The role and function of the sharing and response-tasks provide this safeguard. The facilitator directs the work to spiral up and out, toward the outside world, and may repeat the words of an old North American Indian shaman who said to those who were assembled:

> "If you want to have a good time,
> just go ahead
> and have a good time."

In conclusion

We have now come full circle. From talking about the essential components of a mythmaking structure we moved on to a discussion of the interaction and inter-reaction between these various components. We then described and talked about some of the likely outcomes of mythmaking work to draw your attention to a few of the connections which can be made about the processes we have observed to occur. Finally, we have shared some of the reflections and values of the theory and practice which provide the foundation for our form of mythmaking work.

We can only hope that if you choose to design your own structures, you too will enjoy the process of collecting your own story material and distilling its structural components, and that in the telling or retelling of stories you will allow yourselves to be guided by the words of a Navajo chief:

"My grandmother, father, and grandfather, they told me that if you only hear (or learn) part of it (a chantway), then you have only a wounded deer. You have just wounded a story, you have wounded a prayer or a song. That is the way it is. People will do that. They will hear a portion, get tired of it, and just go away. They just play with it. But it is strong and powerful. It is to learn and to live by. It will help you live a long life. You will protect your people with it. You will stand between the good and the bad, to keep your family and relatives well."*

*A NAVAJO BRINGING-HOME CEREMONY, Museum of Northern Arizona Press, Flagstaff, Arizona 1978.

CHAPTER ELEVEN

WAYS OF MAKING IMAGES

About self-consciousness

Self-consciousness is unpleasant; it inhibits discovery and participation. It is generally caused by the inability to make sense, to connect task with inner meaning. As soon as participants are able to invest a task with personal importance, self-consciousness disappears. It is difficult to be conscious of self and focus on learning at the same time. Inappropriate giggling, strained silence and rolling of the eyes are some of the common signs that group members are working without connection. To ease self-consciousness, the facilitator needs to make sure that participants understand all directions, have appropriate tasks to accomplish goals and purposes, and to know when a task is completed. Specific and clearly articulated steps needed to complete a task or series of tasks lessen discomfort. As participants pay more attention to inner thoughts, ideas and feelings, less focus is given to wondering "what others think". The facilitator also eases self-consciousness by setting a tone that encourages a disciplined, supportive environment in which the discovery is clearly important.

The term "comfort zone" is used in this book to describe a participant's reaction to an activity or experience which feels "natural" and comfortable. When a group member stretches his ability or works in a new way some discomfort is usually experienced. The discomfort can be eased if participants understand that this temporary feeling is an inevitable part of learning. The greater the sense of discomfort, the more a participant is attempting to learn. Too much discomfort hinders learning and can be reduced by limiting the amount or kind of experience being attempted. Discomfort is often eased by encouraging group members to visualize their "comfort zone" expanding as new skills are acquired and old habits are replaced by new choices.

WAYS OF MAKING VISUAL IMAGES

To make a mark is to end a void. All marks or images evoke thoughts and/or feelings in the viewer as well as the creator. In some cases, it is not until we make an image that we know what we are thinking or feeling. Learning to value one's capacity to make images in mythmaking sessions is part of regaining access to personal imagination and primary creativity. The images produced when responding to mythmaking tasks are not made to produce art or artists. Rather, they are developed to concretize inner thoughts, attitudes, ideas and feelings. Individual dexterity or talent enhances visual acuity but it does not determine worth for use in mythmaking sessions.

Definition

Visual images made in mythmaking sessions are primarily made with fingerpaints, pens, pencils, crayons and felt-tipped pens to produce two dimensional responses. Clay, folded paper or material may be used to produce three dimensional objects. The images or objects range from simple marks to complex realistic or abstract symbol and signification.

Developing access to creating visual imagery

In order to make a mark one needs a marker and that which can be marked. Most participants do not feel easy about making visual imagery at first and great care must be taken to create an environment where what is made is valued, as it is, for what it is. If one is free to laugh at someone's first attempts, one knows one can be laughed at, one's work made fun of. Inhibition sets in quickly and the downward spiral which results is difficult to overcome.

    Fingerpaints are often used to make initial images because it is almost impossible to use them precisely. The association with pen and pencil that one might have with paintbrush, crayon or felt-tipped pen is missing when one sticks one's finger into a small pot of fingerpaint. The resulting paintings become the basis for connecting what is made with what is thought or felt regardless of the ease (or lack thereof) with which the image was made.

If participants are extremely self-conscious it often helps to start with group image-making where individual responsibility is hidden or camouflaged. However, no matter how reassuring the facilitator is, only good experience will ease the suspicion, panic and bad memories of the past that most group members associate with having to "make their mark".

When group members make several images at one time it is often useful to hang up each person's images in their order of production so that all images can be looked at at the same time before description or comment is made by group members. The facilitator can start the reflection process by asking the group if anyone notices anything about the images as a group, without singling out any one person's images or collection of images. If no one answers, the group leader may offer suggestions such as: "Do you notice any common themes or patterns? Do you observe any common use of color or shape?" If looking at a series of images the focus might be, "Does one part of a series evoke common thoughts or feelings?" Consider the following example:

> When working with some university students whose first task was to make an image of inside, outside and whatever got them from inside to outside, several students commented that the images of inside seemed more constrained and darker than those of outside. After saying this they looked to the facilitator to confirm their views. The facilitator merely nodded and asked, "Does anyone notice anything else?" This time one person said she noticed that the connecting images often contained a bit of inside and outside. Once again there was silence. Finally one of the group members burst out, "Well, are we right?"

Facilitators take every opportunity to remind the group that what they see or feel is what they see or feel. There is and can be no right or wrong in these regards. As the group is helped to be descriptive and to make "I" statements, accepting responsibility for what they say, participants fears of being ridiculed or being inept ease, and focus goes where it belongs, on what is evoked by a particular image. The ability to differentiate between what the image maker thinks and feels and what a viewer thinks and feels, that there is room for difference in points of view, is an important lesson in the process of learning to express one's own ideas, attitudes, thoughts and feelings.

The use and place of visual imagery

Visual imagery immediately concretizes inner life. It plays an extremely important part in helping group members to develop or improve access to personal resources and expression. Just as metaphors communicate nuance, images create a common point of departure when exploring ideas, attitudes, thoughts and feelings. Individual differences or commonality can be shown through the use of visual imagery that may not be apparent when using other media or forms.

> In a mythmaking group of returning adult university students there were two participants coming from very different backgrounds. One was a married man in his fifties, the father of several children and principal of a high school noted for its commitment to traditional values. The other was a young woman, a mime artist and a committed, active political lesbian. Each thought there was no point in talking to the other, absolutely no way of bridging the gulf which separated them.
>
> Then came the session whose theme was "Sustenance in times of trouble". The woman began to talk about her difficult childhood, recalling incidents of painful sibling fighting while parents were absent. The man virtually echoed her experience. Although they both noticed the similarities in their actual life experiences with a degree of wonder, their essential attitudes and positions did not change.

The surprise occurred when the woman described how her belief system provided her with solace when times grew difficult. The man nodded in agreement. He too found his beliefs a source of comfort. Despite the commonality it was only when the images each painted were shared that the antagonism was suspended and the wide gulf between them narrowed.

The woman painted a solid mountain aglow in the evening sun. The man's painting evoked images of a mountain landscape representing constancy and permanence during times of change. They were the only two people in that group who found solace in visions of mountains. The solidity of their respective positions was revealed in their similar images. Once they recognized this resemblance a dialogue became possible. Neither of them shifted a great deal in their original position but the anger which initially separated them changed into distant but compassionate understanding based on mutual respect for each other's needs to create a firm foundation, a strong belief system to help them through life.

Although their images showed that they shared more than they might have guessed, even from their previous sharing, it was the talking about their images that truly highlighted the extent of their hidden resemblance. The experience of difference was tempered by the awareness of similarity. Had the paintings of "images of sustenance" remained entirely private (not even exposed to the eyes of the group) then an opportunity for increased mutual awareness, and in this case, improved communication would have been missed.

Visual imagery techniques

Aiding the memory: Mnemonic drawing:

Activity: After listening to a story or hearing an experience each group member paints or draws a small image which serves to remind her/him of the essence of the material presented.

What matters is the essence of importance to the listener rather than necessarily capturing the "main point(s)" of what has been told.

Sometimes it helps to divide the paper into as many parts as there will be stories so that all images can be on one piece of paper (on one side).

A few words written near the image may reinforce the image.

Telling/responding in linear fashion:

Activity: Use a roll of brown or white paper that is fairly strong. Roll out enough paper so that each person has a good sized space in which to work.

Each person can respond to a given story or add to what has just been painted (drawn). When everyone has had a chance, the roll should be hung either on a wall or from a line using clothespins to hold it on to the rope.

Hanging the paper gives the group a chance to see their work with perspective. If no roll or wall is available the roll can be placed on the floor, slightly tilted if possible, to give participants a chance to look at their work as part of a whole.

Note: Just as one person can start a story, stop and let the next person continue, each in turn until the story is finished, so the group can tell a story using visual imagery rather than words.

Telling/responding in circumlinear fashion

Activity: Use a large size sheet of paper. If none is available tape many sheets together on one side only. Paint on the untaped side.

Groups of 2 - 4 work simultaneously to paint responses, ideas/thoughts/feelings.

If group tends to talk too much ask that everyone work in silence, to music or while listening to a story.

Note: If silence is difficult the group can be encouraged to chant words relating to the ideas inherent in the task.

When groups look at each other's work, be careful to encourage viewers to walk all around the papers unless the painters decide there is a definite top and bottom.

Multiple imagery:

Activity: Multiple imagery helps participants to record complex ideas, attitudes and feelings showing how these may change or be affected as new information is absorbed. Depending on the situation, group members can divide their paper into a specific number of parts to make even space available for each image.

A second way is achieved by giving each image the space it requires without prior calculation. If all the space is used up before the work is finished, participants can paint over what has already been painted.

A third way requires the use of a separate sheet of paper for each new image. If the images are then hung in order of production viewers can look at and for evidence of change and/or affect.

Note: If separate pieces of paper are used, numbering them keeps the intended order clear.

Collage:

Activity: Working singly or in groups, participants use pre-collected bits of paper, string, wool, cloth etc. to glue, tape or staple onto a heavy piece of paper or cardboard.

Collages can also be three dimensional although using some sort of support/base stabilizes the work.

Collages can be made in response to an idea or story or to create three dimensional images which reveal inner life.

Sharing visual imagery

Gallery walk:

Activity: All images are put in order according to participant (if there are several images) and then group members walk around the space to look at all the images.

Enough time must be available so that group members can take the time they need to look at all work before commentary begins.

However the images are displayed, they remain stationary while participants move.

Looking at images with new perspective:

Activity: Changing perspective often provides viewers with the chance to observe the image separately from the creator and gives the creator a chance to see personal images from other points of view. Ways to achieve this are: hang the images on a wall, board, or from a clothesline (held by tape, wire or clothespins).

If this is not possible, a group member can hold the painting or creation so that the creator can talk about the image while looking at it.

Care must be taken to ensure that all group members see the work. If creator holds image while talking, people directly to each side may have trouble seeing it.

Distance may alter what is seen, thought or felt.

Observing, describing, reflecting

It is very useful to encourage some moments of silence during which people look at images before any commentary is spoken. Beginning mythmakers often need help and encouragement when asked to talk about their images. Past memories of having to explain or defend "art work" makes the experience potentially traumatic. Creators may be asked specific questions by the facilitator such as: "What thoughts (feelings, ideas) are evoked in you as you look at your (the) image?" "What do you see when you look at your image?" "Did you have any thoughts or impressions as you made your image?" "As you look at your image now, does anything surprise or astonish you?" No attempt should be made to ask participants to talk about their work with any notion of judgement.

Observers must use "I" messages when talking about work and take full responsibility for what they say. For example: "That doesn't look like any flower I've ever seen", is better finished by the phrase "It reminds me of..." or "It feels like a..." A participant can also say, "When I look at an image of a flower I expect to see...." This gives the creator and the other group members the chance to listen to someone taking a different position without either person having to defend what is said. What is *not* all right is for the observer to say, "That is not a flower," when the creator has just described the image as a flower.

It is often useful for a group to look at the whole group's work or to note patterns or concepts that are similar and those which are different. Viewing work in this way encourages people to note unique responses to shared tasks. Even after all comments appear to have been uttered, silent reflection may encourage people to absorb what has been said and to check personal perception with ideas expressed by others.

The group should be encouraged (required) to keep a portfolio of their work and to date and label each piece so that private comparison and reflection can be made and patterns or recurring themes noted.

> One group member noticed, after looking at many week's work that there seemed to be no integration in her work, that colors and images did not overlap or appear to be connected. Shortly after the class recessed for vacation she called to say, "The most amazing thing has happened. I was in an automobile accident and while I was recovering a friend suggested I fingerpaint my feelings. All my images are now connected. I feel as if the jolt of the accident connected me up inside."

In any group, the ability to create visual imagery will range from extremely limited to very able, perhaps even to those with talent. Although nothing is said, people notice differences in technical abilities. Only a number of good experiences over a period of time will finally convince participants that talent does not necessarily affect the personal value of a created image. What matters most in mythmaking sessions is that images evoke ideas, attitudes or feelings within the maker and the viewer and these images help to make the participant's world that much more knowable than it was before the image was produced.

WAYS OF MAKING SOUND IMAGES

To utter a sound is to commit oneself to the expression of reaction, intention or feeling. Although it is possible to make disconnected sounds, these usually occur when a person is forced to make a sound or is unclear as to the intention of the task or structure. Learning to value one's capacity to make a variety of sounds with ease, in connection with myth exploration, is part of the process of regaining access to primary creativity and to using all personal resources in the quest for knowledge and understanding without internal and premature judgment.

Definition

Soundmaking, as used in this book, refers to the capacity to make sounds; vocal, physical (i.e.clapping) or instrumental. What we will explore are the primary ways in which human beings communicate through sound and without the use of spoken language. With improved soundmaking capacity comes increased relaxation, resourcefulness and the willingness to play.

Developing access to making and playing with sound

In order to feel truly comfortable while first exploring sound, participants ideally will work in an isolated room so they don't have to hear or fear the reactions of outsiders. If this is not possible, a prior word to colleagues will acquaint them with the planned activity. Participants must begin sound-making carefully to avoid throat strain. Emphasis needs to be placed on exploring variety of sound rather than on paying attention to the quality of sound beyond that of ease. Encourage people to talk about feelings evoked by soundmaking. For example, some men feel uncomfortable when exploring their upper vocal register and may need extra help in gaining ease. Some people may think of soundmaking as an activity associated with young children and will feel more comfortable when they understand how soundmaking aids in relaxation and ease of expression. Shy participants will also need extra reinforcement in order to believe that the capacity to make sound freely is closely tied with spontaneity and ease of reaction.

For beginners, words such as high, low, fast, slow, smooth, rough, light, heavy, front of mouth, top of mouth, give some direction when sound vocabulary is limited. Working with a partner eases self-consciousness as does working with closed eyes. Vocal sounds made with the breath such as a whisper or "ahh" sounds are called wind sounds. When tone is added they are called vocal sounds. Sounds can be varied by changing facial expressions or by sending sound out through various objects such as open cones, boxes, across bottles and through masking.

Sound pictures can be created by participants responding to photographs, events or situations. Sounds can be played with as one might play with a ball, passing it in pairs or as a group. Any game or idea which releases vocal energy without strain will also ease a group's tensions and can serve as a useful way to release emotional energy, particularly in an educational setting where people often go from mythmaking to other classes.

The use and place of warmups

Appropriate warming up will prevent throat strain and forced volume of sound. Warming up with soundmaking will also ease the group into an increased awareness of personal connection and the need for relaxation of the throat in vocal and verbal communication. Both sending and receiving skills are sharpened when soundmaking warmups are regularly included as part of a beginning group's initial activity. Self-consciousness is eased if participants are informed of the purpose for each activity in specific terms (increasing sound vocabulary, exploring size and range of soundmaking capacity etc.). Silence can be frightening and increase fear of soundmaking unless participants are helped to know that silence is part of sound just as "empty" space in a painting allows one to see what is painted. Any fear that is not checked can feed on itself and tie the tongues of group members. Getting people to use their voices in this situation is often painfully difficult. This problem can be eased by sound warmups which start with groups in a circle, move to pairs and then to groups working simultaneously. Some groups may find a games approach produces a relaxed and enjoyable experience.

Teachers and therapists with no special vocal training can still use sound warmups if they do not ask people to make sudden loud sounds, shrieks, screams or other sounds which strain the vocal folds. Participants must be reminded not to push or force sound. If people do hurt their throats, cease all vocal activity for a few minutes and when resumed, keep it soft and to a minimum. Yawns always relax the throat and are a safe activity with which to begin soundmaking or to ease vocal tension.

Warmups: Group

Listening to the wind:

Placement: Group stands in a small circle.

Activity: First person makes a wind sound using breath only and passes it to the next person who repeats it once and then changes it. This person in turn passes it until everyone has had a turn.

Note: People need to be encouraged to work with a variety of sounds. If individuals get stuck, the group can offer suggestions. This is a good activity in those situations where noise levels or self-consciousness is a problem.

Exploring sound:

Placement: Group stands in small circle.

Activity: First person says a word.

Second person makes the first sound or sounds which come to mind after hearing the word.

Second person then selects a new word and gives it to the third person who makes the first sound that comes to mind. Activity is repeated until first person is given a word to make a sound response.

Sound collage:

Placement: Small groups scattered around the room.

Activity: Individuals list on separate pieces of paper scenes which evoke complex sounds (forest at night, mountain top in a windstorm etc.).

Facilitator: Collect papers, shuffle them and allow each small group to pick one scene from pile. It doesn't matter if group picks its own suggestion.

Group looks at scene and begins to make a sound collage around the theme with no prior discussion. Group starts and stops itself.

Sound collages are then shared with other groups.

After each collage is finished, those listening describe images evoked, thoughts and/or feelings which come to mind.

Note: Participants do not guess what the group is describing. What matters are the impressions rather than the accuracy of the sound description.

Sound stories:

Placement: Sit in circle, each person has pen and paper.

Facilitator: Give each person 3 pieces of paper.

Activity: Each person writes the name of a sound word such as whisper, groan, shout, sigh etc. on each of the pieces of paper.

Facilitator: Collect papers, shuffle and place in middle of floor.

Each person picks 3 pieces of paper which become the actions for individual's sound story.

Working as individuals the participants connect their sounds with thoughts and feelings to make a sound story. For example: From the words gasp, squeak and shriek one might make a story about a person seeing a mouse, hearing its sound and shrieking in fright.

When everyone has developed their own sound-story, each person in turn shares their sound-story using any gestures, or movement which enhance the story.

Those watching and listening may echo the sounds to increase the dramatic potential. Repeat until each person has shared his/her soundstory.

Passing sound:

Placement: Stand in circle.

Activity: First person makes a sound and passes it on to the next person as quickly as possible. Second person receives it and passes it on as quickly as possible, repeating until sound reaches first person.

Repeat until each person has had the chance to initiate the sound passes around the circle.

Note: Group helps each individual to work with as great a variety of sounds as possible. Passing speed is of great importance as is the energy with which it is passed. It is best if each person maintains or tops the energy of the previous person's sound.

Warmups : Partner

Add a sound:

Placement: Pairs scattered around the room.

Activity: First person makes a sound. Partner imitates sound and adds a sound. First person repeats first two sounds and adds a third sound.

Partners continue until sequence can no longer be remembered by either partner.

Evoking sounds from images:

Placement: Pairs scattered around the room.

Activity: First person says a word. Partner makes a sound evoked by the word.

First person qualifies the word. Partner responds with sound affected by qualification.

First person adds another qualification. Partner responds in sound.

First person repeats whole sound image. Partner reverberates the sound image varying it (smaller, larger, louder or softer etc.) Activity is repeated with second person giving first person new word.

Change partners and work with at least 3 different partners.

Conversing in gibberish:

Placement: Pairs scattered around the room.

Activity: Partners converse in gibberish until the conversation is finished.

Share conversation while another pair watches.

When conversation is finished second pair shares their impressions of what was said, how partners felt toward each other, what was being said or any other information evoked by conversation. Repeat with pairs sharing places.

Repeat experience sharing with another pair.

Partner sound and movement:

Placement: Pairs scattered around the room.

Activity: First person makes a series of sounds to which partner moves, responding to quality, size and rhythm of sounds.

Second person repeats activity of making sounds while partner moves to the sounds.

Pair works with another pair. First pair makes sounds to which second pair moves, both individually and together. Reverse roles. Work with at least one other pair.

Responding to nonverbal communication:

Placement: Pairs scattered around the room.

Activity: First person faces second person with about 6 feet between them.

First person makes sounds which cause second person to move toward or away from partner.

After 5 or 6 separate sounds, partners share whether signals given were received as intended.

Repeat reversing roles.

Choosing material

Sounds translate inner emotional life into experience which can be shared with others. Although some people may find this frightening, all of us reveal some information about how we are feeling through the way in which we speak. Emphasis, volume, pitch, tone and range all qualify our words whether or not we are conscious of the process. When working with sound in a mythmaking session, material chosen works best when it is highly dramatic, full of action and with many characters. Each character can then be given a different voice although actual words are not used. Choose material where the characters primarily act rather than reflect or think. Work with simple stories which have great power or choose stories on which to focus where the action is clear and direct.

Ways of using sound

When making sound stories, working with closed eyes aids concentration. Initially, most group members will work within a very narrow range of sound and will need help in exploring higher and lower parts of their vocal registers. Encouraging participants to connect sounds to inner visualization decreases self-consciousness and helps them connect soundmaking with inner life. It is sometimes helpful to have participants record their soundmaking on portable tape recorders so they can hear their range of pitch, tone, volume, dynamics and pace. Although the sounds may not sound as they expect, with experience, group members will learn to listen for variety rather than to focus on quality. People will work more effectively if they have specific points of reference such as, "Is what is evoked that which is intended?"

Encourage participants to use as much sound as possible when warming up, before formal sessions begin and when group members are in need of quick releases of tension. If a group member is upset but doesn't want other participants to know details, singing the full story in gibberish often relieves enough emotions to enable the group member to focus on the activity at hand. The more sound the group is able to make easily, the more comfortable participants tend to feel. Groups can take sound breaks as well as tea or coffee breaks; all offer refreshment.

Observing, describing, reflecting

Beginning soundmakers usually have to be encouraged to breathe fully, from the diaphragm rather than by raising shoulders. Observers also want to look for locked joints, particularly the knees. The back must not be hyper-arched which will result in pinched-off sound and fatigue or pain. Heads are best placed in a gentle curve with the back rather than being thrust forward which results in tense, strangulated sound. These and other observations are made gently and with a neutral tone. Group members check observer's comments before any changes are made. Descriptions are nonjudgmental so that participants do not become defensive. Everyone is best encouraged by being helped to work with ease, slowly and gently, avoiding strain, push or pressure. The more comfortable people are physically, psychologically and emotionally, the fuller and richer their soundmaking. It helps to foster a sense of playfulness when making and exploring new ways to make sound. This reduces pressure and relieves anxiety. All reflection is best focused on the pictures created by the soundmaker rather than on an evaluation of the sound itself. Encourage full, relaxed sound expression as part of any emotional, psychological or physical exploration.

WAYS OF MAKING BODILY IMAGES

To move is to reveal. Bodily movement is one of the primary ways we show how we feel. We communicate nonverbally all of the time, regardless of whether we know or intend to do so. If music be the food of love then movement is the dance of life. Sadly, many of us have forgotten the joy of moving that we felt as children. Many of us have forgotten that we already know how to move even though we may have never had a dance class or consider ourselves (are considered) clumsy, awkward or with "two left feet".

Definition

Participants often confuse dance with movement and become afraid of both. Movement and dance lie on a continuum: movement is the least formal, dance the most formal. Movement is the physical action which supports dramatic action, expresses inner thoughts, feelings and ideas, and expresses human relationships to things and people through the informal usage of space, time and force. All living creatures move. Movement as used in this book is the physicalization of inner activity, the externalization of inner life. No two human beings move or think exactly alike. Therefore, the movement structures in this book encourage each participant to explore personal, authentic movement expression which is not dependent on years of formal study or natural talent. Just as professional painters derive benefit from mythmaking, so too will dancers if they use the work to develop increased access to their imagination, creativity and ease of expression.

Developing access to movement

To move freely, participants need a large space free of obstruction and clothes which do not bind or restrain. Beyond this, group members need to be helped to realize that they already know a lot about movement and about interpreting what is expressed through movement. This can be demonstrated by asking people to walk. The walk can then be significantly changed by moving in a variety of ways: on toes, crouching, speeding up, slowing down, going forwards or backwards, moving fluidly or with great restraint. Each change influences the way the walk feels to the walker. Creating a situation such as walking in a dark alley, walking on a narrow wall or walking on ice always affects movement choice.

To avoid clichéd or stereotypical movement which results from movement disconnected from the mover's inner life, create a specific situation or point of view as part of the movement structure. If the level of self-consciousness is high and movement is inhibited suggest that people verbalize their focus and to ask for help if necessary. Encouraging individuals to ask the group for assistance promotes collaboration and cooperation.

The use and place of warmups

Appropriate warmups prevent injury and improve range and ease of movement. Ankles, shoulders, spine, wrists and knees must be moved gently and easily before more active use. Slow and easy stretches, swings, jumps or other types of movement need to precede more vigorous, demanding activity. If the room is cold, the weather is cold outside, or the group is tense, allow extra time for warming up. Pain is the body's signal to stop and reconsider activity choice. Warmups are best when easy, fun, provide for interaction, inter-reaction and prepare participants for mythmaking tasks. While each person's body is different and requires personal choice of movement for warming up, the process is best begun and ended with group activity. If the group has been moving vigorously, allow extra time for winding down and easing up activity. This not only makes possible physical and emotional closure, it also eases participants transitions from mythmaking to what is to come.

Warmups: Group

Rising and falling:

Placement: Stand in circle.

Activity: Sit and stand holding hands without pulling or straining.

Explore at least three different ways to sit and stand. Try exploring with no discussion.

Variation: Begin activity with a group hum or song. Do not let movement affect vocal quality.

Exploring locomotion:

Placement: Everyone is at one end of space.

Activity: In fours, threes, twos then one by one, explore ways to walk, jump, leap and turn. Work with and without sound.

Group motion:

Placement: Individuals scattered throughout the room.

Activity: Start a locomotive activity (walk, skip etc.). Take a partner and continue moving. Pairs now take a pair to become four. Keep moving as fours become eights. Work until everyone is in one group. Work with and without sound.

Variation: Work using space and time in a variety of ways.

Group environment:

Placement: Stand in circle in small groups.

Activity: A participant suggests a place such as a beach, playground, prison or forest. First suggestion is the idea used. Group starts and stops itself.

Group members move in ways that give information to each other. For ideas, participants might think about temperature, what is in the space, amount of light etc. Explore ways to receive information and to show use.

The most difficult task is to end exploration without saying stop.

Variation: Explore variation on theme chosen such as a flood on the beach, accident on the playground, escape from prison, fire in forest etc. All participants find their own responses and interactions.

Each group member chooses a role in which to explore relationship in scene. Roles can be changed at suggestion of group or participant.

Developing movement memory:

Placement: First person makes a sound and a movement which the group repeats as accurately as possible.

Activity: Second person makes a new sound and movement and adds this to first person's. Group repeats two sound and movement sequences. Repeat until group can no longer remember sequence. Start again and continue until everyone has had a turn to make a new sound and movement.

Note: Group helps individuals remember sequence and suggests variation when necessary.

Warmups: Partner

Exploring visual communication:

Placement: Pairs standing about two body lengths from each other.

Activity: Partner one looks at partner two and thinks, "I want him/her to come closer or move further away."

Partner two reads message as transmitted by partner one's eyes and moves accordingly. Repeat at least 3 times before exchanging roles.

When both have played both roles, share experience using "I" messages. If one partner was unable to "read" the other discuss what was done and seen.

Note: Role or sexual identity may interfere with message reception. Base discussion on observation rather than judgment. Work with several partners.

Share experiences with whole group using "I" messages.

Exploring the relationship of sound and movement:

Placement: Pairs in circle.

Activity: Each pair develops distinctive sound for each partner. Partner one closes eyes. Partner two moves away from partner one. Partner two makes agreed sound. Partner one gently moves around room until partner two is found through recognition of sound.

All pairs work simultaneously. When partner two is found, reverse roles and sound.

Note: Facilitator monitors activity to ensure participants safety. Beginning signals are best pitched low and slow.

Exploring movement phrases:

Placement: Pairs scattered around the room.

Activity: Partner one creates a phrase of movement and sound. Partner two copies partner one's phrase as accurately as possible.

Partner two modifies partner one's phrase by changing size, tempo or flow. Partner one repeats modified phrase. Repeat exchanging roles.

Note: Share thoughts and feelings using "I" messages paying particular attention to movement that feels to be outside of personal "comfort zone".

Making sculptures:

Placement: Pairs scattered around the room.

Activity: Partner one sculpts partner two using movement and sound to indicate action and quality. Partner one uses movement to indicate completion of sculpture.

Reverse roles and repeat activity. Each helps other to remember finished sculpture.

Exploring the life of a sculpture:

Placement: Two pairs of four scattered around the room.

Activity: First pair assumes sculptured position (see previous activity). Second pair arranges them in various spatial relationships and selects one for further use.

Note: Beginners work best if they can see each other. Experience makes possible work through sound or touch.

Sculpted pair begin to give birth to themselves by breathing life into their shapes. Working together, use sound and movement to create a phrase of movement with clear beginning and end.

When first pair finishes, reverse roles with second pair.

Note: After both pairs finish, share experiences using "I" messages. Reflect on what was seen, heard, felt and thought. Share memories that come to mind. If total group is less than 12, pairs may work with rest of group watching and sharing observations. Discourage guessing. Encourage personal reflection.

Choosing material

Movement translates inner emotional life into physicalized emotional action which can be seen, heard and shared. Movement provides participants with the opportunity to explore how emotion affects motion. The stories chosen need to have highly dramatic, active material. Stories containing introspection and philosophizing are difficult to use. Stories containing magical transformations can be explored through use of metaphor and often provide exciting material for participants. Use of simulated costumes and props often enhances the experience of physicalization.

Ways of using movement

Participants commonly use only a narrow range of movement possibility. Moving out of this range may cause discomfort and self-consciousness unless the task focus remains clear and understood. Just as a person used to whispering will feel he is shouting with the barest use of voice, so a person inexperienced in moving will not receive accurate information from self monitoring until a fuller range of movement possibility is explored and becomes self-generated.

Movement vocabulary can be developed by understanding aspects of movement just as a fingerpainter is aware of color and texture. The following terms help provide a way to begin: *direction*...the way in which the mover goes; *level*...how high or low the mover moves; *focus*...which way the mover looks or where attention is drawn as the mover moves; *pace*...the rate of movement in each phrase; *rhythm*...the time pattern of each phrase; *dynamics*...the overall shape of the whole movement piece.

In addition, the language of space can be considered. How close or far is one person from another? Who dominates space usage? Are movement patters, linear, circumlinear or diagonal? How are relationships evidenced by spatial inter-relationships? As the picture in the mind's eye changes, so will movement and use of space.

Observing, describing, reflecting

Beginning movers benefit from partner and group observation which concerns itself with that which observers see, hear, feel with no intention to make any single or group observation "correct". The old adage, "What you see is where you look" (how and when) is especially true when looking at movement. Telling a partner, "Your movement is boring," is unacceptable; it helps no one. Telling a partner, "I notice you move in the same rhythm no matter how you move. How would it be if you explored changing the dynamics with which you work?" or "How would it be if you had to finish quickly because you have to go to an important appointment?" give suggestions without personal judgment and provide a clear basis for participant and group consideration. What participants want to know is how their intention relates to their action; whether choices appear to be habit or new possibility.

Although participants often ask (in one form or another), "Do you like my work?" facilitators need to help them reframe the question so that group members learn to value their expression and to concentrate on working with authenticity. Participants often have a long history of feeling inept. Changing deeply rooted attitudes cannot happen overnight. But, when group members focus their comments on observations which enhance, deepen or explore rather than judge, participants come to value their own expression and that of the others in the group.

WAYS OF MAKING DRAMA

To make drama is to work as a community in which all participants are involved in collectively creating a dramatic response, where group members are enabled to experience vicariously, lives and situations different from or similar to their own. When people use the dramatic mode, they work informally to explore the expression of ideas, thoughts and feelings through movement, speech (song), gesture, touch, interaction, inter-reaction and use of space.

Clear directions, well-defined tasks and specific stopping points all help to create a good working environment where group members focus on what is being learned and where participants learn to trust the expression of physical, mental, psychological and emotional action, interaction and inter-reaction.

Definition

Three kinds of dramatic activity will be found in this book. The first group, *warmups*, prepares individuals and groups to participate in more strenuous or complex work. The second group, *making drama*, involves participants in activity where participants create their own scripts (improvisation, oral, written) for their own benefit. Reflection is used to help participants to understand more clearly what they have learned and how this experience connects to personal concerns. The third group, *playmaking*, focuses on the process of making a play for an audience with the help of a director regardless of whether or not the script is written down. Here, reflection serves to connect the interests of the group with the needs of an audience.

The use and place of warmups

Groups are always collections of individual people who come together with differing degrees of interest, need and focus. No group can work well together unless everyone is able to focus on both individual and common purposes and to concentrate on the task at hand (rather than on the past or future). Warmups provide participants with the bridge which connects group members to each other, enables them to focus on the present and prepares participants for tasks requiring physical, psychological, emotional and intellectual access and ease.

Warmups should be used at the beginning of a session, chosen on the basis of the skills to be used in the tasks which follow. If the primary mode will be drama, warmups will include physical and vocal activity, emotional projection and heightened group awareness and appreciation. Special attention needs to be paid to warming up a group if they have been sedentary, if the weather is cold or dreary or if tension is high (exam period, taxes due etc.). It is best if warmups begin and end with a group activity and to emphasize the creation of an environment that is relaxed, accepting, disciplined and safe.

Warmups: Group

Follow the changing leader:

Placement: Stand in circle.

Activity: One participant creates a sound and movement pattern.

The group joins in, repeating the sound and movement pattern. When everyone is sounding and moving together, another group member begins a new sound and movement pattern. Repeat until every group member has a chance to initiate a pattern.

Note: If group is large, work for five minutes and encourage quick changes. Suggest variation using ideas such as change of direction, tempo, rhythm and size.

If group has difficulty it may be a sign that cooperation rather than competition needs to be fostered. Stories which explore themes of working together will be helpful, especially for troubled or inexperienced groups.

Creating, using, sharing:

Placement: Stand in circle.

Activity: First participant creates an object (ball, flower, spinning top etc.) and then uses it. After clearly establishing what it is and qualities it has (weight, size, smell etc.) first participant passes it to next participant.

This person uses the imaginary object in his/her own way and then slowly transforms it into another, totally different object which is used and then shared with next participant. The activity is repeated until everyone has had a turn to use and transform an object.

Note: Encourage clear choices and variety of objects. If a person cannot think of an object, the group is free to make suggestions and to encourage group members to make new choices each time.

Discuss ways to think up new ideas when stuck. Explore different ways to use similar objects.

Creating visual pictures, physicalizing response:

Placement: Stand in circle, one participant in center.

Activity: Group member in center chooses a repeatable action such as walking.

Participants in circle begin to qualify the walking with specific information, one idea at a time, such as *where* the person is, *time of day, purpose of action, why now, environment?*

For example: Participant is walking in woods. It grows dark. The weather turns cold. Participant is searching for wood to make a fire to warm a sick child. The woods are thick. It is difficult to see. Strange sounds are heard.

Participant does not "act" out suggestions. Visual images are created in the "mind's eye". Participant responds to inner imagery. When appropriate, group makes sounds to encourage imagery development (howling wind, bird song etc.)

Note: If participant is given inappropriate information, facilitator should step in, explain why information is inappropriate and give group member a chance to make a new suggestion. After several suggestions have been made and used, a new participant enters into the center to begin a new activity with new suggestions.

Group members will learn in time to focus and contain suggestions so that all information contributes to the dramatic action at hand. It may be important to stress that everyone learns in this activity, not only the participant in the center.

Exploring emotional projection:

Placement: Small groups of 4 - 6, one participant ready to begin, others to watch.

Activity: First group member performs a small action or task such as walking to a chair, sitting on it, getting up and returning to original position.

Each of the other group members creates an inner visual picture of the specific circumstances in which the action is taking place (being scolded, hearing bad news etc.) Keep situations specific rather than general; there is no one way to be angry, happy, sad or frustrated.

Note: If responses seem clichéd or stereotypical, group members help participant to personalize action through asking specific questions. Answers are shown rather than told. Each group member is helped to project the inner emotional life of the character being played in the particular moment.

Creating character: Action and reaction

Placement: Small groups of 4 - 6 scattered around the room.

Activity: First participant creates a character selecting age, historical time, environment etc. With help of group, participant physicalizes character much as a sculptor sculpts.

Note: It is helpful to have a box filled with clothes, props and pieces of material.

Participant creates a life story for character selecting material which can be shown better than told. Members of the group can play roles involved in character's life, make sounds to create an environment or construct obstacles (mountain, busy streets etc.) to give character something and/or someone with whom to react.

After exploring life of character group member selects one aspect to share with larger group. Each group member creates, in turn, a character complete with voice, habitual movement, nervous gestures etc. If total group is large, smaller groups within may share aspects of character creation.

Note: Focus on exploration of many ideas before any are chosen. Reflect on what motivates choice.

Warmups: Partner

Partner stretching

Placement: Work in pairs scattered around the room.

Activity:　Partners hold each other's wrists. (Palms may sweat, making a secure grasp difficult.)

Facing each other, holding wrists, gently and simultaneously lean away from each other, each dependent on the other for support.

Note: Partners of uneven height or weight will need to work slowly and carefully to avoid undue strain.

DO NOT LOCK KNEES. Do not pull or push partner.

Stretch lower back by keeping knees slightly bent, circling torso and rolling head gently around in a circle.

Establish eye contact to use as a signal for starting and stopping.

Variation: Stretching can be varied by facing front, back or side, using one hand and by moving torso forward and backward.

Partner interview:

Placement: Work in pairs scattered around the room.

Activity: First participant asks partner 5 questions which are answered with "Yes" or "No". Repeat exchanging roles. Repeat with at least one other partner.

Form one large circle. Each participant shares what has been learned about the people who have been questioned.

Variation: Ask partner to select a number below chronological age. Ask partner to share something which happened at that time and which can be shared with larger group. Exchange roles.

Note: Emphasize ease of sharing.

Sharing sound and center with partner:

Placement: Work in pairs scattered around the room

Activity: Stand slightly less than arm's length from partner. Place palms facing partner in front of chest. Keep feet on floor.

Keeping torso lifted, lean toward partner catching each other when palms meet. Each partner supports the other and center is shared.

Add sounds. Each partner makes a distinct sound going toward the center. At the center listen to each other's sound. Exchange sounds as partners move away from each other. Complete several cycles before stopping.

Variation: Work in groups of 3 or 4. Sound is taken from participant on right, given to group member on left.

Note: Distance between partners depends on individual height and weight. Begin with less distance, increase as experience is gained.

Action/reaction

Placement: Work in pairs scattered around room.

Activity: Partner one creates the beginning of a sound and movement phrase. Partner two responds by finishing the phrase. Reverse roles several times before working with new partners.

Note: React spontaneously without trying to "make sense" or make a story. Evolve responses without prior planning, continuing until partners agree to stop.

Playing ball

Placement: Work in pairs scattered around the room.

Activity: Partner one creates an imaginary ball, choosing a size, weight and use and throws it to partner two.

Partner two catches ball in accordance with the way it was thrown (kicked). Partner two makes a new ball and throws it to partner one. Continue for several exchanges before working with a new partner.

Note: Concentrate on creating the reality of the ball, being specific about size, weight and manner of throwing.

Variation: A large group can play with 2 or 3 balls at the same time.

Choosing material

Participants employ the dramatic mode as a way of externalizing inner views, impressions and/or feelings derived from hearing a myth or tale through the use of action (physical, mental, emotional, psychological) movement and speech (song). Tales chosen for use in dramatic exploration work best when there is more action than introspection. When doing drama, participants need not worry about preserving every detail, showing every event, using the exact words of the story. Drama requires reflection as well as creation. The power of the story resonates through a group and influences their collective vision which then results in the authentic expression of individual response through communal action and interaction .

Groups may make drama by working with a specific character's point of view, by exploring the emotional life of the myth or tale, or by creating the group's response to the emotional life of the story. However a group chooses, the key word is action. Only through the actions of a character or characters are thoughts, feelings and ideas revealed. Telling is the mode for stories; showing is the mode for drama. Dramatization can begin immediately after a tale is told as a spontaneous reaction to the material or it can be the culminating event after people have worked with images, word associations and personal reflection. In every case, drama is chosen as the mode of expression because group members want to SHOW what is being experienced through movement, speech (song), gesture, action and use of space.

If material chosen is inappropriate for the experience and/or needs of the group, participants may ease inner discomfort through giggling, clowning, eye rolling or "playacting". Should this occur, the facilitator needs to help the group choose ways in which to work with the material that are consonant with the group members level of development. This is why we have ranked both stories and themes in terms of difficulty and complexity. A group can explore any theme as long as the chosen tale connects with their experience. In the long run, especially when doing drama, it is always better to begin simply rather than to overestimate a group's readiness and run the risk of participants getting in over their heads. If individuals within a group experience discomfort, this can be eased by encouraging the group to help them connect through the use of specific questions which refocus response from general to particular. This process is known as personalizing, making the character a "real" person rather than a stereotype, and developing the personal history necessary to support role playing with ease.

Choosing characters and making the drama

Participants volunteer to play particular roles. It is usually not a good idea to assign a role although this may be less true in therapeutic settings than it is in those primarily educational. Drama can still be made when everyone chooses to play the same role. Similarly, no one, neither participant nor facilitator, has the right or responsibility to tell someone else what to do or say if the work is to have personal value. All authentic action and reaction comes from the experience of allowing the tale to resonate within and from working through the story and character needs through exploration motivated by personal response.

Group members develop good working habits best when each group takes responsibility for starting and stopping itself, playing out each sequence until the desired shape and impact is achieved. It is best if no talking about the work occurs among group members until after the story or sequence has been played from beginning to end at least once, preferably twice. Playing is also enhanced if the group does not discuss or plan what will be done beforehand. This tends to dilute the impact of exploration and impairs the integration of head, heart and body response. Premature talk encourages intellectualized response to issues and is a common way of avoiding personal (individual and group) interaction and confrontation with important issues.

Facilitators and/or group members who have more theatre than drama experience may have to watch their tendency to focus on perfecting performance rather than on developing depth of exploration. A drama may work very well for participants yet not be easily accessible to an audience. Clarity of goals and purpose enables appropriate choice regarding focus and task. A drama developed for participant's benefit may always be reworked for sharing with an audience if this proves to be desireable and necessary for meeting a group's needs.

Observing, describing, reflecting

Small groups generally share their work with the larger group. This process of reflection is necessary if individuals and a group are to make personal connection between inner and outer worlds. Yet great care must be taken in the way reflection is structured so that the work's value is not destroyed inadvertently by inappropriate, critical and judgmental commentary. During the reflection process, a few minutes of silence after the end of a scene or play gives everyone time to absorb, digest and take in the experience without being influenced by the reaction of others. When sharing does begin group members talk about what they have seen, heard, thought or felt using "I" rather than "You" messages. Using "I" reinforces awareness that each speaker can only speak from personal perspective, that there is no such thing as *the* truth. When differences arise they are noted but need not necessarily be resolved. If the group sharing intends to continue working on the piece, it often helps if comments are written down for later reference. It also helps if comments are made in question form which can be explored later, in private, by the group. It is usually not helpful if those sharing the work defend, explain or attack. Making a rule of no comment on the commentary prevents discussion not truly related to deepening the work or reflection process. If group members find it difficult to listen without interrupting, it may be helpful to have people comment, each taking a turn while sitting in a circle with the sharing group. If group members have had negative experiences with reflection, time will have to be taken to heal as well as teach helpful ways of observing and describing.

A useful way to deepen the work and enhance participation, particularly when group members feel they have been damaged by previous experiences of being judged, involves no commentary at all. After work has been shown, the facilitator and group ask questions which require the participants, in role, to answer as if the episodes mentioned are indeed part of their experience. All questions asked are intended to deepen the participant's knowledge of the character and situation. For example: Suppose that a group is working with "The Ugly Duckling". The participant playing the mother might be asked, "How did you feel when you first saw the chick who looked so different from the other ducks?" The group member playing the ugly duckling might be asked, "What did you do the first time your brothers and sisters pecked you when you ate food they wanted?" The questions are written down by each person whose role is being discussed and then explored through action not talk. If there is no time for more development, just the asking of the questions, followed by immediate replaying with no discussion, will have a beneficial effect on personal skill and development. The noticeable improvement is always exciting and often appears to be amazing to those watching yet it happens every time a group is committed to the work at hand and is not dependent on talent or previous experience.

.

TASKS WHICH CAN BE EXPLORED AROUND ANY GIVEN STORY OR THEME

Interaction with the material

Retrospective:

1. Fantasies (individual/group - projective identification with a character)

- What happened in the story or to a character before ....?
- How come these events occurred?
- I wish.... (as the character.)
- I wonder what would happen if...? (as the character.)

Parallel:

1. Response

- This is what the story evolves in me/us. Consider:
color; shape; mood; movement; sound; feeling; size; texture.

2. Comment

- I, as a particular character, feel, experience, think, wish.....

3. The left out bit.

- What was not said?
- What was not done?
- What was not seen?

Prospective:

1. Future year
- Where will a character or the characters be at in ...amount of time?

2. Consequences

- What are the consequences of the outcome for one or all of the characters in the story or outsider(s)?

3. Looking forward

- What do I, as a particular character, feel, think, wish about the events after ...number of hours, days, weeks or years?

Personal connection to stories:

1. Memories

- What did I do, experience, feel?
- What happened to me when, where, why, how?

2. Fantasies

- I imagine.....
- I create.....
- I wish.....

3. Knowledge

- I know....
- I believe....
- I value...
- I hope...
- I like (dislike).....

4. Images and associations:

- The story evokes...(words, sounds, ideas, thoughts, gestures, images) expressed through art, movement, drama, storytelling, storymaking.

Initiating discussion through questions and answers

Read, tell, use story: Group members formulate one or more questions on a part or whole of text.

- Question is formulated on part or whole of text which is understood.

- Question is formulated on part or whole of text which is not understood.

- Question is formulated on basis of agreement with text.

- Question is formulated on basis of disagreement with text.

- Formulate basic question(s) that underlie text.

- Formulate basic life assumption(s) that underlie text.

- Formulate question(s) which challenge aspects of the text.

Activity: Write formulated material on piece of paper (one question or statement per paper).

Facilitator: Collect slips, shuffle, pass slips.

Each participant takes one or more pieces of paper.

Each participant formulates an answer or response to question or statement.

Participants share responses with group (or small groups if group is large).

Encourage author of original material to share thoughts. Encourage silence before group discusses other responses. If participants work in small groups, ideas of note can be shared with large group.

Note: This activity leads to general discussion. Only a few questions or assumptions can be dealt with in any one session.

Questions around the process of questioning

- What does it mean to you to ask a question?

- What makes it easier/more difficult to ask a question?

- What kind of environment enhances (inhibits) questioning?

- What sort of question would you never consider asking anyone?

- When questions arise, where do you habitually go to find the answer? Are there special people to whom you might turn?

- What sort of questions do you think are not worth answering?

- How do you feel when you're asked a question and don't know the answer? Are there circumstances which affect your feelings?

- How do you decide something is true or not true?

- What might it take for you to change your mind about your notion of truth?

- Under what circumstances would you deliberately not tell the truth?

- How do you feel when you learn someone has lied to you?

- What makes you curious?

- What did you used to be curious about that no longer excites you? What caused the change?

- What are some things (events, people, ideas) that arouse your curiosity now?

- How do you feel when people continue to ask, "How come?"

- What kinds of questions did you have as a child? Growing up? As an adult?

- How were your questions dealt with (at home, school, etc.)?

- What is the first memory evoked when you think about a time when you asked a question?

- What part in your life does questioning play?

Exploration of a myth

To conclude this chapter, we will show how one myth can be explored by identifying several important issues and working with a variety of modes. Through this process we hope to suggest how rich, diverse, potent and stimulating mythmaking can be.

Myth: CREATION OF MUSIC   *Mexico*

Tezcatlipoca — god of heaven
and the four quarters of the heavens
came to the earth and was sad.
He cried from the uttermost depths of the four quarters:
               "Come, O wind!
                 Come, O wind!
                 Come, O wind!
                 Come, O wind!"

The querulous wind, scattered over earth's sad bosom,
rose higher than all things made;
and, whipping the waters of the oceans
and the manes of the trees,
arrived at the feet of the god of heaven.
There he rested his black wings
and laid aside his endless sorrow.

Then spoke Tezcatlipoca:
               "Wind, the earth is sick from silence.
                 Though we possess light and color and fruit,
                 yet we have no music.
                 We must bestow music upon all creation.
                 To the awakening dawn,
                 to the dreaming man,
                 to the waiting mother,
                 to the passing water and the flying bird,

life should be all music!
Go then through the boundless sadness
between the blue smoke and the spaces
to the high House of the sun.
There the father Sun is surrounded
by makers of music
who blow their flutes sweetly
and, with their burning choir,
scatter light abroad.
Go, bring back to earth a cluster — the most flowering —
of those musicians and singers."

Wind traversed the earth that was plunged in silence
and trod with his strength of breath pursued,
till he reached the heavenly roof of the World
where all melodies lived in a nest of light.
The sun's musicians were clad in four colors.
White were those of the cradle songs;
red were those of the epics of love and war;
sky blue the troubadours of wandering cloud;
yellow the flute players enjoying gold
milled by the Sun from the peaks of the World.
There were no musicians the color of darkness.
All shone translucent and happy, their gaze turned forward.

When the Sun saw the wind approaching he told his musicians:
        "Here comes the bothersome
          wind of earth:
          Stay your music!
          Cease your singing!
          Answer him not!
          Whoever does so will have to follow him
          back down there into silence."
From the stairways of light
of the House of the Sun,
Wind with his dark voice shouted:
        "Come, O musicians!"

None replied.
The clawing wind raised his voice and cried:
     "Musicians, singers!
        The supreme Lord of the World is calling you....!"
Now the musicians were silent colors;
they were a circling dance held fast
in the blinding flame of the Sun.
Then the god — he of the heaven's four quarters —
waxed wroth.

From the remotest places,
whipped by his lightening lash,
flocks of clouds whose blackened wombs
were stabbed and torn by lightening
assembled to besiege the House of the Sun.
His bottomless throat let loose the thunder's roar.
Everything seemed to fall flat in a circle
beneath the World's mad roof, in whose breast
the Sun like a red beast drowned.
Spurred on by fear,
the musicians and singers then ran for shelter
to the wind's lap.

Bearing them gently
lest he should harm their tender melodies,
the wind with that tumult of happiness in his arms
set out on his downward journey, generous and contented.
Below, Earth raised its wide dark eyes to heaven
and its great face shone, and it smiled.
As the arms of the trees were uplifted,
there greeted the wind's wanderers
the awakened voice of its people,
the wings of the quetzal birds,
the face of the flowers
and the cheeks of the fruit.
When all that flutter of happiness landed on earth,
and the Sun's musicians spread to the four quarters,

then Wind ceased his complaining and sang,
caressing the valleys, the forests and seas.
Thus was music born on the bossom of earth.
Thus did all things learn to sing:
the awakening dawn,
the dreaming man
the waiting mother,
the passing water and the flying bird.
Life was all music from that time on.

Nicholson, Irene, ed., MEXICAN AND CENTRAL AMERICAN MYTHOLOGY, Paul Hamlyn, London, 1967, pgs.31-37.

Text:	THE CREATION OF MUSIC
Focus:	The effects of life without music
Length:	1 1/2 hours
Exploratory mode:	Primarily visual/painting
Distribute:	Copies of text.
Read:	First part of "Creation of Music" up to "yet we have no music."
Paint:	Image of a world without music.
Write:	A memory of a time you yearned for music (song) but there was none to be had (found, heard).
Share:	Images and writing.
Read:	Second part of myth up to "where all melodies lived in a nest of light."

386

Paint: Image of wind's journey.

List: Traits wind will need to have and use in order to bring back "a cluster — the most flowering — of those musicians and singers."

Share: Images and words.

Read: Third part of myth up to "The Sun like a red beast drowned."

Remember: A time of struggling to hear.

Paint: Image of how the struggle felt.

Share: As a group, hold up paintings at the same time. Share words and ideas that come to mind.

Sound: As a group, with eyes closed, create sounds of the wind struggling to wrest the musicians and singers from the Sun. The group starts and stops itself.

Read: The last part of the myth to the end, "Life was all music from that time on."

Choose: A phrase of the poem that has great impact on you. Put the phrase into your own words.

Sing: Your words until you can repeat your phrase comfortably and accurately.

Share: In groups of 4-6 share song phrases and put them into an order to make a song. As a group, learn each others' phrases so they can be sung by the group as one song.

Share: Songs with large group.

Reflect: On the impact music makes (has) on your life.

Text: THE CREATION OF MUSIC
Focus: An exploration of conflicting needs (wants)
Length: 1 1/2 hours

Exploratory   Primarily movement
mode:

Distribute: Copies of text.

Read: First part of myth up to "Life should be all music."

Remember: A time when you wanted something that belonged to
someone else.

Response-   As memories are shared, each group member paints a
task: small image of each story to help remember the story. A
few key words for each memory may help reinforce personal impressions. Try to put all images on one paper. If
groups is larger than ten, divide into two smaller groups.

Share: Memories.

Read: Second part of myth up to "All shone translucent and happy, their gaze turned forward."

Move: Divide into groups of three. Each participant chooses one
of three (Sun, Wind, Tezcatlipoca). After choosing a role,
develop one sentence which begins with, "I want ..."

               Using sentence as a kind of musical accompaniment,
create as a group, a movement phrase to show conflicting
desires of Sun, Wind, Tezcatlipoca. Roles can be exchanged.

Share: Movement phrases with group.

Observe: How wants (needs) are expressed. Look at ways in which each person's desires are physicalized.

Read: Third part of myth up to "to the wind's lap".

Paint: Image of moment of greatest impact.

Share: Images.

Read: Fourth part of myth up to, "Life was all music from that time on."

Move: In groups of 4—6 create a movement piece which expresses the groups thoughts and feelings about the myth paying particular attention to how the wants and needs of principals are or are not resolved. Work spontaneously, each person choosing an aspect to focus on such as musician, Sun, Wind, etc. Explore impressions rather than trying to recreate actual myth. Each group starts and stops itself.

Share: Movement impressions.

Reflect: How does it feel to want something someone else has? What are you willing (unwilling) to do to get it? On what do you base your decision?

Text: THE CREATION OF MUSIC
Focus: Ways to use sound to create a community
Length: 50 minutes

Exploratory mode: Primarily sound.

Distribute: Copies of text.

Read: Myth as a group, each participant reading a sentence out loud. Continue until entire myth has been read.

Select: Phrase of greatest impact, beauty or meaning.

Sound: Create a chant for your phrase.

Facilitator: Help participants order their phrases so that they follow the progression of the myth.

Chant: In circle, each group member in turn chants phrase followed by the group echoing the chant. Repeat several times until a rhythm is established.

                    Continue around circle until every group member has had a turn to lead a chant.

Move: Repeat chants with each person creating a simple movement to accompany chant which accents the sounds.

Reflect: On feelings evoked by experience.

Text: THE CREATION OF MUSIC
Focus: Struggle and resolution
Length: 1 1/2 hours

Exploratory   Primarily drama
mode:

Paint: Image of a time of struggle.
                Image of a time of resolution.
                Image that gets you from struggle to resolution.

List: Words that come to mind for each image.

Share: Images and words. If possible, hang up images in order of painting so that group can use them later when reflecting on the structure.

Distribute: Copies of text.

Read: "The Creation of Music."

Share: Images and ideas evoked by myth which have dramatic impact.

Dramatize: Work with groups of 6-8 people. Each person selects role to play. Each person selects key words or phrases to use in dramatization of myth.

Note: Each group plays myth once or twice spontaneously, with no prior discussion or planning. Roles may be changed as desired.

Share: Dramatizations with no discussion before sharing.

Reflect: On dramas and how they explore notion of struggle and resolution.

Discuss: Each group, by itself, shares ideas, feelings, thoughts for about five minutes. The group can make any changes it desires as long as no one tells anyone else what to do or how to do it.

Share: Dramas.

Reflect: Did dramas change? If so, how? Share personal impressions of experience relating to issues of struggle and resolution.

　　　　　If paintings can be looked at by group, reflect on how paintings connect to choices made in creating dramas.

Text:	THE CREATION OF MUSIC
Focus:	Ingenuity
Length:	1 1/2 hours

Exploratory mode:　　Primarily writing

Paint:　　Image of world without sound.

List:　　Words that come to mind.

Paint:　　Image of world filled with sound.

List:　　Words that come to mind.

Write:　　Answers to following questions as quickly as possible. Do not try to think of a "good" answer.

There is a problem. The world is sick from silence.

1. Who sees the problem?
2. What causes the problem?
3. Who can resolve the problem?
4. What would it take for the problem to be resolved?
5. How does hero(ine) solve problem?
6. What happens to the one who sees the problem?
7. What happens to the world after problem is resolved?

Write:　　Story using answers to questions.

Share:　　Stories.

Read:　　"The Creation of Music."

Reflect:　　On experience focusing on part ingenuity plays in stories and how this experience connects to the lives of group members.

BIBLIOGRAPHY

Myth

Campbell, Joseph ed.	Myths, dreams & Religion, 1970, Dutton.
Campbell, Joseph	Hero with a Thousand Faces, 1968, Princeton U. Press.
Campbell, Joseph	The Masks of God, 4 Vols., 1970, Penguin.
Cassirer, Ernst.	Language & Myth, 1946, Dover.
Dundes, Alan ed.	Sacred Narrative: Readings in the theory of Myth, 1985, U. of Cal. Pr.
Eliade, Mircea	The myth of Etcrnal Return, 1974, Princeton/Bollingen.
Eliade, Micrea	Myths, dreams & Mysteries, 1943, Har-Row.
Frazer, James	The Golden Bough, 1975, NAL.
Graves, Robert	The White Goddess, 1983, Peter Smith.
Greenway, John	The Primitive Reader, 1965, Gale.
Leach, Edmund, Ed.	Structural Study of Myth & Totemism, 1968, Meth.
Levi-Strauss, Claude.	From Honey to Ashes, 1973, U. of Chicago Pr.
Levi-Strauss, Claude.	Myth & Meaning, 1979, Schocken.
Sproul, Barbara C.	Primal Myths, 1979, Har-Row.

Folklore and Myth

Bettelheim, Bruno.	The Uses of Enchantment, 1977, Random House.
Binner, Vinal O.	International Folktales Two: A Structured Reader, 1970, Har-Row.
Bulfinch, H.	Bulfinch's Mythology, 1970, T Y Crowell.
Cole, Joanna.	Best Loved Folktales of the World, 1983, Doubleday.
Crossley-Holland, Kevin	The Faber Book of Northern Folktales, 1981, Faber & Faber.
Fine, Elizabeth, C.	The Folklore Text: From performance to print, 1984, Ind. U. Press.
Freud, S. & Oppenheim, D.E.	Dreams in Folklore, 1958, Intl Univ. Pr.
Haviland, Virginia.	Favorite Fairytales Told Around the World, 1985, Little.
Jung, Carl, G. and Kerenyi, Carl.	Essays on a Science of Mythology, 1963, Princeton U. Press.
Kellett, Ernst E.	Story of Myth, 1969, Johnson Repr.
Lee, F. H.	Folktales of all Nations, 1984, Darby Bks.
Raglan, FitzRoy.	The Hero: A Study in Tradition, Myth & Drama, 1975, Greenwood.
Richardson, Alan.	Gate of Moon, 1984, Newcastle Publ.
Robinson, H.S. & Wilson, K.	The Encyclopedia of Myths & Legends of All Nations, 1978, Sportshelf.
Schneiderman, Leo.	The psychology of Myth, Folklore & Religion, 1981, Nelson-Hall.
Schwab, Gustav.	Gods & Heroes, 1977, Pantheon.
Taylor, Benjamin.	Storyology; Essays in Folk-lore, Sea-lore & Plant-lore, 1976, Gordon Pr.
Thomson, Stith.	Motif-Index of Folk-literature, 6 Vols., 1955-58, Ind. U. Press.
Zipes, Jack.	Breaking the Magic Spell; Radical Theories of Folk & Fairy Tales, 1979, Univ. of Tex. Pr.

Storytelling. Bibliography

Greene, Ellin &   Storytelling, A selected and annotated
Shannon, G.   bibliography, 1985, Garland.

Storytelling: Readings, Bibliographies, Resources, 1978, ALA.

Storytelling

Baker, A. &   Storytelling: Art & Technique, 1977, Bowker.
Greene, E.

Bauer, Caroline F.   Handbook for Storytellers, 1977, ALA.

Bausch, William J.   Storytelling, Imagination & Faith, 1984, Twen-
                       tythird.

Bryant, Sara C.   How to tell stories to children. Repr. of 1924 Ed.,
                       Gale.

Burrell, Arthur.   A Guide to Storytelling, Repr. of 1926 Ed., Arden
                       Lib.

Carlsson, Bernice W.   Listen & Help Tell the Story, 1965, Abingdon.

Colwell, Eilleen.   Storytelling, 1983, Merrimack Pub. Cir.

Farrell, Catharine H. Word Weaving: A Storytelling Guide, 1983, SF
                       Study Ctr.

Farrell, C. &   Word Weaving: A Teaching Sourcebook, 1984,
Nessel, D.   Zellerback FF.

Harrell, J. &   A Storyteller's Treasury, 1977, York Hse.
Harrell, M.

Lyman, Edna Pseud.   Storytelling. What to Tell & How to tell it. Repr. of
                       1911 ed., Gale.

Maguire, J.   Creative Storytelling, 1985, McGraw.

Mitchell, D.G.   About Old Story-Tellers, Repr. of 1877 ed., Gale.

Nowlin, Clifford H.   The Storyteller & His Pack, Repr. of 1929 ed.,
                       Darby Bks.

Ransome, Arthur.   A History of Story-Telling, Repr. of 1909 ed. Folcroft.

Savater, Fernando.   Regained: the Art of the Storyteller, 1982, Columbia U. Press.

Sawyer, Ruth.   The Way of the Storyteller, 1977, Penguin.

Shimmel, Nancy.   Just enough to make a story. Natl. Assn. Preserv. & Perpet. Storytelling.

Vivian, Francis.   Story-weaving, Repr. of 1940 Ed., Arden Libr.

Wilson, Jane B.   The Story Experience, 1979, Scarecrow.

Themes and motives in Folk-literature

Baughman, Ernest, W. Type & Motif Index of the Folktales of England & North America, 1966, Mouton.

Newall, Venetia J., Ed. Folklore Studies in the Twentieth Century, 1980, Rowman.

Propp, Vladimir.   Theory & History of Folklore, 1984, University of Minn. Press.

Toelken, Barre.   The Dynamics of Folklore, 1979, HM.

Williams, Paul V., ed. The Fool & The Trickster: Studies in Honour of Enid Wolsford, 1979, Rowman.

Folklore - Dictionaries

Bonnerjea, Biren.   Dictionary of Superstition & Mythology. 1969, Gale.

Jobes, Gertrude.   Dictionary of Mythology, Folklore & Symbols, 3 Vols. 1961, Scarecrow.

Leach, ed. Funk & Wagnalls.   Standard Dictionary of Folklore, Mythology & Legend, 1984, Har-Row.

Folklore, theory and methods

Bassett, Fletcher S.	The Folk-lore Manual, 1976, Folcroft.
Ben-Amos, Dan, ed.	Folklore Genres, 1975, University of Texas Press.
Dundes, Allan.	Analytic Essays in Folklore, 1975, Mouton.
Jackson, Bruce	Teaching Folklore, 1985, Documentary Res.
Zipes, Jack.	The trials & tribulations of Little Red Riding Hood, 1983, Bergin & Garvey.

Folklore & Mythology African.

Abrahams, Roger D.	African Folktales, 1983, Random House.
Arndt, Kathleen	African Myths and Legends, 1962, Oxford Univ. Press.
Beier, Ulli.	The origin of Life & Death, 1966, Heinemann Ed.
Feldmann, Susan Ed.	African Myths & Tales, 1975, Dell Publ. Co.
Green, Lila	Tales from Africa, 1979, Silver.
Jablow, Alta.	Yes & No, The Intimate Folklore of Africa, 1973, Greenwood.
Knappert, Jan.	Myths & Legends of the Swahili, 1970, Heinemann Ed.
Lester, Julius.	Black Folktales, 1970, Grove.
Radin, Paul.	African Folktales, 1970, BKS Demand.
Todd, Loreto.	Tortoise, the trickster. 1985, Routledge & Kegan.
Umeasiegbu, R.	Words are Sweet, 1982, E.J. Brill Holland.

Folklore & Mythology Ancient Greece and Rome

Baker, Douglas	Greek & Roman Mythology, 4 Vols., 1982, State Mutual Bk.
Berens, E.M.	The Myths & Legends of Ancient Greece & Rome, Repr. of 1880 Ed., Longwood Publ Gr.

Burkert, Walter	Structure & History in Greek Mythology & Ritual, 1980, U. of Cal.Pr.
Downing, Christine.	The Goddess: Mythological Images of the Feminine, 1984, Crossroad NY.
Graves, Robert	Greek Myths, 1982, Doubleday.
Harrison, Jane E.	Myths of Greece & Rome, Repr. of 1927 Ed., Folcroft
Keightley, T.	Classical Mythology, Ares.
Kingsley, Charles	The Heroes: or Greek Fairy Tales, Repr. of 1882 Ed., Quality Lib.
Pinsent, John	Greek Mythology, 1983, P. Bedrick Bks.
Slater, P.E.	Glory of Hera, 1985, Beacon Pr.
Zimmerman, J.E.	Dictionary of Classical Mythology, 1964, Har-Row.

Folklore & Mythology Asian

Asian Cultural Centre for Unesco	Folktales from Asia for Children Everywhere, 1976, Weatherhill.
Coomaraswamy, A.K. & Noble, M.E.	Myths of the Hindus & Buddhists, P. Smith.
Dawood, N.Y.	Tales from the Thousand & One Nights, 1973, Penguin.
Hillebrandt, Alfred.	Vedic Mythology, 1980, Orient. Bk. Distr.
Htin, Augn.	Burmese Folktales, Repr. of 1948 Ed., AMS Pr.
Jons, Veronica	Indian Mythology, 1967, Hamlyn.
MacDonell, Arthur A.	Vedic Mythology, Gordon Press.
McCulloch, W.	Bengali Household Tales, Repr. of 1912 Ed., AMS Pr.
Monteiro, Irene-Anne	Favorite Stories from Central Asia, 1984, Heinemann Educ.

O'Flaherty, Wendy tr.	Hindu Myths, 1975, Penguin.
Toth, Marian D.	Tales from Thailand, 1983, C.E. Tuttle.
Viadya, Kraunakar.	Folktales of Nepal, South-Asia Bks.

Folklore & Mythology Assyro-Babylonian/Semitic

Hooke, S.H.	Middle Eastern Mythology, 1963, Penguin.
Kramer, Samuel N.	Sumerian Mythology, 1972, U. of Pa. Pr.
MacKenzie, Donald A.	Myths of Babylonia & Assyria, Repr. of 1915 ed., Longwood Publ. Gr.
Spence, Lewis	Myths & Legens of Babylonia & Assyria, Repr. of 1916 Ed., Gale.

Folklore & Mythology Australian/Aboriginal

Reed, A.W.	Myths & Legends of Australia, 1973, Taplinger.
Hiatt, L.R. ed.	Australian Aboriginal Mythology, 1975, Humanities.
Langloh, Parker K.	Tales of the Dreamtime, 1975, Angus & Robertson Publ.
Levy-Bruel, Lucien	Primitive Mythology, 1984, U. of Queensland Pr.
Mountford, C.P.	Before Time Began, 1976, Nelson.

Folklore & Mythology Caribbean

Smith, Pamela C.	Annancy Stories, Repr. of 1899 Ed., AMS Pr.
Wolkstein, Diane	The Magic Orange Tree & Other Haitian Folktales, 1980, Schocken.

Folklore & Mythology Central America

Alexander, Hartley B.	Latin American Mythology, Repr. of 1932 Ed., Cooper Sq.
Bierhorst, John	The Hungry Woman, Myths & Legends of the Aztecs, 1984, Morrow.
Spence, Lewis	The Myths of Mexico & Peru, Repr. of 1914 Ed., Longwood Publ. Gr.
Spence, Lewis	Popul Vuh: Mythic & Heroic Sagas of the Kiches of Central America, Repr. of 1908 Ed., AMS Pr.

Folklore & Mythology Chinese

Bergeret, Annie & Tenaille, Mabel	Tales from China, Silver.
Birch, Cyril	Chinese Myths and Fantasies, 1962, Oxford Univ. Press.
Ching Wen.	More Tales About Other Wise Men. Oriental Book Store.
Christie, Antony	Chinese Mythology, 1968, Hamlyn.
Eberhard, Wolfram	Chinese Fairy Tales & Folk Tales, 1937, Folcroft.
Hertz, Ellen, Ed.	The Magic Bird, 1985, China Books.
Jest Books	Journey to the Sun, 1981, China Books.
Ku Wan-Chuan	The Fisherman's Love, Oriental Book Store.
MacGowan, John	Chinese Folktales, Repr. of 1910 Ed., Folcroft.
Mackenzie, Donald A.	The Myths of China & Japan, Repr. of 1923 Ed. Longwood Publ. Gr.
A.N.	Peacock Maiden: Folktales from China, China Bks.

Radin, Paul.	The Golden Mountain, 1971, Oriental Book Store.
Yijun, Fang, et al.	Ancient Chinese Fables, 6 Vols. 1982, China Bks.
Werner, E.T.	Myths & Legends of China, Repr. of 1922 Ed., Ayer Co Publ.

Folklore & Mythology Egyptian

Budge, E.A.	The Gods of the Egyptians, 2 Vols. 1969, Dover.
Green, Roger L.	Tales of Ancient Egypt, 1972, Penguin.
Harris, Geraldine	Gods & Pharaos from Egyptian Mythology, 1983, Schocken.
Ions, Veronica	Egyptian Mythology, 1983, P. Bedrick Bks.
Shorter, Alan W.	The Egyptian Gods, 1985, Borgo Pr.

Folklore & Mythology Eskimo

Garber, Clark M.	Stories and Legends of the Bering Street Eskimos, Repr. of 1940, AMS Pr.
Hall, Edwin S., Jr.	The Eskimo Storyteller: Folktales from Noatak, Alaska, 1975, Univ. of Tenn. Pr.
Rasmussen, Knud J.	The Netsilik Eskimos, Repr. of 1931 Ed., AMS Pr.

Folklore & Mythology Japanese

Davis, F Hadland	Myths & Legends of Japan, Repr. of 1912 Ed., Arden Libr.
Mackenzie, Donald A.	The Myths of China & Japan, Repr. of 1923 Ed., Longwood Publ. Gr.
Piggott, Juliet	Japanese Mythology, 1983, P. Bedrick Bks.

Folklore & Mythology North American Indian

Alexander, Hartley B.	North American Indian Mythology, Repr. of 1932 Ed., Cooper Sq.
Benister, M.	Thirty Indian Legends of Canada, 1983, Merrimack Publ. Gr.
Benedict, Ruth	Tales of the Cochiti Indians, Repr. of 1931 Edition, Scholarly.
Bierhorst, John Ed.	The Red Swan, 1985, F.S. & G.
Boas, Franz	Bella Bella Texts, Repr. of 1928 Ed., AMS Pr.
Brinton, Daniel G.	The Myths of the New World, Repr. of 1876 ed, Scholarly.
Coffin, Tristram P. Ed.	Indian Tales of North America, 1961, U. of Texas Pr.
Emerson, Ellen	Indian Myths, Gordon Pr.
Erodes, Richard & Ortiz, Alfonso	American Indian Myths & Legends, 1984, Pantheon.
Grinnell, George B.	Pawnee Hero Stories & Folktales, 1961, Univ. of Nebraska Pr.
Kroeber, Alfred L.	Yurok Myths, 1976, Univ. of Cal. Pr.
Malotki, Ekkehart & Lomatuwayima, Michael	Gullible Coyote, Una'ihu, 1985, Univ. of Ariz. Pr.
Mooney, James	Myths of the Cherokee, Repr. of 1900 Ed., Scholarly.
Marriott, Alice & Rachlin, Carol	Plains Indian Mythology, 1972, T.Y. Crowell
Marriott, Alice & Rachlin, Carol	American Indian Mythology, 1972, NAL.
Parker, Arthur C.	Seneca Myths & Folktales, Repr. of 1923 Ed., AMS Pr.

Radin, Paul	Literary Aspects of North American Mythology, Repr. of 1915 Ed., Arden Lib.
Radin, Paul	Trickster, Repr. of 1926 Ed., Greenwood.
Rice, Stanley P.	Ancient Indian Fables & Stories, Repr. of 1924 Ed., R. West.
Thompson, Stith Ed.	Tales of the North American Indians. 1966, Ind. U. Pr.

Folklore & Mythology Oceanic

Anderson, J.C.	The Maori Tohunga & His Spirit World. Repr. of 1948 Ed., AMS Pr.
Beckwith, M.W.	Hawayan Mythology, 1977, U.H. Pr.
Clark, Kate M.	Maori Tales & Legends, Repr. of 1896 Ed., AMS Pr.
Cowan, James	Fairy Folktales of the Maori, Repr. of 1930 Ed., AMS Pr.
Dixon, R.B.	Oceanic Mythology, Repr. of 1932 Ed., Cooper Sq.
Grey, George	Polynesean Mythology & Ancient Tradition, History of the New Zealanders as furnished by their Priests and Chiefs. Repr. of 1906 Ed., AMS Pr.
Shortland, E.	Maori Religion & Mythology, Repr. of 1882 Ed., AMS Pr.
Melville, Leinan	Children of the Rainbow, 1969, Theos. Pub. Hse.
Kirtley, Basil F.	Index of Polynesian, Melanesian & Micronesian Narratives, 1980, Ayer Co. Pubs.

Folklore & Mythology Scandinavian

Branston, Brian	Gods & Heroes from Viking Mythology, 1982, Schocken.
Crossley-Holland, Kevin	The Norse Myths, 1981, Pantheon.
Davidson, H. Ellis	Gods & Myths of Northern Europe, 1965, Penguin.
Kaufman, Friedrich	Northern Mythology, Repr. of 1903 Ed., Darby Bks.
Sturluson, Snorri	The Prose Edda of Snorri Sturluson, 1964, U. of Cal. Pr.

Folklore & Mythology Siberian/Slavic

Curtin, Jeremiah	Myths & Folktales of the Russians, Western Slavs & Magyars, 1977, Gordon Pr.
Holmberg, Uno	Finno-Ugric, Siberian Mythology, Repr. of 1932 Ed., Cooper Sq.
Ralston, W.R.	Songs of the Russian People, Repr. of 1872 Ed,. Haskell.
Sartakov, S.	Siberian Stories, Progress Pubs. (USSR)

Folklore & Mythology South American

Alexander, Hartley B.	Latin American Mythology, Repr. of 1932 Ed., Cooper Sq.
Brett, William H.	Legends & Myths of the Aboriginal Indians of British Guiana, Repr. of 1880 Ed., AMS Pr.
Cole, Fay C.	Traditions of the Tinguian, Repr. of 1915 Ed. AMS Pr.
Hartt, Charles F.	Amazonian Tortoise Myths, Repr. of 1875 Ed., AMS Pr.

Rohmer, Harriet	The mighty God Viracocha, 1976, Childrens Book Pr.
Teit, James A.	Mythology of the Thompson Indians, Repr. of 1912 Ed., AMS Pr.
Urton, G. ed.	Animal Myths & Metaphors in South America, 1985, U. of Utah Pr.
Willber, J & Simoneau, K. eds.	Folkliterature of the Chorote Indians, 1985, UCLA Lat Am Ctr.

Folklore & Mythology Tibetan

O'Connor, W.F.	Folktales from Tibet, Norwood Edns.
Timpanelli, Gioi	Tales from the Roof of the World, 1984, Viking.

Folklore & Mythology W. European

Baudis. J.	Csech Folktales. Repr. of 1917, Kraus Repr.
Balfour, C.M.	County Folklore Vol IV Kraus Repr.
Briggs, Katherine M.	British Folktales, 1977, Ayer Publ.
Calvino, Italo	Italian Folktales, 1981, Pantheon.
Cousins, H. James.	Irish Mythology, Gordon Press.
Green, Lila	Tales from Hispanic Lands, 1979, Silver.
Grimm, Jacob.	Teutonic Mythology, 4 Vols., Peter Smith.
Jackson, K.H.	A Celtic Miscellary, 1971, Penguin.
Jacobs, J.	More Celtic Fairy Tales, Peter Smith.
Jacobs, J. Ed.	Celtic Fairy Tales, 1968, Dover.
Hull, Eleanor.	Folklore of the British Isles, 1974, Folcroft.
Kavanagh, Peter.	Irish Mythology, Kavanagh.

MacKenzie, Donald A.	Teutonic Myth & Legend, Repr. of 1912 Ed., Longwood Publ. Gr.
Macinnes, D.	Folk & Hero Tales, Kraus Repr.
Nasr Al-Din	Tales of Nasr-ed-Din., 1977, AMS Pr.
Rhys, John.	Celtic Folklore, 2 vols. Gordon Pr.
Segovia, Gertrudis	The Spanish Fairy Book, Repr. of 1918 Ed., Core Collection
Tregarthen, Enys.	The doll who came alive, 1972, Har-Row.

Group-Counseling & Group Psychotherapy

Anderson, Joseph	Counseling through group process, 1984, Springer Publ.
Corey, G.	Theory & Practice of Group Counseling, 1984, Brooks-Cole.
Gazda, G.M.	Basic approaches to Group Psychotherapy, and Group Counseling,,1982, C.C. Thomas.
Gazda, G.M.	Group Counseling, a Developmental Approach, 1984, Allan.
Lifton, W.	Groups: Facillitating Individual Growth & Societal Change, 1972, Wiley.
Seligman, M.	Group Counseling & Group Psychotherapy with special populations, 1982, Pro Ed.
Yalom, I.D.	The Theory and Practice of Group Psychotherapy 1976, Basic Books.
Whittaker, D.S. & Lieberman, M.A.	Psychotherapy through group process, 1965, Tavistock Publ.

The Group Psychotherapy literature: 1981, Silver, Robert J, Miller, Ross D: Lubin, Bernard: Dobson, Nancy H.,
Austin State Hosp Dept of Psychology TX.
International Journal of Group Psychotherapy, 1982, Oct. Vol. 32 (4) 481-554 ISSN: 00207284.

Group Work in Education

Bates, Marilyn et al.	Group Leadership. A Manual for Group Counseling Leaders, 1981, Love Publ. Co.
Cooper, Cary L.	Learning from Others in Groups: Experimental. Learning Approaches, 1979, Greenwood.
Hamon, Philip G.	Learning through groups: A Trainer's Basic Guide, 1981, Univ. Assocs.
Jacques, David	Learning in Groups, 1984, Longwood Publ. Gr.
King, Nancy	Giving Form to Feeling, 1975, Drama Book Specialists, N.Y.
Miel, Alice	Cooperative Procedures in Learning, Repr. of 1952 Ed., Greenwood.
Robinson, Russell D.	Group Dynamics for Student Activities, 1977, Natl. Assn. Principals.
Turney, C. et al.	Micro Skills, Series 4 Handbook, 1976, Sydney Univ. Pr.